Aboriginal Convicts

KRISTYN HARMAN is a historian who lectures in Aboriginal Studies in the Faculty of Arts at the University of Tasmania.

In memory of all aboriginal people incorporated into the convict system in the Australian penal colonies and for those affected by their incarceration.

Aboriginal Convicts

*Australian, Khoisan
and Māori Exiles*

Kristyn Harman

UNSW PRESS

A UNSW Press book

Published by
NewSouth Publishing
University of New South Wales Press Ltd
University of New South Wales
Sydney NSW 2052
AUSTRALIA
newsouthpublishing.com

National Library of Australia Cataloguing-in-Publication entry
       Author: Harman, Kristyn.
       Title: Aboriginal convicts: Australian, Khoisan and Māori exiles/Kristyn Harman.
       ISBN: 978 174223 323 9 (pbk.)
       ISBN: 978 174224 608 6 (ePDF)
       ISBN: 978 174224 118 0 (ePub)
       ISBN: 978 174224 376 4 (Kindle)
       Notes: Includes index.
       Subjects: Convicts – Australia.
       Prisoners, Aboriginal Australian.
       Prisoners – Australia.
       Prisoners, Khoisan (African people) – Australia.
       Prisoners, Māori – Australia.
       Exiles – Africa.
       Exiles – New Zealand.
       Dewey Number: 994.02

Design Josephine Pajor-Markus
Front cover Portait of Musquito, who was transported to Norfolk Island with Bull Dog, and
hanged in Hobart in 1825. (National Library of Australia an7573663)
Back cover 'Etablissement penitentiaire de Port Arthur, Terre de Van-Diemen', engraving,
Paris 1854. (National Library of Australia 22319)
Printer Griffin

Contents

Acknowledgments

My warm appreciation is due to family, friends and colleagues whose generous assistance has contributed to this project. Ian Duffield was the first to highlight the existence of numerous 'coloured' people from many different places who ended up labouring as convicts in the Antipodes. Cassandra Pybus detailed the lives of black convicts on the First Fleet that weighed anchor at Botany Bay in 1788 and encouraged me in my research from the outset. Vertrees Malherbe researched extensively the circumstances at the Cape that saw numerous Khoisan civilians and soldiers transported to New South Wales and Van Diemen's Land in the early decades of the nineteenth century, providing a solid foundation on which I could build. Research by John Tattersall, Jeff Hopkins-Weise and Leslie Duly has also been particularly useful for me to draw on in investigating the lives of aboriginal convicts.

Particularly in the earlier stages of my research, I benefitted greatly from discussions with Hamish Maxwell-Stewart, Mitchell Rolls, Nigel Penn, Henry Reynolds, Peter Chapman and Anna Johnston on topics ranging from the colonial practice of publicly displaying corpses in chains hanging from trees to the missionary Reverend Lancelot Threlkeld's role as an 'interpreter' for Aboriginal defendants in the Supreme Court of New South Wales. Several people deserve a special vote of thanks for their generosity in sourcing and sharing archival records with me. Tim Causer kindly shared information he uncovered as he trawled the archive to revise our understandings of the convict past at Norfolk Island. Phil Hilton generously brought back from London records of several courts mar-

tial involving Khoisan convicts located as he researched the dispro-
portionately high numbers of soldiers transported to the Antipodes
as convicts. These records enriched my understanding of this aspect
of the Khoisan convicts' history. Thanks are also due to Tony Stagg
and Eleanor Cave whose sharp eyes helped decipher seemingly
unreadable convict records.

The staff at numerous institutions including the Allport Library
and Museum of Fine Arts, Public Record Office of Victoria, Victorian Parliamentary Library, State Records of New South Wales, State
Library of New South Wales, Mitchell Library, National Library of
Australia, National Gallery of Australia, Archives New Zealand,
Alexander Turnbull Library, British Museum and Museum Africa
have provided me with generous assistance. Special votes of thanks
are due to the staff at the Tasmanian Archive and Heritage Office for
their assistance over a prolonged period and to those who staff the
document delivery service at the University of Tasmania who never
failed to deliver on my straightforward and more complex requests.
Institutionally, the University of Tasmania also deserves recognition
for endowing me with a scholarship, which made possible much of
the research incorporated into *Aboriginal Convicts*.

On a more personal note, my parents Alister and Pam Harman
strongly encouraged me to pursue an education, for which I am very
grateful. Friends such as Basil Sansom and Pat Baines and their
extended family, Carol and Denis Pybus, Ian McFarlane, Patrick
Ball and Kaz Ross have been generous with their encouragement and
good company along the way. Lex and Susan Brodie provided much
appreciated hospitality in several locations at various stages of this
project. Nicholas Brodie has always been unstinting in his support,
for which I am very appreciative. My daughter, Eleanor Murrell,
deserves a special mention, too, for her tolerance of my immersion
over the past eight years in the research that has culminated in this
book.

Acknowledgments

Finally, I have enjoyed a warm relationship with staff at UNSW Press including Phillipa McGuinness, Melita Rogowsky, Heather Cam and Marie-Louise Taylor whose encouragement and professionalism have made the process of publishing this book and sharing the stories it contains nothing short of a pleasure.

Plate credits

1 'Nouvelle-Hollande, Nlle. Galles du Sud, Ourou-mare, dit Bull-dog par les Anglais, jeune guerrier de la tribu des Gwea-Gal', Barthelemy Roger, reproduced with kind permission from the National Library of Australia, an7569776.
2 'Nouvelle-Hollande, Y-erran-gou-la-ga', Barthelemy Roger, reproduced with kind permission from the National Library of Australia, an7573663.
3 'Aboriginal Troopers, Melbourne police with English corporal', William Strutt, reproduced with kind permission from the Victorian Parliamentary Library.
4 Yanem Goona, Convict Conduct Record, CON37/1/2, p. 588, reproduced with kind permission from the Tasmanian Archive and Heritage Office.
5 'Port Arthur, VDL', John Skinner Prout, reproduced with kind permission from the Allport Library and Museum of Fine Arts, Tasmanian Archive and Heritage Office, AUTAS001124073305.
6 'Hyde Park Barracks, N S Wales' in Collection of Views Predominantly of Sydney, Liverpool, and the Sunda Straits, and Portraits, ca 1807, 1829-1847, 1887, owned by AWF Fuller, reproduced with kind permission from the Mitchell Library, State Library of NSW [PX*D 41/5].
7 'Hottentot Convict', Charles Bell, reproduced with kind permission from Museum Africa, Johannesburg, accession number MA1954-568, Catalogue of Pictures no. B754.

8   Volume of Indents from the *William Glen Anderson*, CON14/1/2, reproduced with kind permission from the Tasmanian Archive and Heritage Office.

9   'Boulcott's Stockade in the Hutt Valley N.Z. 1846. Graves of soldiers 58th Reg.', George Hyde Page, reproduced with kind permission from the Alexander Turnbull Library, Wellington, New Zealand, Reference No. B-081-002.

10 'Hohepa Te Umuroa 1846', William Duke (1814 Ireland–Australia 1853), oil on canvas, 70.6 cm x 60.35 cm, reproduced with kind permission from the National Gallery of Australia, Canberra. Purchased with the assistance of the Catherine Margaret Frohlich Memorial Fund, 2011; 2011.937.

11 'Hohepa Teumuroa [Hohepa Te Umuroa], New Zealand', John Skinner Prout, reproduced with kind permission from the Trustees of the British Museum, Reg. No. Oc2006, Drg.29; PRN. EOC83205.

12 'Ku Me Te [Te Kumete], New Zealand', John Skinner Prout, reproduced with kind permission from the Trustees of the British Museum, Reg. No. Oc2006, Drg.30; PRN. EOC83206.

13 'Te Waretea [Te Waretiti], New Zealand', John Skinner Prout, reproduced with kind permission from the Trustees of the British Museum, Reg. No. Oc2006, Drg.31; PRN. EOC83207.

14 'Ko Pi Ta Ma, Te Ra Ni [Te Rahui], New Zealand', John Skinner Prout, reproduced with kind permission from the Trustees of the British Museum, Reg. No. Oc2006, Drg.27; PRN. EOC83203.

15 'Martiu Tikiahi [Matiu Tikiahki], New Zealand', John Skinner Prout, reproduced with kind permission from the Trustees of the British Museum, Reg. No. Oc2006, Drg.28; PRN. EOC83204.

16 Plate supplied by the author.

–MAPS–

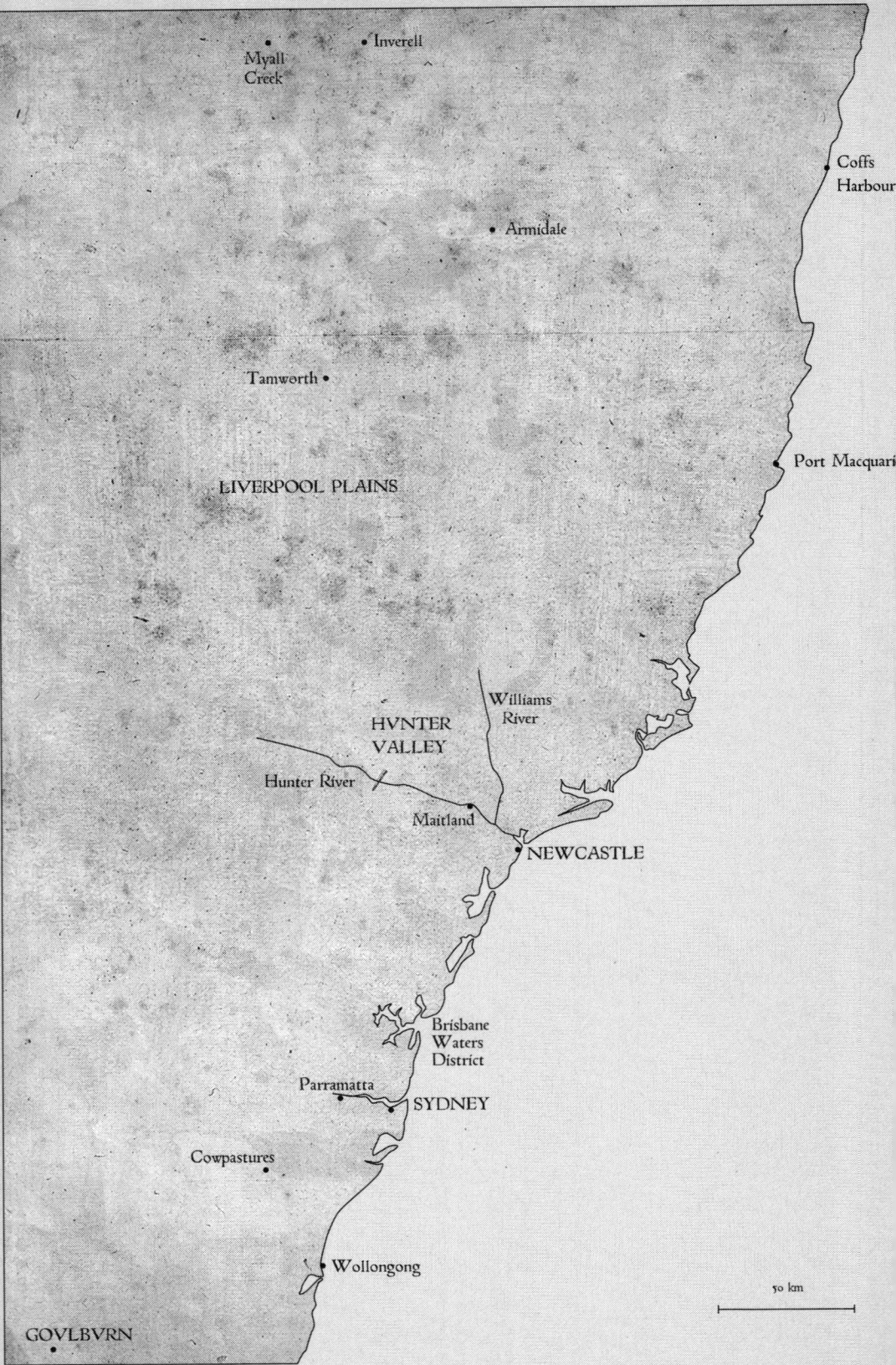

Inverell

Myall
Creek

Coffs
Harbour

Armidale

Tamworth •

Port Macquarie

LIVERPOOL PLAINS

Williams
River

HVNTER
VALLEY

Hunter River

Maitland

NEWCASTLE

Brisbane
Waters
District

Parramatta

SYDNEY

Cowpastures

Wollongong

GOVLBVRN

50 km

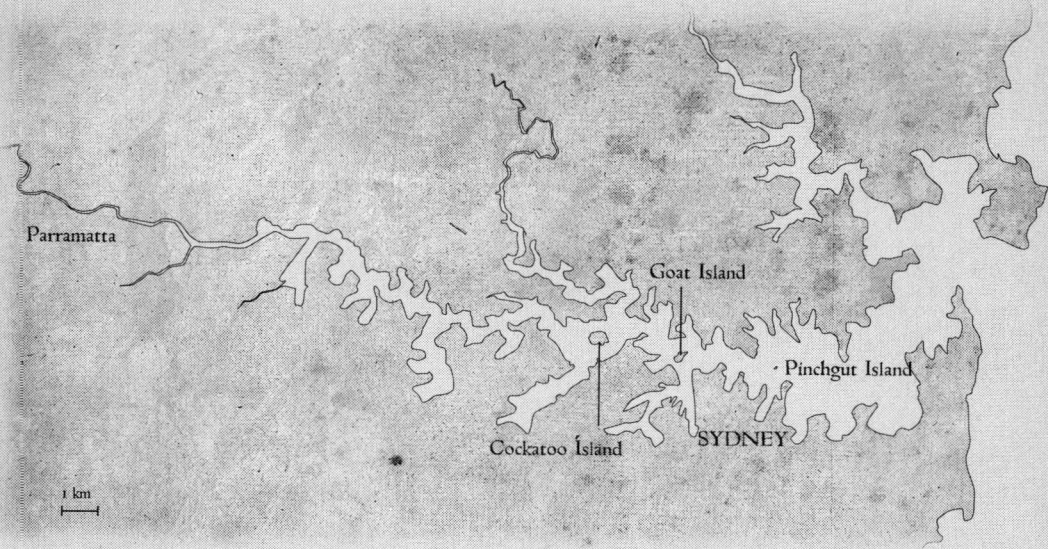

Parramatta

Goat Island

Pinchgut Island

Cockatoo Island

SYDNEY

1 km

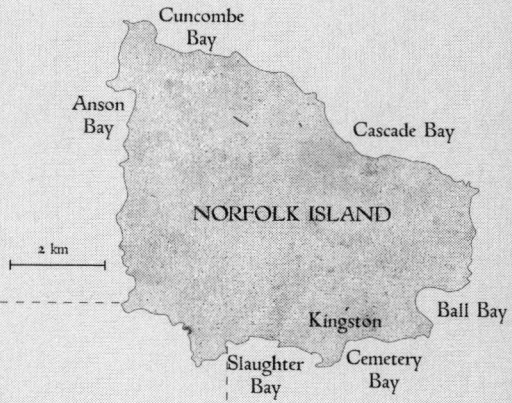

Cuncombe
Bay

Anson
Bay

Cascade Bay

NORFOLK ISLAND

2 km

Kingston

Ball Bay

Slaughter
Bay

Cemetery
Bay

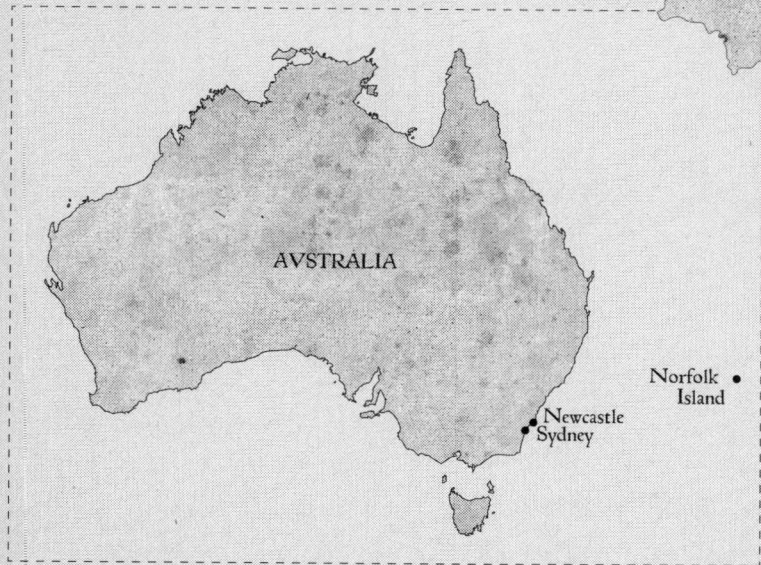

AVSTRALIA

Norfolk
Island

Newcastle
Sydney

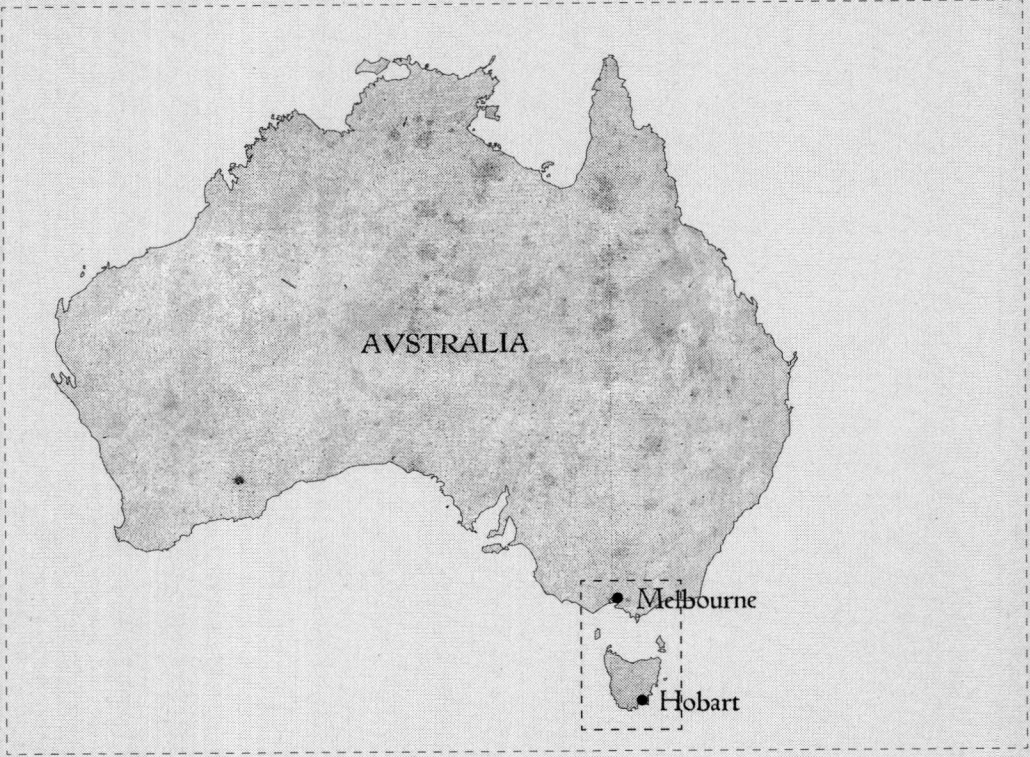

AVSTRALIA

Melbourne

Hobart

Mt Arapiles

GRAMPIANS

MELBOVRNE
•Narre Narre Warren
GEELONG •
•Western Port
Port Fairy •

KING
ISLAND

FLINDERS
ISLAND

LAVNCESTON
(Prisoners' Barracks) •
Westbury •   •
Longford •

Campbelltown •
Ross •   Eastern
Strahan •   Marshes   Oyster
MACQVARIE   Jericho •   Bay
HARBOVR Bothwell •   Musquito
Plains
Parsons Pass •   Darlington
Buckland •   MARIA
New Norfolk •   ISLAND
• Sorell
HOBART
TOWN •
(Prisoners' Barracks Cascades)
Port Arthur
Lymington •   TASMAN'S
Southport •   PENINSVLA

BRVNY
ISLAND

50 km

CAPE COLONY

Colesberg

Beaufort
West

Graaff-Reinet

Somerset

Fort Beaufort

Trompetter's Drift

Georgetown

CAPE TOWN

Stellenbosch

Swellendam

Bethelsdorp Mission

Port Elizabeth

Caledon

Cape of
Good Hope

100 km

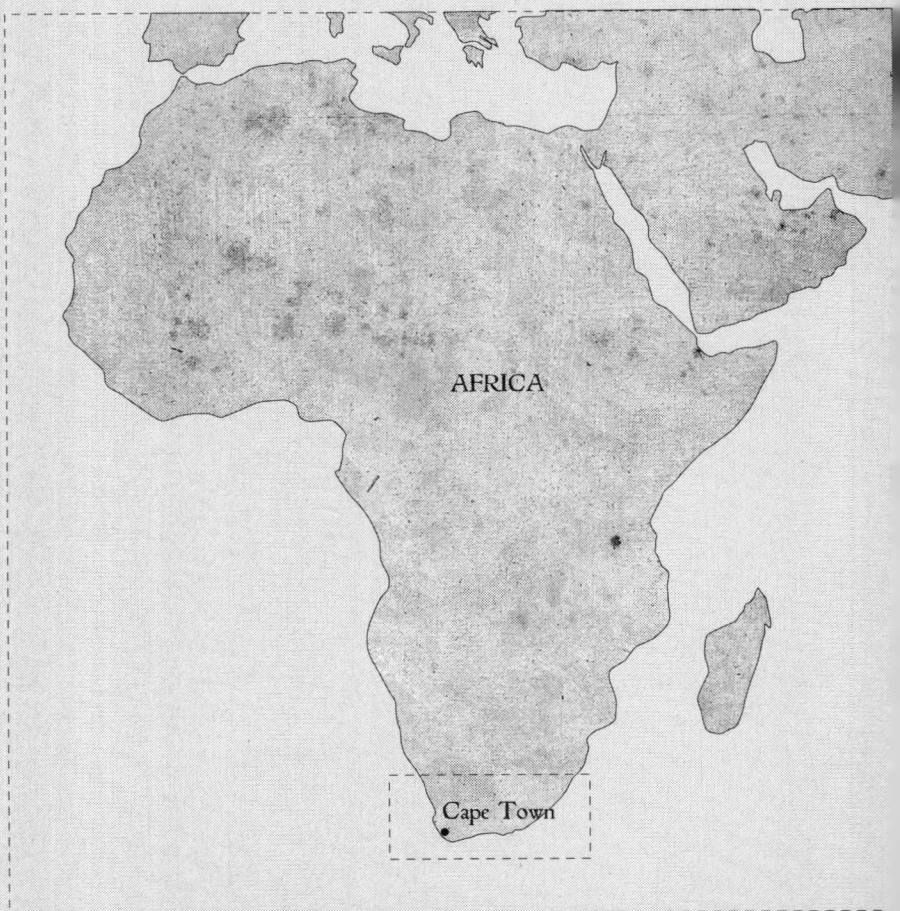

AFRICA

Cape Town

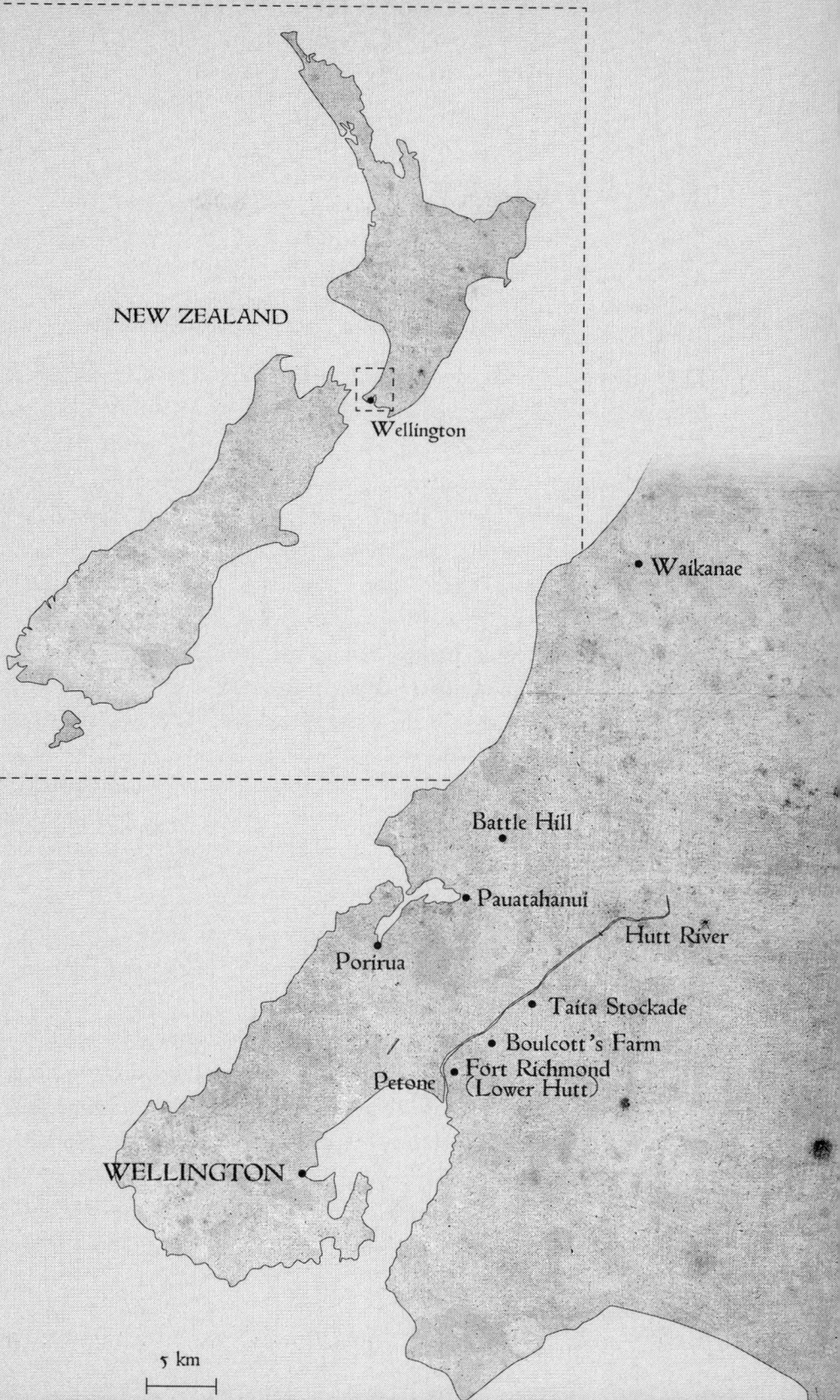

NEW ZEALAND

Wellington

Waikanae

Battle Hill

Pauatahanui

Hutt River

Porirua

Taita Stockade

Boulcott's Farm

Petone

Fort Richmond
(Lower Hutt)

WELLINGTON

5 km

Terminology

Throughout this book, the phrase 'aboriginal convicts' has been used to refer collectively to indigenous people from New South Wales, the Cape Colony and New Zealand who were sentenced to transportation or whose death sentences were commuted to transportation. When referring to people from specific colonies, I have used 'Aboriginal' or 'Australian Aboriginal' to denote those from New South Wales, 'Khoisan' in reference to Khoi (also known as Khoikhoi or Khoekhoe) and San people from the Cape, and Māori to describe those from New Zealand. In the colonial period, San people were known as 'bushmen' with Khoi and San collectively called 'Hottentots'.

The usage of personal names and place names is consistent with their usage throughout the period to which this book refers. As a result, some names may appear with different spellings than those with which a present-day readership might be more familiar. During the times in which the events described are set, spelling variants were common particularly in relation to aboriginal personal names. At times, some aboriginal personal names appear with inconsistent spellings, as in the use of direct quotations. Such names have been reproduced as they originally appeared.

To reflect the colonial setting, imperial measurements are used for both distances and currency. The spellings adopted during the early era of colonial contact are also conserved so that, for example, colonial judges are referred to as His Honor rather than His Honour. Other terminology has also been preserved to reflect something of the character of the times albeit at the risk of offending present-day sensibilities. For example, Australian Aboriginal actions against colonists were often referred to as 'outrages' or 'depredations' and Aboriginal people were considered to belong to 'tribes'.

Preface

One of the more unusual artefacts surviving from the convict period in Tasmania is a tall, weatherworn headstone standing in the cemetery at Darlington on Maria Island. After moving to Tasmania from New Zealand in 1994, I visited Maria Island for the first time over the weekend before the Christmas of that year. The steep, mountainous island is a national park, home to kangaroo, wombats, bluetongue lizards and other marsupials as well as abundant bird and marine life. The north and south of Maria Island are connected by a narrow isthmus. Accessing the island involves a trip by catamaran that takes somewhere between twenty and forty minutes depending on the weather, or a flight in a light plane that buzzes the grassy airstrip before landing to clear away the Cape Barren geese.

Aside from close encounters with Tasmanian wildlife, Maria Island is also renowned for unusual geological features: the enchanting Painted Cliffs with layers of differently hued sandstone; and the Fossil Cliffs on the far side of the island, embedded with fossilised shells from eons ago. The built environment is similarly striking. One of the first buildings visible from the jetty is the convict-built brick Commissariat Store, now used as a reception area by the National Park rangers welcoming visitors to the island. The main settlement at Darlington comprises convict-built buildings dominated by the Penitentiary, home to a productive community of forced convict labourers in the mid-nineteenth century but now temporary shelter for tourists who hire bunkrooms for a few dollars per night.

As the crowd from the ferry disperses by bicycle – a popular mode of transport as only the rangers are allowed vehicles on the island –

and on foot, it is time to explore. Further afield from Darlington, other architectural relics from the convict period are nestled in the bush. The brickworks stand not far from the reservoir that continues to provide water to the settlement. In the opposite direction, not far from the Painted Cliffs facing the main island of Tasmania, an oast house can still be found. Several buildings lie up the hills rising steeply beyond the Commissariat Store, a huge bat-infested barn with a rambling collection of rusty farm machinery, and, much further up, the miller's cottage with views across to Freycinet Peninsula.

Also up the hills behind the Commissariat Store are the basic yet serviceable airfield and a small, iron-fenced cemetery. Almost all of the headstones, in various states of disrepair, commemorate settlers from the convict period and subsequent periods of occupation on Maria Island. But the one that moved me most was the headstone standing separately from the rest, inscribed in Te Reo Māori and English, commemorating Hohepa Te Umuroa. What, I wondered, was a fellow New Zealander doing so far from home in the 1840s? What was a Māori doing in Van Diemen's Land, as it was then known, in the colonial period? And how did he come to die here?

These questions remained unanswered for a number of years. In 2004, as I was completing undergraduate studies begun in New Zealand at the University of Tasmania, I decided these questions would inform my doctoral research. Directing a few questions to people in the know soon revealed that Te Umuroa was one of a small group of Māori transported from New Zealand to Van Diemen's Land as a convict. That he was given a headstone is extraordinary – almost all of the men and women who died within the convict system were buried in unmarked graves or provided to hospitals for dissection. I began to wonder whether any Australian Aboriginal people had also become convicts. Other scholars seriously doubted I would find any Aboriginal people among the tens of thousands of convicts in the Australian penal colonies, although a few knew about some Khoisan convicts shipped to New South Wales and Van Diemen's Land from the colony of the Cape of Good Hope.

By 2008, I discovered that more than sixty Aboriginal men from New South Wales (which originally included the present-day states of Victoria, Queensland and Tasmania) were incorporated into the convict system. The stories of these men became my doctoral thesis. Through writing this book, I hope their stories and those of other Aboriginal convicts I have since discovered will become much more widely known. It has also allowed me to include the stories of Khoisan civilians and soldiers sent halfway around the world to the Antipodes to labour in the Australian penal colonies, and of Māori warriors transported from New Zealand for rebelling against Queen and country. Collectively, these people were known in the nineteenth century as 'aborigines', hence the book title *Aboriginal Convicts*. Very, very few aboriginal convicts ever returned home.

Introduction

The Australian penal colonies were much more ethnically diverse than most people realise. Places like Tasmania's Port Arthur or the more distant Norfolk Island are often thought of as prisons for reluctant transportees from England. Men who stole a loaf of bread from somewhere in London's East End to feed their starving families, or women who took a scrap of fabric to stitch together something a little better than rags to cover their children as they ran along chilly, grey city streets. The majority of prisoners labouring in the Australian penal colonies were indeed convicts transported from England, Ireland and Scotland. Yet in their midst were men and women from a diverse range of places including, but not limited to, Antigua, Barbados, Calcutta, Canada, the Cape Colony, China, Denmark, Egypt, France, Gibraltar, Guadalupe, Hawaii, India, Iraq, Italy, Jamaica, Madagascar, Malaya, Mauritius, New Zealand, Poland, Russia, Sierra Leone, Spain and Sweden.

This book is the first written about aboriginal convicts. It uncovers the life narratives of aboriginal convicts from three British settler colonies: New South Wales, the Cape Colony and New Zealand. A small settlement was established at Sydney Cove in New South Wales in 1788 primarily to cater for convicts. British gaols were overcrowded, and following the American Revolution the North American continent was no longer available to take the overflow of prisoners. The Cape Colony at the Cape of Good Hope (now part of South Africa) was taken over from the Dutch by the British between 1795 and 1803 because the Netherlands were occupied by France over this period. Several years after handing it back to the Dutch, the British resumed control in 1806 amid fears that French Emperor Napoleon would seize it. The Cape was strategically important, being located on a major shipping route from Europe to the New World. Given its proximity to the Australian colonies, by the early nineteenth century New Zealand was being unofficially colonised by convict absconders, timber getters, sealing gangs and whalers. Missionaries followed. It was not until the 1830s that Britain sought to formalise its relationship with New Zealand's aboriginal people, culminating in the Crown and some Māori signing the Treaty of Waitangi in 1840.

Aboriginal convicts came from vastly different backgrounds. Different cultural beliefs and practices reflected their different geographies. Australian Aborigines were hunter-gatherers with highly developed land and sea management practices. In the Cape, Khoi were predominantly cattle herders, while San hunted and gathered. Māori lived in settlements and tended extensive agricultural cultivations and also fished and hunted. They were renowned for their warriorship and highly developed defensive systems. Despite these marked differences, aboriginal convicts shared harrowing experiences of British colonisation, including intrusion onto their lands, co-option of their resources, and impingement on their lifestyles. The transportation of aborigines to, and within, the Australian penal colonies was one of the outcomes of these cultural collisions.

Aboriginal convicts ranged in age from early teens to elderly, with stories including night raids, pitched battles, collaboration with settlers, punitive expeditions, mutiny, punishments, rewards, bushranging and pauperism. Between 1800 and the mid-1860s, more than ninety Aboriginal men from New South Wales were incorporated into the convict system. From the late 1820s until the early 1850s, at least thirty-four Khoisan prisoners were transported to the Australian penal colonies. This cohort was predominantly male but, unusually, included a woman. Between the mid-1840s and the early 1850s, six Māori convicts were transported to Van Diemen's Land from the recently annexed colony of New Zealand. Like the vast majority of other aboriginal convicts, all the transported Māori were men.

That almost all aboriginal convicts were male is a function of their having been captured, for the most part, during frontier wars. The arrests of Aboriginal men across New South Wales followed the frontier as it advanced inland and then to the north and south of Sydney. In the early decades of colonisation, the colony of New South Wales included Van Diemen's Land (now Tasmania), the Port Phillip District (now Victoria) and Queensland. Men from all these locations were incorporated into the convict system, with those nearest to Sydney and from Van Diemen's Land (colonised in 1804) being transported between 1805 and the mid-1830s, those from the Brisbane Water district north of Sydney in the mid-1830s, those from Maitland and from the Port Phillip District in the 1840s, and others from outlying areas and from Queensland into the 1850s and 1860s. Khoisan convicts were transported from the Cape Colony during times of rising tensions during and between the sixth and seventh frontier wars fought between the Xhosa and the English. Some of these men had been incorporated by the English into a military regiment comprised solely of 'Hottentot' soldiers under white officers, formed to supplement the regular troops stationed at the Cape. The majority of the Māori convicts were transported to Van Diemen's Land following their involvement in the Lower Hutt War in the mid-1840s in the lower North Island of New Zealand, just a few short years after the signing of the Treaty of Waitangi.

While the advent of bitterly contested frontier wars became part of New Zealand and South African history, memories of warfare in the Australian colonies faded over time. Nineteenth-century newspapers and correspondence are replete with examples of settler Australians acknowledging warfare between colonists and Aborigines. However, the Australian colonies were officially acquired through being empty land or *terra nullius*. In the twentieth century, the notion that frontier wars were fought across Australia became contested in the nation's understanding of itself and its inception. Former Prime Minister John Howard branded versions of Australian history acknowledging frontier warfare as 'black armband' views of the past, while those promulgating revisionist histories counterclaimed people who would not see the evidence for warfare were wearing 'white blindfolds'.[1]

Despite most Australian Aboriginal and Māori men being taken prisoner within a context of frontier warfare, they were not treated as prisoners of war. Their actions were criminalised and they were dealt with either by the Governor, or through the criminal courts or military tribunals established by the colonists. Khoisan people were similarly dealt with through the court system or military tribunals. The phenomenon of criminalising aboriginal resistance arose principally through indigenous people being construed as protected by, yet answerable under, the same English-derived colonial laws as the colonising population. These laws gradually superseded prior laws and practices across the three colonies. Because aboriginal people were considered to be British subjects, the colonial judiciary could not conceptualise one part of Her Majesty's subjects being at war against another.

Civil or military trials involving aboriginal defendants were described by some as farcical. Prisoners not conversant with colonial laws or the English language were at an enormous disadvantage. Some failed to understand the charges brought against them. For example, in a Supreme Court case heard before Chief Justice Dowling in Sydney on 9 November 1840, seven Aboriginal men from the vicinity of the Macquarie River faced charges of cattle stealing. Six denied the charge, but the seventh, Tommy Boker, 'said the beef was good'. Confusion over whether the men understood the charge resulted in a verdict of 'not guilty', following which the prisoners were discharged to the Benevolent Asylum.[2]

Introduction

Across all three colonies, the lack of aboriginal defendants' fluency in English led to their being allocated court-appointed interpreters. In instances where a suitable interpreter could not be procured, prisoners were eventually released, but often only after spending far more time in gaol than the law allowed. In the Australian colonies, Aboriginal defendants were further disadvantaged through mostly not being Christian. As pagans, Australian Aborigines could not swear the required oath to provide evidence in court or to participate as members of a jury. Excluding Aboriginal people from providing evidence 'encouraged the continued reprisals between Aborigines and the colonists ... When whites stuck together, their superior weaponry was matched by the legal tool of this rule of evidence and reinforced by the general cultural gap between blacks and whites'.[3]

Because of the length of time involved in communicating between London and the colonies, and also because practicalities of life at the peripheries of Empire were sometimes at odds with ideologies espoused at the centre, events unfolding at the colonial frontier were dealt with in ways that did not always elicit Imperial approval. Hence judges at the Cape treated Khoisan subjects more harshly than their London-based superiors decreed. They took advantage of a window of opportunity to ship Khoisan prisoners halfway around the world to Van Diemen's Land, knowing in all likelihood they would never return. Transporting Khoisan to the Australian penal colonies only came to an end after an edict was issued from London demanding a halt to the practice of transporting 'Negroes' there. This was not, however, motivated by any undue concern over the fate of the transportees, but was predicated on concerns for the potentially negative impacts such convicts would have in the Australian colonies.

New Zealand took advantage of its proximity to the Australian penal colonies to make examples of Māori warriors fighting against British redcoats through transporting them across the Tasman Sea. Within a decade, Tasmania (as it became known) made it clear to the

New Zealand and Imperial authorities that it would not accept any further aboriginal convicts because of the costs involved in meeting new requirements to house them entirely separately from the rest of the convict population. This edict, which had been handed down in relation to the Swan River colony (now part of Western Australia), was interpreted by the Tasmanian authorities as also applying to the island colony.

Despite transportation of convicts from Britain to New South Wales ending in 1850 after strong opposition to the practice from the Anti-Transportation League in England since the 1830s and increasing opposition from within the Australian colonies, the colonial judiciary continued to use the convict system as a repository for Australian Aboriginal prisoners. This practice continued until at least the mid-1860s. By then, those being incarcerated were the dispossessed rather than resistance fighters at the frontier. This is reflected in the types of offences for which they were being charged, which tended to be public order offences.

The majority of Australian Aboriginal convicts appear to have been transported from the mid-1830s until the mid-1860s. This was in part due to significant changes in the colony of New South Wales over time. What was in effect a 'beach-head frontier' at Sydney with restricted British settlement in terms of numbers and weaponry gradually expanded inland and along the coast until British sovereignty extended over a far greater tract of land than originally envisaged by either colonists or Aborigines. Battles over land and resources were waged in the process. Over time, pressures from London and demographic changes locally triggered resulting changes to social, political, economic and judicial systems in the colony.[4]

The apparently lower number of Australian Aborigines transported during the early colonial era may reflect the survival of less complete records. For example, in November 1818 two Aboriginal men, James Tedbury and George Frederick, 'who have long been among the inhabitants' were sentenced in Van Diemen's Land to three years' transportation for theft. No records survive to indicate whether this sentence was carried out, but given that numerous other Aboriginal men were incorporated into the convict system it is likely they shared this fate. Even as late as the mid-1830s through until 1840, the names of five Australian Aboriginal men about whom nothing else is known were entered into the convict death register. Jimmy, aged 35, died in the General Hospital in Sydney in December 1835. The following year, Paddy, aged 34 and originally from the Patrick Plains, died at the same location. In December 1839, 22-year-old Jemmy died at the General Hospital, as did two men both known as Jackey the following year. One, aged 60, died on 1 April 1840 and the other, aged only 15, died on 28 November 1840.[5]

Aside from the convict death registers, a number of other convict records reveal a lot about individual lives. The indents prepared on board convict transports (ships) name each prisoner and provide details about their age and occupation, place of origin, where and when they were sentenced, the offence for which they were sentenced, and the term of imprisonment imposed. Other details sometimes include the prisoner's marital status and whether they had children. Description lists, as the name suggests, provide detailed physical descriptions of each prisoner. These were referred to if convicts absconded. Their description could be circulated, and their identity confirmed, with a reward usually offered for their return. Assignment lists reveal details about where the convict was sent, either into service with private individuals or to labour on public works during the early decades of the convict period. Appropriation lists also detailed the locations to which convicts were sent to labour. A particularly detailed account of a convict's life in captivity is contained within their conduct record. This replicates much of the material located in other records, yet also lists any further offences committed while a convict including details of punishments meted out.

This book goes beyond the convict records to draw on material including newspaper reports, trial records, personal diaries, official journals and reports, biographies, art and correspondence to situate each aboriginal convict's personal story. Piecing together the life narratives of these aboriginal convicts has been painstaking work involving countless hours learning to read, and then transcribing, nineteenth-century texts. What can be known about these aboriginal convicts is of course limited to those points in their lives at which they collided with the colonial world in such a way that a record was made, and also relies on those records having survived. Sitting behind their experiences in captivity are their indigenous worlds, which are inaccessible to present-day historians.

While the life narratives of Australian Aboriginal, Khoisan and Māori convicts are the principal focus of *Aboriginal Convicts*, their life events are situated within broader colonial contexts to facilitate a more complete understanding of their interactions with, and captivity within, colonial societies. The first section of the book, focusing on Australian Aboriginal convicts, follows the encroachment of colonial intruders onto Aboriginal country and traces the processes through which colonists and Aborigines came into conflict. The gradual imposition of English-derived colonial laws onto Aboriginal defendants unfolds, culminating in colonial court cases over matters solely involving Aborigines. Its principal focus is on how Aborigines came to be incorporated into the convict system. The second section focuses on Khoisan convicts. Because many of these prisoners survived for lengthy periods within and after being discharged from the convict system, these chapters focus principally on their convict experiences after explaining how they came to enter into captivity. The third and final section is about Māori convicts, mostly a small group of warriors transported to Van Diemen's Land following a court martial. It follows their journey into captivity, reveals details of their time spent at a convict probation station at Maria Island off the coast of Van Diemen's Land, and concludes with the repatriation of the remains in 1988 of one of the warriors who died in captivity.

- I -
NEW SOVTH WALES

1

Banishing Musquito, Bull Dog and Duall

The first Aboriginal convicts were exiled at the Governor's behest. During Governor Philip Gidley King's administration in New South Wales, Musquito and Bull Dog were captured in 1805 following conflict at the Hawkesbury River. Duall was taken prisoner, in 1816, after Governor Lachlan Macquarie ordered a punitive expedition against Aborigines at the Cowpastures. In these early decades, the colony's laws were overseen by the Governor and his Judge Advocate. The Supreme Court of New South Wales was yet to be established. The conflicts that formed a backdrop to the men's captivity were not simply a matter of black against white. Instead, their stories reveal delicate, fraught and complex negotiations within and between various colonising and indigenous groups.

From the mid-1790s, colonial population numbers along the banks of the fecund Hawkesbury River exploded. The colonists' cultivations extended for more than 30 miles along the riverbanks, depriving local Aborigines of essential access to fresh water and impacting on the availability of traditional food resources. Competition over land use escalated to the point where violent encounters became increasingly commonplace. Hawkesbury colonist Jonas Archer, a former convict turned struggling farmer, described how between 1795 and 1800 about twelve colonists and twenty Aborigines were killed in conflicts.[1]

On 13 May 1805 settlers from the outlying districts of Sydney with constables from Parramatta 'went in quest of the natives in the neighbourhood of Pendant [sic] Hills in order to disperse them'. They returned with Aboriginal warrior Tedbury in their custody. Son of resistance leader Pemulwuy, Tedbury had been incriminated in murdering stockmen at Prospect, near Sydney. His captors coerced him into revealing the hiding place of weapons used in the attack. While they were about this business, the vigilantes came across a small group of Aborigines including Musquito. According to a report in the *Sydney Gazette*, Musquito 'saluted them in good English' and declared 'a determination to continue' his actions against the colonists.[2]

Musquito favoured economic sabotage as a tactic. He used it against farmer Abraham Young at Portland Head on 15 June 1805. He and his supporters set fire to Young's 'Barn and Stacks', a flagrant act of war that saw Musquito held responsible by colonists for 'keeping the flames [of conflict] alive'. Aboriginal use of fire as a weapon signalled an innovative departure from the usual technologies of warfare – the spear, shield and stones.[3]

Several of Tedbury's kin were also under lock and key. Knowing how desperate the colonists were to get their hands on Musquito and wanting to redeem Tedbury, on their release from Parramatta Gaol on 1 July 1805 some of them volunteered to search for Musquito. On 6 July 1805, they handed over Musquito and his compatriot Bull Dog (men from a different tribe from them) to the colonists. These two, who were sketched by Nicolas-Martin Petit when the Baudin expedition visited Sydney in 1802, were implicated in the murders of two settlers and several stockmen at the Hawkesbury. In exchange, the former Aboriginal prisoners successfully negotiated the release of Tedbury.

Once King had Musquito and Bull Dog safely in custody, he was faced with the difficult decision of what to do with them. The

Governor felt sure there was enough evidence against the men to demonstrate their guilt in court. There were problems, though, when it came to staging a trial. Judge Advocate Richard Atkins told the Governor that while he appreciated the necessity of making examples of Musquito and Bull Dog, he could not see how the Court of Criminal Jurisdiction would be able to uphold its oath 'to give a true Verdict according to the *Evidence*' if a trial were held. Not being Christians, the prisoners could not swear the required oath. Their evidence would therefore be inadmissible.[4]

As Atkins deliberated over his advice to King, Musquito and Bull Dog did not merely sit contentedly in gaol waiting to learn their fate. Instead, they 'ingeniously contrived to loosen some of the stone work by the help of a spike nail' and plotted to burn Parramatta Gaol and all the white men within it. Their plan was foiled, though, when their discussions were overheard and reported to the turnkey. Musquito and Bull Dog attacked the informant while he was still in gaol. Soon afterwards, the man received a pardon for his role in preventing the escape attempt.[5]

As a trial seemed out of the question, King decided on a course of action that would see Musquito and Bull Dog removed from the scene and curtail any further participation on their part in the ongoing conflict. He exiled them to one of the colony's harshest penal settlements, Norfolk Island, where the least desirable officers and worst of the convict offenders were being shipped from New South Wales. Convict labour on the island produced food to supply Sydney, which struggled to feed itself in its early years. In a letter dated 8 August 1805 to Acting Commandant John Piper, the Governor wrote:

> The two Natives Bull Dog and Musquito having been given up
> by the other Natives as principals in their late Outrages are sent
> to Norfolk Island where they are to be kept, and if they can be
> brought to Labour will earn their Food – but as they must not

be let to starve for want of subsistence – they are to be victualled from the Stores.[6]

Musquito and Bull Dog arrived at Norfolk Island on 5 September 1805 where they spent more than seven years relegated to the lowest ranks of the convicts, labouring as assistants to a charcoal burner. While lowly, this job was nevertheless important to the daily functioning of the penal station. Charcoal was essential to the process of infusing iron with carbon. This was a necessary step in manufacturing processes where iron needed to be 'given an edge', as in, for example, 'to make sturdy pins that could be sunk into the keel of a ship, or to forge pick heads sharp enough to dress a block of sandstone'.[7]

In 1806 the colonial administration decided to close Norfolk Island because it was expensive to administer, difficult to communicate with, and awkward to approach safely by water. Over several years, numerous convicts from Norfolk Island were shipped to Port Dalrymple in the north of Van Diemen's Land. On 20 January 1813, Musquito boarded the *Minstrel II* to be relocated. Sometime after August 1812, Bull Dog (also known as Roy Bull) seems to have been returned to Port Jackson along with another Aboriginal convict, Jackson.[8]

Musquito arrived at Van Diemen's Land during a period when convicts were assigned to private individuals to work as servants. In return for shelter and 'rations and cloathes equal to that issued from the [Government] stores', a convict's master or mistress could expect labour equivalent to 'a full government task'. Failure to carry out their duties, or being absent without leave, landed a convict before the local magistrate. Musquito's contemporary, Danish convict Jorgen Jorgenson, claimed the Aboriginal convict was assigned as a stockkeeper to farmer Edward Kimberly of Antill's Ponds. Jorgenson suggested Musquito took a Tasmanian Aboriginal wife known as 'Gooseberry of Oyster Bay', but later 'killed the poor creature in the Government paddock'. There is no evidence to support this assertion, and Jorgenson was known for gross exaggeration. For example, he claimed himself to be a king of the Danes.[9]

Diplomatic efforts were made to have Musquito repatriated. On 17 August 1814, New South Wales Colonial Secretary Thomas Campbell wrote to Lieutenant Governor Davey in Van Diemen's Land:

> Application having been made by some of the Natives of this District on behalf of A Native formerly banished ... by the late Governor King to Norfolk Island and who was lately removed from thence to Port Dalrymple on the final evacuation of that Island, soliciting that He might be returned to his Native Place, His Excellency has been pleased to Accede to said Solicitation.

Davey was asked to send Musquito back to Sydney and told Musquito's brother Phillip was travelling to Van Diemen's Land on board the *Kangaroo* to arrange his repatriation. For unknown reasons, Davey did not return Musquito to Sydney. It is possible Musquito, described as 'an admirable bloodhound', was too valuable for his tracking skills to be lost to the colonial outpost. Instead, by the time Lieutenant Governor William Sorell replaced Davey, Musquito was a stockman employed by wealthy pastoralist and former marine Edward Lord. He was also working as a blacktracker to locate escaped convicts and bushrangers.[10]

Musquito was one of two servants described as 'natives of these Colonies' in Lord's employ. At the time, he was looked upon favourably both as a stockkeeper and as an explorer of sorts. While moving Lord's cattle, Musquito, Lord's 'faithful servant', 'discovered' Lawrenny Plains. The plains, located in the south-east of Van Diemen's Land inland from the town of Buckland, were identified on colonial maps as 'Mosquito Plains'.[11]

When Lord planned to visit Mauritius, he advertised his intention in the *Hobart Town Gazette* so that creditors could present their claims prior to his departure. In the same edition of the newspaper, 24 February 1818, he placed another notice that read 'Muskitoo and James Brown (Natives of these Colonies) proceeding to the Isle of France [Mauritius] with Mr. E Lord, all claims are desired to be presented at his house in Macquarie-street'. Lord apparently took two other servants with him instead of Musquito and James Brown, perhaps because Lieutenant Governor Sorell would not allow them to accompany their master on his cattle-buying expedition. In any case, Musquito was in Van Diemen's Land in 1818 where he and another Aboriginal convict, Duall, were utilised to track bushrangers. The latter was banished to Port Dalrymple in Van Diemen's Land in 1816 from country around Camden, New South Wales, called Muringong by Aborigines and the Cowpastures by colonists.[12]

By the time Duall was born in the mid-1790s most of the yam beds Aboriginal people in the greater Sydney area had previously relied on for food were destroyed. The land was being planted with crops by the settlers and conflict was escalating. In the 1790s, Dharawal people to the west of Sydney were yet to feel the full impact of the British arrival, as were their Darug neighbours north of the Nepean River and the Gundungurra who lived in the Blue Mountains. All three peoples shared a common hunting ground, a bountiful plain situated about 30 miles inland from Sydney. The first of the newcomers to intrude onto this country were 'bovine pioneers'.[13]

Two bulls and six cows strayed from the Government Herd five months after Sydney was established in January 1788. The sudden appearance of these 'beings with spears on the head' must have been very disconcerting for Dharawal people. Their 'sense of terror' was conveyed through a Dharawal representation of a bull that dominated the wall of Bull Cave to the north of present-day Campbelltown. The bull was 'so different in size to the soft-pawed kangaroo' to which local Aboriginal people were accustomed.[14]

The loss of the black cattle brought by the First Fleet from Cape Town while en route from England to Sydney was a devastating blow for a small colony struggling to feed itself. Seven years later, a large herd of cattle descended from the runaways was spotted more than 20 miles inland from Sydney Cove. Details of who relocated the herd, and the original number of animals that strayed, change with the teller of the tale. After the cattle were relocated, Governor John Hunter led an expedition to the area and renamed it the Cowpastures. In a contemporary account the escaped herd of cattle were said to be 'extremely wild and vicious'. The animals had 'taken possession of a most fertile valley'. The bovine coloniser that formed the most memorable impression was undoubtedly a particularly large and ferocious bull:

> A bull, fierce and of great size, made an attack on the party with such obstinacy that they were obliged to shoot him. He took six balls through the body before they durst approach him; but in revenge they eat [sic] a beef-steak cut from his rump on the spot.

A correlation could be drawn between the attitudes displayed by the Governor's party towards the wild bull who stood in their way, and actions taken by some colonists towards Aborigines. While some maintained good relations, many settlers along the Hawkesbury River 'shot any Aborigines they saw on their land'. On some occasions, these actions were officially sanctioned. People living beyond the bounds of Europe were often 'identified with the land they occupied' and 'imagined as being part of the natural world'. Just as a bull perceived to have gone wild could be shot, so too could Aboriginal people who were seen as being as wild as the lands they inhabited. Aborigines were described as 'wild men of the woods' or 'children of nature' well into the middle of the nineteenth century.[15]

After the cattle strayed, 'a fear of venturing far amongst the natives, then somewhat hostile, repressed all attempts to regain them'. The author of an account of their rediscovery could not fathom why 'in the almost starving state of the colony' the land where the cattle were found had not been explored previously in the hope of relocating the beasts. However, vestiges of the reluctance to traverse territory thought to be inhabited by hostile natives remained embedded within the psyches of the settler population of New South Wales for several decades following settlement.[16]

Duall enters the colonial records for the first time in 1814 as the expedition guide who accompanied the later famous explorer Hamilton Hume on his first exploratory journey. With Hume's brother, they travelled south from the Cowpastures to Berrima. Hume later claimed he and his brother 'discovered' the County of Argyle where Berrima is situated. However, it seems Hume's uncle John Kennedy, a man who featured prominently in Duall's life, preceded his nephews to Berrima. In his obituary, Kennedy was said to have been 'the first European who entered the new county of Argyle by the Bargo Brush, in the early part of the present century (if not before)'.[17]

By the time Duall and the Hume brothers returned from their 1814 journey, the colony was experiencing a severe drought that did not break until March 1816. It caused 'a very great Mortality amongst the Horned Cattle and Sheep throughout the colony' and 'greatly Injured the Crops'. The already stressed Districts of Airds and Appin, adjacent to, and including the Cowpastures, came under increasing strain from an influx of settlers that further displaced Aboriginal people and put pressure on resources. Conflict resulted between some colonists and Gundungurra people who traditionally came down from the Blue Mountains seeking food at the Cowpastures.[18]

The escalation in hostilities led Governor Macquarie to order a magisterial investigation. The magistrates found that 'cruel acts' were 'reciprocally perpetrated by each party'. There was adequate evidence 'to convince any unprejudiced man that the first personal attacks were made on the part of the settlers'. However, the available evidence was considered insufficient to warrant criminal prosecutions. Macquarie resolved that those involved in the hostilities would receive 'the most exemplary punishment', but because of the lack of prosecutions this ended up applying only to 'hostile natives' and not to colonists.[19]

The Governor ordered a punitive expedition against 'hostile' Aborigines at the Cowpastures. Settler John Warby was instructed to lead it. At about the same time that Musquito and Bull Dog were shipped to Norfolk Island, Warby became the first colonist officially sanctioned to reside at the Cowpastures. His role was 'Superintendent of the Wild Cattle'. The local knowledge Warby acquired and the relationships he fostered led to demand for his services as a European guide. On more than one occasion, this placed him in the awkward position of being ordered to assist in punitive expeditions against Aboriginal people he had befriended while other Aboriginal friends were commandeered as guides under his supervision.[20]

On the 1814 punitive expedition, Warby was accompanied by thirteen armed settlers and four 'friendly native' Darug guides. They pursued five Gundungurra men accused of murdering two white children. Those deaths, in turn, were in retaliation for the murder of an Aboriginal woman and child at settler William Broughton's farm in Appin. While the ultimately unsuccessful expedition was under way, local Dharawal sought refuge with some of the Cowpastures settlers. Dharawal leader Gogy frightened settlers with accounts of Gundungurra acts of cannibalism. The veracity of such claims is unproven, but these stories effectively distanced in colonists' eyes Dharawal from the Gundungurra, thus aiding in their protection.[21]

After the 1814 punitive expedition, tensions escalated. Macquarie noted a disturbing change in the 'disposition' of 'the Natives'. They began to take 'a portion of the maize and other grain' from the colonists just as it was becoming ripe and ready to harvest. The increasing numbers of Gundungurra descending from the mountains alarmed colonists. Aborigines seemed less frightened of firearms than previously. Under such volatile conditions, some Aborigines once thought 'friendly' were considered by some to have become 'hostile'. Duall, who in 1814 was a 'friendly' native, was identified as a 'hostile native' on the basis of information supplied to Macquarie by Cowpastures resident William Macarthur in 1816. A list was prepared identifying Aboriginal leaders fomenting ongoing hostility towards colonists.[22]

Macquarie's list of hostile natives was circulated to the 'fittest and best troops' from the colonial garrison. Where British troops were engaged in fighting indigenous peoples, they 'generally deployed as light infantry – that is, as skirmishers who moved and fired individually'. On 9 April 1816, in what was 'one of the most elaborate operations ever carried out by the British Army on the Australian frontier', the Governor instructed the colonial garrison, the 46th (South Devonshire) Regiment, to undertake punitive expeditions against Aborigines in the Nepean, Hawkesbury and Grose river valleys. Captain G B W Schaw proceeded with his light infantry to Windsor. Captain James Wallis and the grenadiers marched to Liverpool. Lieutenant Charles Dawe with his light infantry was directed to the Cowpastures.[23]

Documents in Macquarie's own handwriting survive in the present-day archives. He wrote to his military leaders that he wanted them to inflict 'exemplary punishments' on 'which of the guilty natives as you may be able to take alive'. He told them to 'make prisoners of all the natives of both sexes whom you may see … delivering them over in charge of the magistrates'. Horses and carts, he wrote, could be used to convey prisoners 'tied two and two together with ropes'. If people refused to surrender, the military was to 'fire upon and compel them to surrender, breaking and destroying the spears, clubs, and waddies of all those you take prisoners'. Any men killed, instructed Macquarie, were to be 'hanged up on trees in conspicuous situations, to strike the survivors with the greater terror'. Women and children were also to be taken prisoner. If killed, Macquarie wrote they were to be 'interred wherever they may happen to fall'. Macquarie asked the punitive expedition leaders to 'procure twelve boys and six girls ... for the Native Institution at Parramatta ... 'fine healthy good looking children ... aged between four and six years'. White guides accompanied each party. Friendly native guides were commandeered to point out the 'hostile' Aborigines.[24]

Warby was ordered to accompany Wallis's detachment to Airds and Appin with two Dharawal guides, Boodbury and Bundell. These men had been sheltering at *Glenfield*, the home of settler Dr Charles Throsby, since the previous month along with other local Aborigines, Gogy, Nighgingull and their families. Dharawal families sought refuge at *Glenfield* as early as February 1816.[25]

Throsby arrived in New South Wales in 1802 on board the *Coromandel* on which he served as Naval Surgeon. His skills were much needed in the new colony. He replaced the Medical Officer at Castle Hill while the incumbent took a year's leave. In 1804, Throsby was appointed Assistant Surgeon to the then newly established penal station at Newcastle. When the Commandant resigned and his replacement became insane, Throsby took over. He remained in charge until 1808, at which point he retired due to failing health. Throsby received several land grants, some of which were later rescinded, and eventually settled at Upper Minto (to the north of the Cowpastures and Campbelltown) where *Glenfield* was built in 1810. In his retirement, Throsby became an advocate for Aboriginal people and was also an explorer.[26]

As tensions escalated in the districts west of Sydney, Throsby wrote 'lengthy missives' to Macquarie 'to complain frequently about the maltreatment [of local Aborigines] by other settlers'. When he

learned of the Governor's plans to send in the soldiers, he was concerned that those at *Glenfield* would wrongly be held to account for
others' actions. Rather than invoking Macquarie's empathy, Throsby's
letters aroused the Governor's suspicions. Throsby was denounced
in a secret report of malcontents dated 1 December 1817 in which
Macquarie named 'Persons residing at present in the Colony of New
South Wales, who have always manifested an Opposition to the
Measures and Administration of Governor Macquarie'.[27]

As per the Governor's instructions, Wallis and his men marched
to Liverpool on 10 April 1816 and then, on the following day, to
an outlying farm. On their arrival, Warby refused to take responsibility for Boodbury and Bundell. Wallis agreed to keep the indigenous guides under surveillance. While he was distracted by having
to humour his drenched and exhausted troops, the Dharawal men
absconded. The loss of the Aboriginal guides was the only circum-
stance on which Wallis commented specifically in the covering letter
to his official report on the punitive expedition. Yet the events that
transpired over the course of the coming week have since become
notorious.

Initially, Wallis gathered intelligence about the activities of Aborigines in the area. He heard on 14 April about a group of Gundungurra being nearby and organised an attack on the camp at
Broughton's farm near Appin during the night of 17 April. Being
woken by the intrusion of armed soldiers was terrifying. The noise
and the darkness confused people, and in their terror at the ensuing
violence at least fourteen Gundungurra fled over nearby cliffs, falling to their deaths below. According to Wallis's report, he ordered
his men 'to make as many prisoners as possible and to be careful in
sparing and saving the women and children'. Yet in the Gundungurra
camp, only two women and three children remained. The rest were
shot by the military or rushed 'in despair over the precipice'. This
tragedy has since become commonly known as the Appin Massacre.

Among the dead lay Durelle and Kinabygal, two of 'the most hostile of the natives'. Complying with Macquarie's instructions, Wallis had Lieutenant Parker take the men's bodies 'to be hanged' in a conspicuous position. Wallis hoped in vain this might entice their Aboriginal guides to reappear.[28]

Wallis apparently sanctioned the post-mortem removal of Kinabygal's head. In an 'unplanned and largely unimagined consequence of complex negotiations, accommodations, and conflicts that characterized relations between colonists and Indigenous peoples', Kinabygal's severed head left the colony secreted in the luggage of the Naval Surgeon Patrick Hill. On his return to Britain, Hill gave Kinabygal's skull to Sir George Mackenzie, a mineralogist with a strong interest in the emerging field of phrenology, a pseudo science based on measurements and characteristics of the skull. Mackenzie put it to extensive use in his 1820 *Illustrations of Phrenology* using his analysis of Kinabygal's skull as evidence of a lack of linguistic and mathematical ability. He claimed Kinabygal would have been incapable of showing compassion towards colonists. Mackenzie concluded that although 'the progress of these people may be slow … much may be done for these miserable race of beings'.[29]

Four days after the bodies were publicly displayed, Parker went to the settler Woodhouse's farm 'to receive the same evening Duall and Quiet [Quayat] two hostile natives who had been taken on Mr Kennedy's farm in the morning'. Broughton's neighbour, Kennedy, was a known sympathiser towards Aboriginal people. Several years earlier, in 1814, Yellooming and Bitugally were implicated in a payback killing (aided by Duall) in retribution for the murders of their family members. When they were found hiding at Kennedy's farm, Kennedy and his nephew had successfully persuaded Wallis not to arrest the fugitives. This time, though, the soldiers were not going to be deterred. Guards were posted at Kennedy's farm and on 22 April 1816 Parker arrested Duall and Quiet. The next morning Duall was taken under police escort to Liverpool. Quiet was detained by Parker to show him the location of 'that body of natives to which he belong'd' before being taken to Liverpool Gaol.[30]

Macquarie recalled the three military detachments to Sydney at the end of April 1816, leaving behind a few soldiers at Macarthur's farm at the Cowpastures. The *Sydney Gazette* reported their return, suggesting the punitive expedition was not 'altogether so successful as might have been wished'. Dawe's detachment, from which the 'friendly native guides' had also absconded, was the only force to encounter a significant number of Gundungurra.[31]

Regardless of the limited success, the participants were amply rewarded. Schaw and Wallis each received 15 gallons of spirits while three junior-ranking officers, including Parker and the Assistant Surgeon, got 10 gallons. Each of the sixty-eight soldiers was given a pair of new shoes and half a pint of spirits. White guides were paid £12 each and issued with slops (clothing), blankets and some stores. In contrast, Aboriginal guides were not given any money but were instead issued with slops, provisions to last four days, a blanket, half a pound of tobacco, and half a pint of spirits. The disparity in payment demonstrates the men's different status on the fringes of colonial society. Despite the relatively meagre reward bestowed by the colonial administration, the Aboriginal guides had the gratitude of their people because they had for the most part managed to keep the military away from those most sought.[32]

The punitive expeditionary parties took only a handful of Aboriginal prisoners. All except Duall were released from custody after one month's confinement.[33] Duall was left in gaol awaiting the Governor's pleasure. A full three months passed before his fate was made public by Macquarie in the *Sydney Gazette*. The Governor described Duall as 'dangerous to the peace and good order of the community'. He mentioned that Duall was initially sentenced to death, but that he was overturning the sentence:

By virtue therefore of the power vested in me, as Governor in Chief of this Territory, and moved with compassion towards the said criminal, in consideration of his ignorance of the laws and duties of civilized nations, I do hereby remit the punishment of death, which his repeated crimes and offences had justly merited and incurred, and commute the same into banishment from this part of His Majesty's Territory of New South Wales to Port Dalrymple, in Van Diemen's Land, for the full term of seven years.

Banishing Duall, reasoned Macquarie, would deter other Aboriginal people from committing similar 'flagrant and sanguinary acts'. Macquarie's policy of exclusion saw Duall removed not only from colonial society but also from his tribe. The punishment was meant to be exemplary, as explained in the *Sydney Gazette* on the same day Duall's banishment was announced. The editor George Howe referred to the anticipated outcome of pacifying the 'hostile' natives through the use of fear and intimidation:

> The banishment of the native *Dewal* … may possibly produce a greater dread in the minds of his predatory associates than if he had been killed when in the act of plunder. The doubt of what may be his fate, when absent, is likely to excite a dread which may render them less liable to a similar treatment, the justness of which they cannot at the same time challenge, as they are sensible that the crimes of this offender were enormous.[34]

Macquarie's strategy had economic consequences. Aboriginal people traditionally lived in small groups. Depriving a group of a young man like Duall reduced its capacity to hunt and to defend itself. Within the context of sporadic frontier conflict, Duall's absence also deprived Dharawal of a strategist and a man of fighting age and capacity.

Given that Duall enjoyed long-established relationships with key colonists at the Cowpastures, banishing him removed one of the significant cultural brokers from the district. Such a move may have been intended to break down what Macquarie viewed as opposition from men like Throsby and Kennedy who had formed associations with Duall, Gogy and other significant Dharawal leaders.

By the time Duall's fate was revealed in the columns of the *Sydney Gazette*, he was already on board the brig *Kangaroo* with one hundred other male convicts bound for Van Diemen's Land. Also on board the ship was a letter from Macquarie to the Commandant at Port Dalrymple, Brevet Major James Stewart, informing him that the 'Black Native' Duall was 'to be kept at Hard Labour and to be fed in the same manner as the other Convicts'.[35]

2

Diverging destinies

In 1816 Van Diemen's Land was in a state of chaos. In the letter conveyed along with Duall on the *Kangaroo*, Macquarie apologised to Lieutenant Governor Davey for being unable to provide badly needed stores and clothing 'there being very few of the former, and none at all of the latter now remaining in the King's Stores here'. The following year, Davey's replacement, Lieutenant Governor William Sorell, petitioned Macquarie for relief. Sorell told him that many Van Diemen's Land convicts were 'totally without bedding'. Many of the convicts had 'not had Jackets, etc., for three Years'. Two years later, the Government stores at Port Dalrymple remained in a state of 'complete destitution'. No more than 200 convict labourers could be victualled there.[1]

These hardships led to anarchy within the ranks of the colonial administration and the garrison. In 1814, 'bands of runaway convicts' known as bushrangers or banditti plagued Van Diemen's Land. The term 'bushranger' had been used in the Australian colonies from 1805 onwards and was borrowed from the North American context where it referred to skilled frontiersmen. Over time, its meaning in the Australian penal colonies changed. By 1814, 'bushranger' and 'banditti' denoted an escaped convict who was living off his wits in the bush, or a criminal living in the bush and getting by through robbing others. Such men functioned symbolically as 'a personification of all the convict system's evils'. The former Acting Deputy Surveyor of Lands Peter Mills and George Williams, the former Acting Deputy

Commissary of Provisions at Port Dalrymple, led bands of such men. As Macquarie observed, Mills and Williams had until recently 'held official and credible Situations under this Government'. They took to the bush to avoid paying their debts.[2]

Soldiers from the colonial garrison at Port Dalrymple descended into a 'state of intoxication and insubordination'. They set fire to their barracks, burnt their fences and those of their officers, and destroyed the Commandant's gardens. The soldiers also robbed the Assistant Pilot and Acting Chief Constable before driving them from their respective stations. The situation at Port Dalrymple was exacerbated by the 'highly insubordinate and unmilitary' conduct of their Commandant, James Stewart. Stewart was recalled, and most of his men were redeployed to India. In March 1818 the more orderly 48th Regiment replaced the unruly 46th.[3]

When Sorell took office in Hobart Town on 9 April 1817 he was expected to 'restore order and bring direction and organization into the government' of Van Diemen's Land. One of his tasks was to address the challenge posed to the authority of his administration by bushrangers. One man who particularly vexed Sorell was Michael Howe, a convict who arrived in the colony on 19 October 1812 on the *Indefatigable* to serve a sentence of seven years' transportation for highway robbery. In 1815, Howe took over leadership of a gang of bushrangers that had formed about five years earlier. An audacious man, Howe wrote letters to both Davey and his replacement Sorell in which he styled himself variously as the 'Lieutenant-Governor of the Woods' and 'Governor of the Ranges'.[4]

In 1818, the reward promised in return for Howe's capture was raised after he murdered one of his would-be captors William Drew, also known as Slambow. Originally set at one hundred guineas, the incentive was increased to include Sorell's recommendation to the Governor of a free pardon and a passage to England for 'any Crown Prisoner who shall be the means of apprehending the said Michael

Howe'. Sorell regularly sent out detachments of the colonial garrison to scour the countryside for Howe. He also called for volunteers to track the wanted man.[5]

Historian Christine Wise stated that 'amongst the "volunteers" were Musquito, another Aborigine from Sydney called Dual [sic] and two convicts named Worrell and McGill'. If Duall did indeed volunteer, there seems to be no surviving evidence in the archive to confirm this. What is apparent, however, was that a number of blacktrackers were utilised in the search for the elusive bushranger. One of the trackers was Howe's former companion Mary Cockerill, a Tasmanian Aboriginal woman also known as Black Mary. Another Aboriginal woman (unnamed) is also referred to as working with Cockerill and a contingent of the 46th Regiment to track bushrangers.[6]

Thomas 'Jack' Worrell later reminisced about life in Van Diemen's Land, recalling how the search party after Howe went out with a blacktracker, 'a native that lived in the service of Mr Carlisle, and who had been ill-treated by the Bush-rangers but a few days before, when they were plundering his master's house'. Howe and his gang, which at that stage included Cockerill, robbed several properties in New Norfolk in April 1815 where they killed several local settlers, including Carlisle. Worrell's story predates Duall's arrival in Van Diemen's Land by a year, suggesting that the unnamed blacktracker was probably Musquito.[7]

On 13 October 1817, Sorell wrote to Macquarie about shipping Carlisle's alleged murderers to Sydney on the *Jupiter* together with witnesses. One of the Crown evidences, or witnesses, was Cockerill. Sorell told Macquarie the 'native Woman ... had lived three Years in the Woods with Howe' and that since being 'taken' by the military had 'been the Constant Guide of Serjt. McCarthy's party, which has, through her Capacity for tracking foot-marks, been enabled so often to come up with Bush-rangers'. McCarthy, of the 46th Regiment, led one of several military parties pursuing the bushrangers who plagued

Van Diemen's Land. In the same letter, Sorell petitioned Macquarie on behalf of Musquito:

> a native of Port Jackson, who has been some years in this
> Settlement and who has also served constantly as a guide with
> one of the parties, and has been extremely useful and well
> conducted, also at his own desire goes to Sydney. I beg leave
> further to solicit Your Excellency's humane consideration of him
> on account of his useful Services.[8]

It has often been suggested that Sorell sought to repatriate Musquito because his work as a blacktracker led to some Van Diemen's Land convicts resenting and taunting him. This notion seems to have arisen through a misreading of the Lieutenant Governor's letter to Macquarie. In the letter in question, Sorell also sought a pardon for McGill, 'a prisoner for life' from England. He stated that McGill, because of his 'very great service against the Bush-rangers', had become 'unavoidably odious amongst the prisoners' in Van Diemen's Land. So it seems it was McGill rather than Musquito who attracted the convicts' opprobrium.[9]

In September 1818, McGill and Musquito nearly apprehended Howe. McGill was kangaroo hunting at the Fat Doe River when Howe robbed his hut. McGill later set out with Musquito to track the bushranger. They followed him for several days and saw Howe receiving flour from one of Lord's stockkeepers, William Davis, who later denied having seen the man. Surreptitious help was essential to men like Howe who evaded the law for lengthy periods.[10]

Commenting on Howe's long career, Carl Canteri suggested that it owed something to the patronage of Lord, a powerful player in Vandemonian colonial society whose economic competitors suffered losses at the hands of Howe and his gang. Lord's stockkeeper's ready assistance to Howe suggests the servant may have had his master's support in this. It also raises questions about whether Musquito, also a servant of Lord's, allowed Howe to slip through his grasp when he and McGill found the bushranger at his campfire. McGill later claimed that he and Musquito fired their fowling-pieces at Howe as he fled the scene but failed to hit him. The following month, a military party came across Howe and he was shot dead. When the reward for Howe was shared out, Worrell received £40 and was subsequently granted a free pardon. However, Sorell's intention to repatriate Musquito to Sydney was never carried out.[11]

Two months after Howe's death, Macquarie's secretary, John Campbell, wrote to Sorell regarding several matters including passengers embarking on the *Prince Leopold* about to sail from Sydney. Cockerill, the woman he referred to as 'Black Mary', was to have been on board but at the last minute sickness saw her return to Van Diemen's Land delayed while her passage was allocated to someone else. In the same letter, Campbell wrote that 'the Governor requests that you will please to send hither by the earliest opportunity, a Native Black Man called Dicall [sic] who was Transported about two years ago to Port Dalrymple'. Duall was returned to Sydney aboard the *Sindbad*, arriving a few days prior to 30 January 1819.[12]

Duall's early recall from Van Diemen's Land was arranged to suit Dr Charles Throsby, who requested his old friend's assistance as an interpreter on an exploratory journey. Macquarie compelled colonial diarists such as Throsby to focus on ascertaining the suitability or otherwise of the land being traversed for pastoral and agricultural purposes. He also expected them to advise him on the extent to which local Aborigines might resist intruding colonists. With their focus on these imperatives, colonial explorers set out with a few friends, Aboriginal guides, provisions and horses, and kept journals of their journeys of 'discovery' to meet the Governor's demands.

Throsby and his party, including Duall, set out from Airds on 25 April 1819 to find a direct route from the Cowpastures to

Bathurst. They were accompanied by another interpreter, Bian, and guided by Coocoogong who was a Gundungurra man. Throsby maintained good working relationships with the Aboriginal guides and interpreters who accompanied him. He saw to it that they were adequately provisioned, even risking such provisioning being at his expense despite being on official business. He also sought rewards for the men. Throsby asked that Coocoogong be designated 'Chief of the Burrakburrak Tribe, of which place he is a Native', suggesting that this 'may be the means of tranquilizing the Natives about Bathurst', an area that the settlers intended for more intensive occupation. In addition, Throsby asked that 'a Plate as a Reward of Merit' be bestowed upon Duall and Bian.[13]

On receiving news of the successful conclusion of Throsby's expedition, Macquarie ordered that the proposed titles and breastplates be bestowed upon Coocoogong and Duall (no further mention was made of Bian). Throsby was rewarded with a land grant of 1000 acres in what the Governor termed the new country. The remaining white members of the expeditionary party received smaller land grants in recognition for their services. Duall went on to have a distinguished career as an interpreter and guide to numerous exploratory expeditions and was one of the 'sable gentry' at the Governor's annual feast for Aborigines at Parramatta on 17 January 1826. He sat at the head of his tribe who 'raised three cheers' when they were served soup, beef, plum pudding and grog. Duall was last mentioned in the colonial records as receiving a blanket in the annual distribution in 1833 along with his kinsman Quiet. At the time, Duall was aged around 40 and was living at the Cowpastures with his wife and child.[14]

Sometime after Duall's departure from Van Diemen's Land, Musquito withdrew from colonial society, exchanging his stockman's position for life in the bush with a group of Aboriginal people known as the 'tame mob'. This group of around twenty to thirty had 'absconded from their proper tribes' and lived within the settled districts surrounding Hobart Town. The group was thought of as being inoffensive and quite distinct from 'the wild natives in the bush'. Wesleyan missionary Reverend William Horton noted that 'though they have been accustomed for several years to behold the superior comforts and pursuits of civilized man, they have not advanced one step from their original barbarism'. They preferred instead to remain 'perfectly naked' around their campfires in the bush. Musquito claimed he 'should like it very well' to 'till the ground and live as the English do' but assured Horton none of his companions would be interested in doing likewise.[15]

As well as consorting with the tame mob, Musquito formed an association with the Oyster Bay people. During late 1823 and 1824, they attacked settlers' properties on the east coast of Van Diemen's Land and killed several men. The 10 June 1824 spearing of Matthew Osborne was described in lurid detail in the *Hobart Town Gazette* with more than a full column given over to a vivid account of the incident. The editor blamed the 'mischief' on Musquito for corrupting local Aboriginal people having 'taught them a portion of his own villainy, and incited them time after time to join in his delinquencies'. By July 1824, the military and constabulary had been 'actively pursuing' Musquito and his cohort for some time. The following month, Musquito reportedly speared a man at Pittwater, a place to the north-east of Hobart Town. Three weeks later he was apprehended by a local Aboriginal man called Tegg, who shot him. Musquito 'ran a considerable distance' before succumbing to his wounds and being taken into captivity. He was taken to the Colonial Hospital in Hobart Town where the Lieutenant Governor went to see him.[16]

By December 1824, Musquito was sufficiently recovered from his wounds to stand trial in Hobart Town alongside 'Black Jack', an Aboriginal man from Van Diemen's Land. Without the aid of any legal counsel they were arraigned before the Supreme Court of Van

Diemen's Land. The men entered pleas of not guilty in relation to a charge of 'aiding and abetting in the wilful murder of William Holly-oak, at Grindstone Bay, on the 15th of November, 1823' and to a further charge of 'being principals in the second degree for aiding and abetting in the wilful murder of Mammoa, … [a] Otaheitean'. As the defendants were not Christians and were therefore unable to take the oath required of witnesses, they were unable to tender any evidence to the court on their own behalf. They were further disadvantaged through not being provided with an interpreter. As newspaperman Henry Melville later explained in relation to the trial:

> What mockery! The wretched prisoners were not aware of one tittle of evidence adduced against them, were totally ignorant of having committed crime, and knew not why or wherefore they were placed in the criminal's dock, and so many eyes fixed upon them.[17]

After hearing evidence from white witnesses, the jury found Musquito guilty of the first charge, while Black Jack was found not guilty. Both men were acquitted of murdering Mammoa. Black Jack was later charged with murdering Patrick McCarthy at Sorell Plains and was found guilty. Musquito and Black Jack were sentenced to hang. In a frequently cited exchange that was said to have taken place between Musquito and his gaoler after the sentence was announced, the condemned man apparently said 'hanging no good for black fellow … very good for white fellow, for *he* used to it'.[18]

On 25 February 1825, eight men including Musquito and Black Jack were hanged at Hobart Town. The *Hobart Town Gazette* reported that 'for the first time, the scaffold was erected within the Gaol-walls, but in view of the town'. The condemned men joined in a hymn and prayers while assembled together on the platform awaiting their deaths. The Reverend William Bedford addressed the assembled crowd on behalf of the prisoners to 'acknowledge for them the justice of their condemnation'. Following this, 'the hapless offenders after a short interval were launched into eternity'. Not everyone in Hobart Town concurred with Bedford's assertion that justice was being done, or at least being seen to be done in the case of Musquito and Black Jack. Black Jack was said to have known 'scarcely ... half-a-dozen English words, and the whole of these were most horrid imprecations, taught him by the bushrangers and stock-keepers', while both men had not been acquainted with English law. Controversy surrounded their trial and some considered it 'a mere mockery of justice, placing warriors on their trial for murder, when they were only defending themselves from the attacks of the men who were about to become judges [jurors] in their own cause'.[19]

While colonial commentators showed some sympathy towards Black Jack, the Aboriginal convicts transported to Van Diemen's Land from New South Wales were seen in a very different light. An extraordinary story circulated that Duall had been 'transported from Sydney, for chopping off the right arm of his wife: he said she should "make no more dough-boy"', which was an oblique reference to miscegenation. Equally extraordinary stories circulated about Musquito who was said to have been transported for the rape and murder of a woman, or because he killed his Aboriginal wife. Earlier celebratory accounts of Musquito as a blacktracker responsible for apprehending bushrangers and as the 'discoverer' of Lawrenny Plains were superseded by myths after his death. He was relegated to the position of 'violent, treacherous, murderous, hostile native' until becoming rehabilitated as an Aboriginal resistance leader in post-colonial renditions of his life story.[20]

3

Jackey's pitiful state

As the steamer *William IV* left Newcastle in April 1834, an Aboriginal passenger known simply as Jackey cried bitterly. It was very unlikely that he would ever see his kin or country again. Convict irons cut deeply into the man's flesh. Entirely naked, Jackey was left exposed to the elements on the wooden deck, restrained by convict chains that weighed heavily on his limbs. The chains were a matter of course for Aboriginal prisoners, who showed a remarkable propensity for escape. And a glance at these restraints would suffice to reassure cabin passengers that Jackey would pose no threat on the journey south.[1]

William IV regularly conveyed prisoners down the coast to Sydney, the site of the colony's Supreme Court. The sturdy wooden vessel was affectionately known to locals as 'Little Billy'. She was a symbol of progress: the colony's first ocean-going paddle steamer. Built at the Deptford Shipyards just up the William's River from Newcastle, at Clarence Town, she was launched on 14 November 1831, setting off under sail for Sydney where her engines were to be fitted. Her arrival marked the beginning of a regular freight and passenger service along the south coast of New South Wales.[2]

Over the four decades following its founding, the canvas characterising early colonial Sydney gave way to more substantial buildings. The sandstone structures lent the burgeoning town an air of permanence and gentility. In the early decades of the nineteenth century, convict workers sweated and bled as they hewed blocks of sandstone out of the natural quarry down at the Rocks by the waterfront. Many workers lived alongside the quarry in a haphazard network of small cottages, where they birthed the next generation and from where they buried their dead. Their forced labour gradually transformed the town. Churches glowing in the golden hues of the locally quarried sandstone began to adorn Sydney streets. The colonial town's other most necessary structure was forged from the same solid material. Sydney Gaol opened for business in 1801.

Sydney Gaol was a far cry from the open-air prison that was early Sydney. The convict settlement had leaked like a sieve. It was most likely a boatload of absconders who were the first Europeans to intrude on Jackey's traditional lands. Their clandestine departure from Sydney Cove at the end of the eighteenth century was followed by a sojourn up the coast, probably to what was later Newcastle. The escapees then sailed off to Timor, apparently in a bid to flee to China, before being retaken. Others followed, and fights began to break out between the colonial intruders and local Aboriginal people.[3]

A particularly violent altercation took place between some fishermen and Aborigines at Port Stephens in 1796, several years before Jackey's birth. The fishermen were accused of molesting Aboriginal people, and the Aborigines sought retribution. This series of violent exchanges set the tone for ongoing interactions between the two groups. Following the fight, it became common practice around Port Stephens for these early colonial intruders to 'fire upon the natives whenever they approached, and to deprive them of their women whenever the opportunity offered'.[4]

By the time Jackey was born, around 1800, speculators were arriving in the region to seek their fortunes in coal. In 1804, a small settlement called King's Town was established at the site of present-day Newcastle. Diplomacy ensured smoother relations between local Aborigines and the newcomers. The main negotiator was a leader of the Broken Bay Tribe, Bungaree. Wearing a cocked hat and eclectic second-hand military uniforms, Bungaree was a familiar sight around Sydney. Some colonists respected his intelligence and good humour, but others mocked him. Celebrated as the first Aborigine to circumnavigate Australia (he accompanied Matthew Flinders' expedition in the *Investigator* in 1801–02), Bungaree was well travelled. He was favoured by a succession of colonial governors, whom he was adept at mimicking. When an escort was needed to accompany an Aboriginal group from Port Stephens back to their country from Sydney in 1804, Bungaree was the obvious choice. Once there, he acted as an interpreter between the colonists and local Aborigines and helped establish friendly relations.[5]

King's Town was separated from Sydney by an eight-hour sea journey and surrounded by steep hills. Its relative isolation made it an ideal location to ship the more troublesome among Sydney's convicts. The burgeoning but ill-housed, under-fed and poorly dressed convict population was kept occupied mining coal, harvesting timber and salt, lime burning, and engaging in public works. From 1805 to 1808, the convict workers at Newcastle were overseen by Colonial Surgeon Dr Charles Throsby who acted as Commandant at the penal station. Captain James Wallis, the man who commanded the soldiers who apprehended Duall, later served as Commandant at Newcastle following the 1816 punitive expedition.[6]

Despite the uninviting countryside, many convicts chanced their luck in the unknown. After Captain Wallis assured the convicts of their death or recapture at the hands of local Aborigines if they tried to escape, the number of escape attempts declined. To heighten convicts' fears of Aborigines, the Commandant ensured that no action was taken against any locals who killed escaped convicts. The authorities were also keen to restrict contact between Aborigines and escaped convicts in case convict absconders encouraged the locals to violence against the colonists.[7]

Aboriginal men were encouraged to take on a policing role for the penal station. John Thomas Bigge, the Oxford-educated judge sent as a Commissioner by the British Government to New South Wales in 1817 to report on the colony, watched Aborigines working as blacktrackers for the Newcastle penal station. Bigge's favourable impression of the trackers led to Aboriginal people being employed as blacktrackers for convict establishments at Bathurst, Wellington Valley, Port Macquarie and Moreton Bay. Intriguingly, Aborigines distinguished between convicts and free people. The missionary Reverend Lancelot Threlkeld told the New South Wales Supreme Court that in his opinion the practice of rewarding Aborigines with the clothing of runaway convicts they apprehended led to Aborigines drawing 'a distinction between free settlers and what they call "*croppies*" – that is, prisoners'. They treated convicts more harshly. 'If they met a free man in the bush they would not hurt him', explained Threlkeld, 'but if they met a prisoner they would probably strip him'.[8]

By the time Jackey reached adulthood, local convict attitudes towards Aborigines had hardened. A number of convicts received the lash in 1819 for assaulting Aborigines. Tensions increased following the execution in 1820 of the convict absconder John Kirby following the death of King Burrigan (also known as Jack, Chief of the Newcastle Tribe). Kirby stabbed King Burrigan while some Aboriginal men were trying to capture him. He became the only white man to hang for the death of an Aborigine prior to the contentious hangings following the Myall Creek Massacre almost two decades later. Although Edward Colthurst was hanged in 1826 after being tried for murdering an Aboriginal man, Tommy, he was capitally convicted for piracy rather than murder. When Macquarie assented to hanging Kirby, Attorney General Saxe Bannister, remembered for his 'humane and philanthropic disposition', concluded that 'the law of jurisdiction in the Colonial Courts was well settled'. White people could and would be punished capitally for taking the lives of Aboriginal people.[9]

By the mid-1820s, the free population in New South Wales was growing. Many convicts' terms had expired. The Newcastle penal station closed down in 1823. The first two generations of children born free in the colony were grown to adulthood. To create new opportunities, Bigge recommended the development of a capitalist pastoralist economy in New South Wales. His proposal made sense. The colony had a growing reputation for raising fine wool. Plenty of convict labour was available. Involving convicts in the pastoral industry could offset the costs of feeding, clothing and housing them. The only question that remained was from where the finance would come.[10]

Early in 1824, meetings held in London resulted in the Australian Agricultural Company and the Van Diemen's Land Company being formed. With a company charter modelled on the English East India Company, the Australian Agricultural Company received royal assent in 1824. The November 1825 arrival of the Australian Agricultural Company's inaugural Executive Resident, Robert Dawson, at Port Stephens with 79 settlers, 720 sheep, 12 head of cattle and seven horses heralded a new phase in relations between Aborigines and colonists. Aboriginal people were among the most productive of the Company's employees. They tended the sheep and cattle, worked as surveyors and hutkeepers, and acted as messengers and envoys. Aboriginal men also rowed boats and worked as builders and constables. They were very well adapted to local conditions, whereas imported convict labourers struggled to adjust to the ferocious summers.[11]

The treatment meted out to Company convicts by local Aborigines was very different from the way they dealt with convict absconders from Port Macquarie. Convicts who escaped from the northern penal settlement tried to make their way down to Newcastle. Company Executive Resident Dawson described how 'the few that arrive alive' were 'stripped and speared in some parts of the body by the Natives'. He also saw a man 'who came across naked and speared through both legs'. These men did not realise there were protocols to follow when travelling across Aboriginal land. The locals were far less forgiving of these strangers' transgressions than they were of Company convicts.[12]

The Australian Agricultural Company followed the Newcastle penal station in using Aborigines as police. It cost a fraction of the expense incurred in using convict constables. Yet not everyone agreed with the practice. In his 1828 report on the settlement, Dr Alexander Nesbit recommended Aborigines be used only for tracing stolen property or apprehending convict absconders. He thought Aboriginal men too ignorant of European customs to be useful. He thought them too inconsistent to be reliable employees. But Nesbit also admitted the Company was doing a fine job in exciting Aboriginal interest in European goods. By creating Aboriginal demand for manufactured items, the Company ensured that Aborigines remained willing to work to gratify their newly stimulated desires.[13]

As the 1820s drew to a close, options available to Aborigines not associated with the Australian Agricultural Company were increasingly limited. By the time Jackey was arrested in 1834, the number of sheep run by the Company had increased from 720 to 36 615. The Company took up major land grants adjacent to the William's River. The Church and School Corporation also occupied a large tract of land. An influx of free settlers added to the large-scale expropriation of Aboriginal land.[14]

The influx of free settlers into the Hunter Valley and the establishment of large, privately operated pastoral runs transformed the social order at the William's River. Aboriginal people were no longer viewed as trading partners. Those outside the Australian Agricultural Company became fringe dwellers. Pushed to the margins of society, they were left to eke out a living as best they could. Many were reduced to begging for food. 'Domesticated' Aborigines such as

Jackey sometimes traded their labour with the free men and convict workers employed on the stations. For fetching wood and water, they received small quantities of tobacco or other European commodities such as tea, flour and sugar. Aboriginal women and children were constantly to be seen about the colonists' huts in Newcastle: 'it was quite common to see a black woman dressed up with an old gown or cap, and dandling in her arms the infant of a white woman; while others, especially young girls, frequently assisted their white neighbours at the wash-tub', Dawson wrote. They received food and cast-off clothing in return for their labour.[15]

The colonial mindset evident in Dawson's writings led him to justify Company interference in the lives of local Aboriginal people. He saw Aborigines as 'untutored children of nature' who deserved to be treated kindly, but firmly. Aborigines, Dawson thought, were unable to control themselves in their apparent pursuit of selfish pleasures. By way of contrast, the colonists pictured themselves as well-mannered intellectuals who could show restraint. This colonial mindset was shared by many, including local landowners George Mackenzie and Archibald Mossman who occupied large tracts of Jackey's traditional lands. Both men were intimately involved in the events surrounding Jackey's arrest and deportation.[16]

Mackenzie and Mossman were part of a wider colonial network that extended well beyond New South Wales. Mackenzie was the son and namesake of Sir George Mackenzie, the Scottish phrenologist who received Kinabygal's severed head following the 1816 punitive expedition. A decade after receiving the Aboriginal skull, the elder Mackenzie wrote to fellow Scot John Gladstone, a wealthy merchant and slave owner who lived in Liverpool, England, to seek his endorsement for Mackenzie's son George who was departing for New South Wales. Gladstone wrote to the Colonial Secretary, Huskisson, who provided a letter of recommendation to facilitate the younger Mackenzie's entry into colonial society.[17]

When young George left Dublin for New South Wales, he carried Huskisson's letter of recommendation and £500 from his father. The capital put up by Sir George entitled his son to a land grant immediately upon his arrival. The young man was keen to take up land near two friends who had made successes of themselves in the colony. It is likely that these two were fellow Scots, the Mossman twins, Archibald and George.[18] Like Mackenzie, the Mossmans benefitted from patronage. When the brothers had tired of their tin mining and cotton plantations in the West Indies, they moved to New South Wales. When Archibald Mossman arrived in the colony in 1828, he was recommended to the 'notice and protection' of Governor Darling in a letter from Under-Secretary Stanley. In orders dated 6 February 1829, he and his brother received grants of 2560 acres of Crown land. Archibald Mossman submitted his selection in June 1829. It was on the north bank of the William's River, upstream from Mr Justice Dowling's grant, and to the east of the Government Surveyor's land. George Mossman's grant ran along the east boundary of his brother's property.[19]

By the 1830s, the contrast between Aboriginal lives and the colonial fortunes enjoyed by gentlemen settlers could hardly have been greater. Men such as Mackenzie and the Mossmans at the William's River celebrated clement weather that increased the yield of milk from their dairy cows and improved their pastures. Aboriginal numbers were dwindling rapidly. There were only about 500 remaining in the region, just a fraction of the estimated population at first contact. Many who survived the introduced diseases and frontier violence retreated to the hills at the upper reaches of the William's River. From there Aborigines, sometimes with convict absconders and bushrangers, attacked colonists who were usurping their ancestral lands.[20]

During the night of 2 April 1834, a group of Aboriginal men targeted some convict servants assigned to Archibald Mossman and robbed the workers' hut. Nobody was killed. However, Mossman's men feared the Aborigines would return to murder them. Two convicts rode over to get help from George Mackenzie's station. When Mackenzie heard about the night's events, he gave his overseer Thomas Rodwell some guns loaded with powder and buckshot. He told Rodwell to get together a party of men from his and Mossman's stations to arrest some of the Aborigines.

When Rodwell and eight others rode into the Aboriginal camp, they did not conceal their weapons. The overseer saw one of Mossman's convict servants, John Flynn, hit by a spear. It pierced the man's body just beneath the shoulder blade. Flynn immediately pulled out the spear then chased Jackey, the man thought to have thrown it. Jackey was well known to Rodwell because he occasionally laboured at Mackenzie's station. After a brief chase, Jackey was taken into captivity. The overseer inspected Flynn's wound in front of the prisoner. He did not notice much blood and therefore thought the wound was not dangerous to the convict worker's health.

It took Flynn two days to walk the 22 miles to the nearest courthouse at William's River with the prisoner Jackey to report the attack. Flynn's deposition was sworn before station owner George Mackenzie. Jackey was compelled to watch as Flynn made his mark upon the document that led to the Aboriginal prisoner being charged with assault and gaoled. Two unnamed 'native blacks' were present to 'explain to the prisoner the nature of the accusation against him'.

Because of the considerable distance from Sydney, law and order at a mundane level was a local concern. Regional landowners sat on the bench of magistrates and acted as Justices of the Peace. Constables came from within the lower ranks of the local community. At the William's River, the constable was Thomas Rodwell, Mackenzie's station overseer.

With local landowners doubling as the local judiciary, conflicts of interest could arise. But the British population in outlying regional areas was small and economic circumstances harsh. These fledgling settlements could not afford dedicated, and therefore disinterested, upholders of the law. This did not mean, though, that practices at a local level were beyond censure. Mackenzie was later forced to defend before the Supreme Court his and Rodwell's actions against local Aborigines. He argued their actions were based on a need to enforce the law. Yet in 1834 Rodwell was temporarily relieved of his duties as a constable after eleven years of service. He was not reappointed until 3 February 1838. While Mackenzie remained beyond reproach, having his man removed temporarily from his position as a constable would have been disadvantageous to a station owner with local interests to protect.

Flynn's health unexpectedly worsened. The convict set out on foot for Newcastle the day after handing Jackey over to Mackenzie to have his spear wound treated. Along the way, his health began to deteriorate rapidly. Fortunately, an Australian Agricultural Company dray was on the road. Company men found Flynn, took him to the *Settler's Arms* at Paterson's River, and summoned the Colonial Surgeon Dr Isaac Scott Nind. Nind later claimed in court that Flynn was in a dying state when he first saw him. When the patient died that evening, the charge against Jackey was upgraded from assault to wilful murder.

The gravity of the charge meant that Jackey's case had to be heard before the Supreme Court in Sydney. The first step involved an arduous walk from the William's River to Newcastle Gaol. The two-storeyed stone and brick gaol was built in 1818 when Wallis was Commandant at the Newcastle penal station. When Jackey was led across the gaol yard to his cell he would have been confronted by the sight of numerous 'instruments of torture', for the interior yard was the site where prisoners were tortured and executed. His surroundings were daunting for a man unused to built structures and European methods of punishment and coercion. Within days, the tearful prisoner was transferred to *William IV* for the journey to Sydney.[21]

When *William IV* docked in Sydney on 1 May 1834, the prisoner Jackey was in a pitiful state. His legs were badly lacerated, and his health clearly impaired. The *Sydney Monitor* declared that his condition reflected badly on the police. The 'constables who had charge of the man', reported the newspaper, 'valued the black's flesh at a less price than a piece of old rag, or a bit of old sugee bag [sack]'. The suffering prisoner was transferred to Sydney Gaol. At the time, the gaol was badly overcrowded and falling into a state of disrepair. Conditions deteriorated to the point that on 1 March 1834 the Chief Justice of the Supreme Court introduced rules to allow debtors to stay in private lodgings while they waited for their cases to be heard. They could lodge at private houses within a prescribed area around the prison, but not at a public house.[22]

Conditions within Sydney Gaol took an awful toll on the inmates' health. With so many sick prisoners, night lights were often needed. A lamp affixed to the Gaol wall provided a reliable source from which torches could be lit. But solving one problem caused another. Having a lamp burning all night in such crowded conditions made the air even more fetid. By day, summertime temperatures could top 110 degrees Fahrenheit in the cells. Even when a refreshing breeze blew across nearby Church Hill, the air remained foul inside Sydney Gaol. Jackey endured these difficult conditions for three long months before his case came before the Supreme Court.[23]

Strong class and racial divisions characterised Sydney society at the time of Jackey's arrival. By 1830 Aboriginal people living in Sydney no longer practiced many of their traditional skills. This, according to historian Bob Reece, led to colonists finding Aboriginal culture 'of no more interest or significance than the antics of animals'. Visitors to Sydney were taken aback by the extent to which alcohol, disease and malnutrition were impacting on local Aboriginal people.[24]

These distinctions are abundantly clear in a newspaper article published in 1834 where an anonymous overseas visitor described an upper class that included public servants, doctors, lawyers, British invalids retired from India, and people such as himself. Merchants and landholders occupied the next class. Beneath these came the emancipated convicts. Prisoners of the Crown were at the bottom of society while Aborigines were outside the social strata. The columnist wrote:

> There is a further feature which gives a novel tone to the mind
> in parading the streets of Sydney, which is, the groupes [sic] of
> Blacks which are to be met at every corner … They are often
> in a state of perfect nudity; and their almost inhuman facial
> conformation and expression, their dark and coarse texture of
> skin, and frightful contour of limb, produce upon the mind
> the most revolting impressions. These unfortunate beings are,
> however, the most interesting in other respects, of any other of
> the savage tribes. In disposition they are artless, confiding, and
> sociable; and, without the slightest exaggeration of terms, they
> may be said to possess the kindliest of affections. They speak
> English with surprising volubility and enchanting sweetness,
> and are as full of mimicry as monkeys. I could write a volume
> in description of them, but I am travelling out of the proposed
> scope of my observations in making reference to them at all.[25]

Reduced to an entertaining aside in a newspaper column, Sydney's Aboriginal population was seen as the antithesis of what it was to be civilised. Their living conditions were considered the result of inherent savagery rather than a visible outcome of the processes of colonisation.

Despite the hardships that they endured, local Aborigines did not necessarily accept an inferior position in Sydney's colonial society. Instead, their behaviour towards white people was often described as confident or impudent. Like Aboriginal people around Newcastle and the William's River, Aboriginal adults were reduced to begging from colonists. They let their children mix with white people, who sometimes fed, clothed and schooled them. Parents drew the line, though, at having their children taken into white households as domestic servants. Being put to work as domestics and farm labourers was later imposed on Aboriginal youth by law as Aboriginal Protection Acts were passed in the states across mainland Australia in the late nineteenth and early twentieth centuries.[26]

The arrival of a naked, manacled Aboriginal prisoner in the colony's capital grabbed the attention of the colonial press. Jackey's poor condition was condemned not only by the more radical *Sydney Monitor*, but also in the conservative *Australian* newspaper. Media attention was also focused on the man's trial when he appeared before Chief Justice Francis Forbes, Justice James Dowling and a civil jury three months later. The trial was reported in *The Australian* and the *Sydney Gazette*, although the *Sydney Herald* did not cover Jackey's case. When Jackey was brought before the Supreme Court on 8 August 1834, it was to answer a charge of having wilfully murdered John Flynn 'by wounding him with a spear at William's River on the 3rd April last, of which wound he lingered until the 6th following, and then died'. Forbes asked Jackey by what jury he would be tried, to which the defendant answered 'black-fellows'.[27]

The vexed question as to whether Aboriginal defendants were entitled to be tried before Aboriginal jurymen was dealt with in an earlier case heard by Dowling, *R v Binge Mhulto 1828*. Binge Mhulto had been sent to Sydney from Moreton Bay to face a murder charge. Under the rule of law, a prisoner was entitled to be tried by a jury comprising one half of his own countrymen. This implied that Aboriginal defendants' cases ought to be heard before a jury composed one-half Europeans and one-half Aborigines. However, Attorney General Alexander Baxter argued in Binge Mhulto's case that this would be almost impossible to effect given 'the present untutored and savage state of the natives'. Ultimately, Dowling opined that if he 'were to try this savage, in his utterly defenceless situation, I should be at once departing from the spirit and letter of the British law'.[28]

The arrangements made for Binge Mhulto after his trial was abandoned demonstrate a trajectory from the early banishment of Aboriginal men such as Musquito, Bull Dog and Duall to the later sentences of transportation handed down on Aboriginal prisoners. In December 1828, Baxter wrote to the Colonial Secretary in relation to Binge Mhulto and another Aboriginal man, Willimore from Port Stephens, held in Sydney Gaol. Because of 'the impracticability of enabling these men to take their Trials under all or any advantages of British Law or Justice', the Attorney General recommended foregoing prosecution. He suggested instead that the men be 'removed to some part of the Colony distant from their former abodes'. The Colonial Secretary's approval of Baxter's recommendation is annotated on Baxter's letter along with arrangements for their transfer.[29]

Consistent with the judge's ruling in *R v Binge Mhulto 1828*, Jackey's request to have a jury of blackfellows was declined. A uniformed soldier was shown to him to signify a military jury, but when he said 'no soldier' a civil jury was empanelled. The formalities continued as missionary Reverend Lancelot Threlkeld was sworn in as the court's interpreter. The Sydney-born, English-educated lawyer George Nichols was on hand to defend Jackey.[30]

Nichols was outspoken in his criticism of putting Jackey on trial, telling the court that it was 'manifestly a mere mockery to call upon the prisoner to make his defence before persons by whom he could not be understood'. He then requested the court's leave to address the jury on Jackey's behalf. This would have been a departure from

British law as it stood at the time and Forbes refused to set such a precedent.

Nichols' key strategy was to challenge the legality of the colonists' attack on Jackey's camp. He argued that Jackey was entitled to his acquittal in point of law. Aborigines were 'the primary tenants of this soil', he told the court, who 'subsisted in the woods by fishing and hunting'. He asserted that it was illegal for anyone 'to disturb them in the possession of these natural rights'. The attack by the settlers, said Nichols, was not covered by a warrant. This made it an act of open warfare. It followed that any actions arising from the affray were not indictable under civil law. Forbes rejected Nichol's line of argument. He simply responded that a sufficient case existed to be put to the jury.

The defence produced no witnesses. This was queried by the Solicitor General. Nichols responded with a practical demonstration. The well-known Aboriginal companion and informant to the missionary Threlkeld, Biraban *alias* Johnny McGill was present in the court. Nichols had him put on the witness stand. Threlkeld then told the court that Biraban believed in the existence of a divinity only on his, the missionary's, say so and was a pagan. Like any other Aboriginal people Nichols might have called, Biraban was precluded from taking the required oath and therefore could not give evidence in court. This had further ramifications for Biraban. While he was present in court as an assistant to the sworn interpreter, Threlkeld, it was really Biraban who performed this function.

After Biraban stepped down from the witness stand, Forbes addressed the jury. He told them Jackey was to be treated the same as any other of His Majesty's subjects principally because 'the enjoyment and protection of life is as much the law of nature as the law of England'. He extrapolated this point: 'If in a newly inhabited country, there be no municipal law, then the law of nature comes into operation; for if it were not so, the law of retaliation or self-defence would be acted upon'. Forbes's argument was that it was as much for the protection of the black community as of the white that the protection of the law was equally afforded to Aborigines. Because of the provocation apparent in armed men pursuing Aborigines, the Chief Justice instructed the jury to consider a verdict of manslaughter rather than wilful murder.[31]

Despite doubts raised during Nichols' cross-examination over the correct identification of the accused and the actual cause of Flynn's death, the jury found Jackey guilty. He was sentenced to transportation for the term of his natural life. The *Sydney Gazette* reported that 'the unhappy creature seemed totally unconscious of what was passing while he was being sentenced to perpetual exile.' Jackey was transported to Van Diemen's Land on 20 September 1834 on the *Currency Lass*. He was described in the convict records as being 5'4" tall with a black complexion. On 29 October 1834, little more than a month following Jackey's arrival in Van Diemen's Land, the Colonial Surgeon certified the man's death.[32]

Complex interwoven factors contributed to the prisoner's death. These include the devastating impact of his removal from family and country, the march to Newcastle Gaol, and his incarceration in Sydney Gaol. However, the most immediate cause of death was likely to have been a deep wound on Jackey's leg. As historian Satadru Sen pointed out in a different colonial context, 'irons caused abrasions which quickly became festering sores, leading to amputations, general debilitation, and not infrequently, death'. In Jackey's case, the irons on his legs en route from Newcastle to Sydney had cut through his flesh and exposed his ankle bone. It is hard to imagine that conditions in Sydney Gaol were conducive to the wound healing. Following his death, it is likely that Jackey's body was given over to the surgeons at Hobart's Colonial Hospital for dissection. Aboriginal cadavers are known to have stimulated significant colonial curiosity at the time.[33]

4

Dancing in defiance

Within Australia, it has generally been believed that 'the non-hierarchical organisation of Aboriginal society meant that they were unable to unite against the invaders, and each Aboriginal group fought the British on its own'. Evidence from numerous Aboriginal attacks on Brisbane Water colonists to the north of Sydney during 1834 proves otherwise. Aboriginal men from different tribes throughout the wider region met to plan an orchestrated campaign against the settlers who were flocking into the Brisbane Water district in ever-increasing numbers. Sustained conflict resulted, with Aboriginal warriors having the upper hand throughout the early months of engagement.[1]

On 25 October 1834, sixty Aboriginal men surrounded settler Alfred Jaques' house at Brisbane Water as Jaques and his convict servant barricaded themselves inside. When three of the men demanded food and tried to enter the house, Jaques opened a window and thrust out his double-barrelled piece. His convict servant William Rust guarded the doorway with an adze. The Aborigines coo-eed (called out). More joined the assembled force. Jaques and Rust were now confronted by about 150 men armed with stones and spears. Hobby, one of the Aboriginal men, boasted to Rust that 'black fellow was best fellow' and that 'Black fellow master now rob every body – white fellow eat bandicoots and black snakes now'.[2]

As the house was battered and Rust speared, Jaques decided they should flee. 'By dint of hard running', the men reached the neighbouring farm and took refuge. Jaques' house was ransacked, adding to the property losses he had already sustained at Aboriginal hands during the preceding nine months. In all, his losses totalled about £100. Jaques and his brother went to Sydney to apply to the Governor to send a police force to protect them from the 'native blacks'. They were 'terrified by the atrocities of those savages'. Some Aboriginal men warned Jaques they would return when the wheat was ripe and spear the colonists. As a gesture of defiance, they took the landlord's clothes and watches and wore the articles themselves. Jaques thought the Aborigines were encouraged by 'prisoners of the crown' or bushrangers. While Aborigines and bushrangers reportedly worked together on some occasions, Jaques provided no evidence to support his view.[3]

The attack on Jaques' farm was not an isolated incident. The same year, around thirty Aboriginal men, 'the same party from Brisbane Water', attacked some Aborigines attached to Reverend Lancelot Threlkeld's mission at Lake Macquarie and 'plundered our huts, threw their spears, which nearly wounded two of our servants and fell in the yard where my wife and children were standing'. Provisions, clothing and blankets were taken. Some of the Aboriginal raiders who stripped the huts of their contents mocked the colonists as they 'danced in the men's clothes in defiance'. Threlkeld petitioned Colonial Secretary Alexander McLeay to send mounted police to the district to dissuade Aborigines from committing further 'depredations'. In a letter to McLeay dated 26 May 1834, he described the men who were committing violent acts throughout the district as 'belonging to Newcastle, The Swamps, and these Parts'.[4]

In November 1834, several groups of Aboriginal men including Mickey Mickey, Charley Muscle and Toby approached John Lynch's farm at Sugarloaf Creek in the Brisbane Water district. The Lynchs and their servants were alarmed as no women or children were with the men, a sure sign of war. As they came under attack, Mickey

Mickey told Lynch's wife that she 'must go with them and become his gin'. Eleven of the men took the convict servant Margaret Hanshall about 3 miles 'into the bush, where they ... all, severally perpetrated the crime of Rape'. Whether their purpose was to intimidate, retaliate, satiate curiosity or engage in a ritual is difficult to gauge. However, *The Australian* suggested that what colonists considered to be rape was 'a *custom* amongst these ... savages; this is the first step in their courtship – and it is hopeless to expect to inspire them with our estimation of offences of this nature, till they participate with us in the blessings of knowledge'. While the newspaper's interpretation of Aboriginal customary practice was somewhat crude, it is nevertheless consistent with the anthropologists Ronald and Catherine Berndt's description of female initiation practices in parts of the south-east of the continent:

> A girl may not know when her marriage is to be consummated, although her parents and other relatives may have come to some arrangement about it. She may go out food-collecting as usual, perhaps with an older woman, and be seized by a group of men comprising her future husband and several others whom he calls 'brother'; she therefore calls them husband too, and they have temporary rights of access to her before she finally settles down in her husband's camp.

Lynch later told the Supreme Court one of the Aborigines said that he wanted to take Lynch's child 'to do what he liked with'. He said the man 'also laid hold of my wife, and told me he wanted to take her into the bush to ravish her'. Armed with a scythe, the settler attacked three of the Aboriginal intruders, including a man who was carrying off his child. When Lynch 'split his face and breast open' the man dropped the child and 'ran from the house screaming'. Lynch later heard that one of the men died from wounds received during the raid.[5]

By 1834 there were about 315 colonists in the Brisbane Water district. The majority were male, with 144 of the 271 men being assigned convict servants. There were 44 females, including eight convict servants. Law and order in the district was upheld by a local constabulary comprising three men with an armoury of two muskets, two cutdown muskets, four pistols, one sword and scabbard, two bayonets and scabbards, 40 musket cartridges and 40 pistol cartridges. Following the Aboriginal attacks, resident settlers such as the Jaques brothers and absentee landlords like Sydney schoolmaster William Cape lobbied the Government to send mounted police and the military to strengthen their protection. Such responses demonstrate the effectiveness of Aboriginal campaigns because fighting had risen above a level with which local colonists could cope unaided.[6]

Successive colonial governments deployed the military against Aboriginal people, and Governor Richard Bourke followed suit when he sent a 'liberal force of armed men' to the troubled district. A description of the violence that ensued was published in the *Town and Country Journal* several decades later:

> In the middle of the night, camp after camp was surprised and the occupants, men, women and children, shot down like native dogs. The poor friendly blacks fared no better than the others; and the whole affair was a horrible satire upon our civilization.[7]

While the activities of the military were later looked back on shamefully, at the time disgruntled colonists bickered over whether the soldiers were deployed to the areas of greatest need. Differing opinions were aired about the actual numbers of Aborigines involved. 'A Dreadful Sufferer' wrote to the *Sydney Herald* that an Aboriginal force had gathered from the Hunter River, Wollombi, Newcastle and Port Stephens to supplement 'the straggling few belonging to Brisbane Water'. They were, he stated, engaged in 'warfare'. Settler James

Smith of Blue Gum Flats, on the basis of having been visited by 'the whole body of them', informed the *Sydney Herald* that 'A Dreadful Sufferer' magnified the number involved.[8]

The large Aboriginal contingent at Brisbane Water was well aware of the movements of the soldiers. Despite the presence of the military and mounted police, Aboriginal attacks became increasingly audacious. On one occasion, Aboriginal warriors confounded a small contingent of soldiers trying to make a river crossing. They would not let the soldiers land, even though the military had a police guard. A correspondent reported how 'outrages are actually committed in the face of the troops'. The *Sydney Herald* printed extracts from an unnamed writer participating in the conflict who claimed Aboriginal men went to a Mr Bloodsworth's farm only one hour after the troops who'd been sent to guard it had left. The contingent ransacked the house and speared the farmer's stock. The writer said he was 'fatigued both in body and mind' but was 'off again at daybreak' as news of the whereabouts of another Aboriginal camp had been received.[9]

Meanwhile in Sydney, public debate continued over how to curb Aboriginal aggressions at the Brisbane Water district. Discussions broadened to include strategies to resolve 'the Aboriginal problem' generally. One proposal was to send Aboriginal people to an offshore island. In 1826, several magistrates 'up the river' from the missionary Threlkeld tried to persuade the Governor to send an Aboriginal man 'Billy the black' to Norfolk Island, which reopened as a penal station in the mid-1820s. According to Threlkeld, Billy had already spent a considerable period of time in gaol. In 1828, Binge Mhulto and Willimore were sent into exile and, earlier, Musquito, Bull Dog, Jackson, Duall and Jackey had all been shipped elsewhere. Some proposed the entire Aboriginal population of New South Wales ought to be sent to an offshore island, demonstrating that colonists had little idea of the actual numbers of Aboriginal inhabitants in the colony.[10]

Interest in this approach could have been triggered by news that most of the remaining Aboriginal population of Van Diemen's Land had been shipped to Flinders Island. On 31 October 1834 Cape, who frequently complained of insufficient action on the part of the colonial administration to curb Aboriginal attacks, informed the Under-Secretary to the Colonial Office that:

> I did hear but I can hardly believe it, that Jonathon Warner Esq. [a magistrate] has given orders for Constables and the men sent after the ignorant Blacks to shoot them, this would be going to the other extreme. I hope they may all be moved to some distant land as in the sister colony.

Despite the extremely high death toll among Aboriginal people at Wybalenna — by 1842 more than 150 people of the 200 exiled to Flinders Island had died — the popularity of the idea of exiling mainland Aboriginal people to offshore islands persisted well into the later decades of the nineteenth century.[11]

Financial incentives were offered to encourage colonists to risk trying to capture the wanted men at the Brisbane Water district. In November and December 1834, the Government gazetted a reward of £10 per Aboriginal 'ringleader' in the 'various Robberies and other Outrages'. The wanted men were identified by their English names with the December advertisement including annotations such as 'Brothers, and very bad characters' and 'always carries a gun'. The absentee landlord Cape, whose son farmed at Brisbane Water, claimed that 'the ringleaders … are all men who have lived for years among the white people, and speak English fluently'. Hobby and his brothers, Molly Morgan and Little Jack were among the alleged offenders.[12]

On 15 January 1835, Visiting Magistrate Jonathon Warner wrote to the Colonial Secretary about a police operation undertaken nine days earlier to capture several of the ringleaders. A constable and three colonists hid inside a hut used by some of the wanted men. When six of the men entered the hut a scuffle ensued and Jack Jones was shot in the neck. During the affray, three Aborigines escaped through a hole in the slabs. The wounded Jones, along with Jago and Nimbo, was taken to the nearest lockup at Brisbane Water.[13]

On the day of their arrest Jago and Nimbo, who were handcuffed together, seized the constable, William Smith, as he brought water to their cell. Jones struck the constable while Jago and Nimbo struggled with Smith for about twenty minutes. The wounded Jones escaped, although he was eventually recaptured and put on trial. Warner sought advice from the Colonial Secretary about how the men who had arrested 'the blacks' were to be rewarded in light of the prisoners' subsequent escape. He bemoaned the fact that leg irons were unavailable as they were already in use on three Aboriginal prisoners en route to Sydney. Aboriginal prisoners, according to Warner, 'are very determined and consequently require more caution to be looked after than white prisoners'. He could have added that Aboriginal people were not used to incarceration as a form of punishment; they had not been socialised into accepting it as a valid means of maintaining social control.[14]

The Aboriginal protagonists in the Brisbane Water 'depredations' were classed as criminals. Those captured were tried in the Supreme Court of New South Wales. Between February and August 1835, eight separate trials took place in relation to the attack on Jaques' dwelling house and his convict servant Rust, and on the property and persons of others at Brisbane Water. These trials involved eighteen Aboriginal defendants: Long Dick, Jack Jones, Tom Jones, Abraham, Gibber Paddy, Monkey, Little Freeman, Currinbong Jemmy, Major, Whip-em-up, Lego'me, Charley Muscle, Little Dick, Mickey Mickey, Toby, Old John, Hobby and Maitland Paddy. These men represented just over ten per cent of the cohort allegedly involved. Dividing these men into smaller groups for the purposes of trial downplayed the scale of the conflict. The spatial and temporal separation affected through instigating criminal proceedings against them effectively transmuted their collaborative acts of resistance into a series of smaller scale criminal activities.

As Aboriginal captives began to arrive in Sydney, local newspapers reported their presence. The following report in *Sydney Monitor* on 4 April 1835 probably referred to some of the men charged with robbing Jaques' house, as four were tried for this offence that month:

> On Thursday, two native blacks arrived in Sydney, ironed, in charge of a constable, committed to take their trials for several robberies perpetrated at Brisbane Water; their heads were not cropped, and both were nearly in a state of nudity.[15]

The Aboriginal prisoners' hair was cropped as a matter of course at Sydney Gaol. This change in appearance created problems for the witnesses who were required to swear to the identity of the prisoners. When nine of the men appeared in the Supreme Court before Justice Burton and a military jury on 11 February 1835 charged with 'burglary in the dwelling-house of Mr. Alfred Hill Jaques', confusion abounded. Threlkeld, the officially sworn interpreter, thought the men 'looked alike and had changed since the time of these events'. Further uncertainty surrounded the men's names because 'they were sometimes called by the place where they were born, and sometimes by the place where they reside'.[16]

Identification problems led to Little Dick, Charley Muscle, Little Freeman, Lego'me and Major being found not guilty. They were remanded to face further charges. Whip-em-up, Monkey, Tom Jones and Currinbong Jemmy were convicted and appeared before Burton for sentencing. The justice told them he 'had heard of many atrocities committed on the natives by the whites' although his enquiries into the matter had not produced any evidence of the defendants being provoked by the settlers. While their crime was 'according to the English laws ... punishable with death', Burton found room for mercy. He passed a sentence of 'death recorded' at which 'the prisoners all expressed their tears of death'.[17]

In light of their tearful response, it is not apparent whether the men understood their punishment. Prisoners under this sentence were not condemned to be hanged. 'Death recorded' was:

> a formal sentence of death without an intention that the
> sentence would be carried out ... If the judge thought that the
> circumstances made the offender fit for the exercise of Royal
> mercy, then instead of sentencing the offender to death, he could
> order that judgment of death be recorded. The effect was the
> same as if judgment of death had been ordered, and the offender
> reprieved.[18]

Given that these sentences were usually commuted into transportation for life, the prisoners had sufficient reason to shed tears. According to *The Australian* the Aboriginal defendants presented 'a melancholy sight'. Its report of their sentencing encapsulates the moral dilemma faced by the colonists:

> it could not but occur to us, that, the prisoners being as
> ignorant as beasts, it was almost a mockery to bring them to the
> unintelligible formality of a trial ... The observations made by
> His Honor in passing sentence were not intended, of course, to
> have any influence upon either the prisoners or their countrymen;
> on the contrary, His Honor expressed a hope that it would be
> generally received amongst them that the five prisoners had been
> put to death – thus preserving one great end of punishment, and
> that not at the expense of an outrage upon humanity.[19]

The Quaker missionary James Backhouse, travelling through New South Wales with George Washington Walker at the time of the court hearings, bemoaned the fact that 'one of the barbarous, white evidences, stated in open court, that he considered the Blacks as no more than the beasts of the field'. Backhouse considered this 'sentiment [is] too prevalent among many of the Whites of the Colony'.[20]

By the late 1820s, the legal dilemma involved in bringing Aboriginal people before the court to answer charges deriving from colonial laws had been resolved in relation to the offences against the white inhabitants of the colony. In *R v Binge Mhulto 1828*, the Attorney General and Dowling agreed that 'the Aboriginal inhabitants of the Colony are most certainly amenable to all the consequences of punishment which the English law affixes'. Dowling, like others after him, argued that Aborigines were entitled to the protection of British law but were obliged to fulfil their responsibilities under the law. To try Aborigines in keeping with the 'spirit and the letter' of British law, Dowling found it necessary to provide Aboriginal defendants with an interpreter. Such was the case, rationalised Dowling, in India where 'trials of this sort are a common occurrence'. The blanket-clad Binge Mhulto, who was described in *The Australian* as being 'in a state of near nature', was remanded in custody for want of a suitable interpreter before being exiled without trial.[21]

The presence in the courtroom of Threlkeld as the sworn interpreter, despite Biraban doing most of the required translating, was essential to the Brisbane Water trials. The figure of Threlkeld salved the moral conscience of the judiciary and provided the legal mechanism through which the practice of trying Aborigines under laws that were foreign to them was legally justified. As Backhouse observed, the judge 'was glad, that through the medium of a respectable Missionary, their causes were capable of being pleaded in that Court'.[22]

On 12 February 1835, Threlkeld and Biraban attended the Supreme Court for three more trials involving four Aboriginal defendants. The prisoners faced charges arising from conflicts at Brisbane Water. Lego'me was indicted for 'highway robbery, and putting in bodily fear Patrick Sheridan, at Brisbane Water, on the 18th January last'. Sheridan described encountering a group including Lego'me in which the latter threw a spear at him and robbed him. Defence counsel Roger Therry, in his cross-examination, posed a question to Sheridan that did not make much sense to the man. The lawyer asked him 'if he was not aware that he had been a squatter for some time on Lego'me's ground, and had frequently committed great depredations on his kangaroos?' Failing to grasp the lawyer's point, Sheridan answered that 'the ground belonged to the Government, and, as for kangaroos, he had something else to do than to look for them'. The jury was unsympathetic to Therry's argument and returned a guilty verdict. Lego'me was sentenced to seven years' transportation for 'stealing a pipe from the person, value one penny'.[23]

Little Dick appeared before Burton on the same day, and was convicted of 'robbing the dwelling house of Mr. William Bloodsworth, and putting the inmates in bodily fear, by presenting his spear at them'. Burton formally recorded a sentence of death against Little Dick although he intended the prisoner to be transported for life. Toby, who also appeared before Burton on 12 February 1835, was found guilty of 'robbery in the house of John Lynch of Sugar Loaf Creek' and sentenced to 'death recorded'. *The Australian* reported that an unnamed Aboriginal defendant was found guilty of 'robbing the house of Patrick Murick [sic] at Wollombi' and that he, too, was sentenced to death recorded. The unnamed man was Little Freeman who was found guilty of 'stealing in a dwelling house and putting in fear' following the robbery of sheets, blankets, shirts and trousers belonging to the overseer Monks from a house owned by his employer George Palmer. The information prepared in relation to the case claimed Little Freeman 'did steal, take and carry away one Patrick Monks then to wit, at the time of committing the felony aforesaid'. Whip-em-up, sentenced to transportation for robbing Jaques' dwelling house, was also involved. Monks' wife Sarah testified that Whip-em-up 'was the person in the party who gave her the greatest ill-usage'. Little Freeman was found not guilty of robbing Jacques' dwelling house, but was sentenced to death recorded in relation to the attack on the property and person of Monks. Toby and Little Freeman were described as 'an aboriginal native labourer'. They were probably labouring for colonists.[24]

News of the Brisbane Water trials reached Van Diemen's Land. The *Launceston Advertiser* reprinted an article from the *Sydney Monitor* that suggested the convicted men were to be sent to 'an island in Bass's Straits', presumably an allusion to Flinders Island where the Van Diemen's Land tribal remnants were living in exile. The *Hobart Town Courier* published a report reprinted from the *Sydney Herald* about the men's response to sentencing:

> The native blacks who have received sentence of transportation
> to Van Diemen's Land have expressed – in their ignorance of
> the manner in which they will be disposed of, supposing that
> they will be turned adrift into the woods – extreme fear of being
> destroyed by the Aborigines of that colony, in revenge for the
> assistance which six of them rendered to the military and police
> in pursuing them about two years ago, having volunteered their
> services from this colony for that purpose.[25]

The Aboriginal convicts clearly knew little about the convict system and did not realise that the tribal remnants from Van Diemen's Land were no longer on the mainland but were living in exile on an offshore island.

In the aftermath of the Brisbane Water trials, *The Australian* newspaper posed a question on the minds of many settlers: 'how are these outrages to be stopped?' Drawing on remarks made by Burton during the Brisbane Water trials, *The Australian* opined:

> it is not the forms of the trial that form the impression – it is
> their removal from their tribe for ever, and the idea that will
> prevail amongst them that they have been put to death; their
> execution at Brisbane Water could scarcely have a greater effect
> upon their minds than the dim uncertainty of their fate, which
> will, perhaps, preserve the circumstances as a tradition, long after
> the lives of the present generation.[26]

The implication that transportation could supplant the scaffold is
indicative of a gradual shift taking place between 1760 and 1840
in the way states deployed power to manage their populaces. In the
mid-nineteenth century the spectacle of the scaffold as an expression
of the power that punished gave way to a disciplinary regime intent
on producing 'docile bodies'. Anybody who deviated from society's
norms was incarcerated in the prison or the mental asylum to be
retrained before re-entering society. Initially, transportation was
touted as being a useful tool for managing Aboriginal people because
it produced inexplicably absent bodies. However, transportation and
incarceration were also state instrumentalities that produced docile
Aboriginal bodies.[27]

The 'great sensation over the whole territory' following these
trials, and the May 1835 trial *R v Long Dick, Jack Jones, Abraham,
and Gibber Paddy* relating to the robbery at Jaques' property, occupied
column inches in the letters to the editors of Sydney newspapers.[28]
While public debate raged, Governor Richard Bourke took steps to
arrange the transportation of the Aboriginal defendants in the Brisbane Water trials sentenced to death recorded or transportation. He
wrote to Lieutenant Governor George Arthur in Van Diemen's Land
on 14 February 1835:

I have been obliged to apprehend and bring to trial several of the Aboriginal Natives for robbery, rape and other crimes. One poor wretch is to suffer capitally for Rape, and there are eight whose sentences are commuted to transportation for life. I propose to send them to V.D. Land if you have no objections. They are more than half civilized and will make decent herdsmen. If for any cause with which I am unacquainted in that it would not lead to their advantage or to the tranquillity of the colony that I should send them to V.D. Land I should thank you to let me know. I will keep them here until I receive your reply.[29]

Bourke's suggestion that Aboriginal convicts could make 'decent herdsmen' may have been inspired by the employment of Aborigines by the Australian Agricultural Company. He was probably also influenced by his experience as Acting Governor of the Cape Colony between March 1826 and September 1828. While at the Cape, Bourke gained firsthand experience of people 'known to generations of European sailors, travellers, writers and colonists as "Hottentots"'. Now known as Khoi, these people had, at the time of European contact, 'an intense involvement with their cattle'.[30]

The 'Aboriginal natives' referred to by Bourke were Lego'me, Toby, Whip-em-up, Currinbong Jemmy, Tom Jones, Little Freeman, Monkey, Little Dick and Charley Muscle. Muscle was indicted for 'committing a rape on one Margaret Hanshall, on the 5th of November last' with Mickey Mickey. Their trial was presided over by Burton on 12 February 1835. During the trial, Hanshall claimed to have been assaulted by eleven men but 'from the strong resemblance the blacks bear to each other' she could identify only Mickey Mickey and Muscle. She failed to recognise Muscle at the gaol, and later identified him solely on account of his having whiter teeth than his companions. When questioned, the Lynchs swore to seeing Mickey Mickey carrying off their servant, but were unable to confirm

Muscle's involvement. The jury retired for half an hour before returning to the courtroom to have Hanshall put back in the witness box where she swore positively as to Muscle's identity. When the jury returned a guilty verdict Burton 'passed the sentence of death on them both, to be executed on such day as His Excellency the Governor shall be pleased to appoint', although Muscle was later reprieved.[31]

In a departure from convention, Muscle and the other Aboriginal prisoners were, at Threlkeld's suggestion, made to witness Mickey Mickey's execution. This was only the second occasion on which an Aborigine had been hanged in Sydney and the execution 'attracted a considerable crowd'. Threlkeld described how the Aboriginal prisoners had 'pale visages' as they watched Mickey Mickey being hanged. Their 'trembling muscles', he said, 'indicated the nervous excitement under which they laboured at the melancholy sight'. Biraban, who accompanied Threlkeld to the execution, exclaimed: 'When the drop fell, I thought he should shed his skin!'. According to Threlkeld, prior to witnessing the hanging, Aboriginal people thought being sent to gaol 'was a matter of Joke'. The missionary suggested any Aborigines under confinement when executions were being carried out ought to be made to watch.[32]

In the meantime, Lieutenant Governor Arthur and his Executive took issue with Bourke's proposal to transport Mickey Mickey's companions to Van Diemen's Land. The Executive Council saw no means of assigning them as servants or putting them to labour in the public works. Incarcerating these Aboriginal men was considered likely to 'bring on disease and perhaps ensure their premature dissolution'. It preferred the option of sending the Aboriginal convicts to Flinders Island where the Van Diemen's Land tribal remnants were living but feared 'they would endeavour to incite discontent among those who had gone there voluntarily'. Port Arthur was ruled out in case the

Aboriginal convicts helped other convicts to escape. But the over-riding concern was the likelihood that Van Diemen's Land colonists would 'entertain strong apprehensions of the outrages which a hostile mob of Aborigines consisting of nine persons might easily perpetrate before they could be retaken'. Allowing Aboriginal convicts from New South Wales to be sent to Van Diemen's Land would, in the Executive's opinion, 'be the more grievously felt as the residents in the interior were now congratulating themselves upon the successful result of the measures which had been adopted for the conciliation and removal of the Native Blacks of Van Diemen's Land'. After a lengthy debate, the Executive Council declined to receive them.[33]

5

Exiled to Goat Island

Governor Bourke exiled Monkey and his kinsmen to Goat Island just off the coast of Sydney. Wesleyan Methodist catechist George Langhorne, with prior missionary experience at the Cape Colony, was hired for £100 per annum to teach those incarcerated on the prison hulk *Phoenix* as well as the 'eight Aboriginal black natives ... placed on Goat Island under a sentence ... for outrages committed on some of the Colonists of the district of Brisbane Water'. He was expected to teach the Aboriginal convicts 'elements of the Christian Religion' and the English language.[1]

In colonial New South Wales the penal station became the site *par excellence* for the state in its endeavours to produce the civilised native. Its potential to succeed where the mission station was failing was encapsulated in two key advantages. Aboriginal people exiled to penal stations were captives in every sense. The heavy irons on their legs, the surveillance they were under, the cellular walls enclosing them at night and, in the case of Goat Island, the sea surrounding them made escape almost impossible. In addition, the suspension of any legal rights that Aboriginal captives had notionally been entitled to claim as free British subjects meant 'the state's power to coerce, to manipulate, and to experiment was relatively unimpeded by its own constructed limits'.[2]

On top of broader public debates over the justice of trying Aboriginal people before the law courts and how to dissuade them from attacking colonists, the government's intended treatment of those

Aborigines consigned to captivity following the Brisbane Water trials was criticised. *The Australian* denounced the Governor's plan:

> To teach religion and literature to these poor wretches is absurd
> – the one it is impossible that they should understand – the
> other cannot be accomplished without putting a force upon the
> inclinations of the adults, to which they would never submit.

Rather than civilising the natives, *The Australian* argued that separating them from the settlers would result in 'the grand remedy' being accomplished more rapidly than by any other means.[3]

While it was understood the Aboriginal prisoners would be sent to Van Diemen's Land, *The Australian* baulked at the notion that the men were to be subjected to a regime of harsh physical punishment and prison discipline:

> It has been supposed by some persons ... that these poor
> wretches are to be worked in irons – or at least subjected to some
> form of 'prison discipline'; the idea is too monstrous for belief; we
> are persuaded that not only useless and uncalled for severity will
> be avoided, but that all that can be done to render their situation
> bearable, will be the aim of both Governments.[4]

Despite these misgivings, Bourke intended to have the men worked in irons for two years on Goat Island and housed in the prison hulk *Phoenix*. By day, the Aboriginal prisoners were taken off the hulk to cut stone on Goat Island 'under charge of one of their own kindred'. Sandstone was required for the construction of a powder magazine that Backhouse and Walker observed was nearly finished by the time of their visit in 1836. Most of the 200 men on the island, Backhouse noted, laboured in irons while a further 200 housed in the prison hulk *Phoenix* were worked in chains.[5]

This harsh existence took its toll. During their first year of captivity, several died. Muscle, whose name is recorded as 'Charley Myrtle', died on 6 July 1835. At the inquest the coroner concluded the deceased 'Died by the Visitation of Divine Providence'. The following month, Langhorne reported that 'one of the most promising of the Black Prisoners' had died in the General Hospital mid-August 1835 of dysentery. Based on the testimony of the other Aboriginal captives, the missionary had formed the opinion that the unnamed deceased convict was probably innocent of the crime for which he was imprisoned and described him as:

A pattern to the others for his good conduct of which perhaps patience under suffering and a strict adherence to the hulk were not the least remarkable features – and I would add – his apparent firm reliance upon a Saviour's atonement for pardon and Salvation, towards the close of his mortal career.

Langhorne held out hopes that he was 'perhaps among the first ... of the New Holland Tribes gathered in to the Kingdom of God'. Before the year's end, another unnamed Aboriginal convict died. In a letter dated 31 December 1835 to Reverend Richard Hill in Sydney, Langhorne described the deceased as a 'very intelligent man and remarkable for his good behaviour on all occasions'. By February 1836, Langhorne told Hill the remaining Aboriginal convicts were 'exceedingly depressed in Spirits' and did 'not receive the instruction with the cheerfulness that formerly characterised their conduct when engaged with me'. The minds of the Aboriginal prisoners, he wrote to Hill, were 'constantly irritated by the sight of their irons, and the guard placed over them'.[6]

By the end of 1835 another Aboriginal prisoner had joined the convicts on Goat Island. On 17 April 1835, Colonial Botanist and Superintendent of the Sydney Botanic Garden, Richard Cunningham, accompanying Sir Thomas Mitchell's Darling River expedition, wandered away from his travelling companions at the Bogan River beyond Bathurst. When the remains of his belongings and his dead horse were discovered, Cunningham was presumed murdered. The Mounted Police arrested three Aborigines in relation to the alleged murder. Two escaped. The remaining captive was sent to Goat Island, where Langhorne had a severely limited capacity to communicate with him. The man could not speak English. The other Aboriginal convicts communicated with him using sign language.[7]

Late in 1836, the Attorney General sent Threlkeld to Goat Island to question Cunningham's alleged murderer. The other Aboriginal captives had become sufficiently versed in the man's dialect to translate for the missionary. The man, Purimal, had also learned some 'broken English'. Purimal denied involvement in Cunningham's murder, insisting two others had carried out the crime. Suspicion had fallen on Purimal when he had guided the search party seeking Cunningham to the remains of the man's material possessions. Because of a lack of evidence, Purimal was not put on trial, but was nevertheless detained on Goat Island. Langhorne drew on a vocabulary provided to him by the missionary William Watson at the Wellington Valley mission station to assist him in their communications. He thought befriending the 'exceedingly docile' Purimal could be useful because the man, Langhorne hoped, might be willing to promote the missionary's works among his own people should the occasion ever arise.[8]

His visit to Goat Island gave Threlkeld a chance to assess the Aboriginal convicts' progress. He found 'under the superintendence of Mr Langhorne they were improving fast in their English reading'. Langhorne told him 'on asking the Blacks who made all things, one of them immediately to his surprise replied, God! and on being further questioned as to his source of knowledge he replied it was at Lake Macquarie'. This gratified Threlkeld and demonstrated to him and his wider colonial audience that the Aboriginal prisoners were closing the substantive gap between their former selves and the normative behaviour demanded of British subjects. Further plans were under way to continue narrowing this gap. With their sentences about to expire, the surviving Aboriginal convicts were transferred to Threlkeld's mission station at Lake Macquarie in November 1836 to undergo further coercive instruction.[9]

The cohort of prisoners comprised those surviving captives from the Brisbane Water trials and probably Purimal as well. Little Freeman had, in the meantime, died in the General Hospital in Sydney on 14 August. Local Aboriginal people led by Biraban guided the party from Goat Island to Threlkeld's mission where the missionary 'heard their lessons'. The Brisbane Water prisoners could 'repeat the Lord's prayer in their own Language, and three could read', Threlkeld wrote to the Reverend William Parker, Secretary to the Society for Promoting Christian Knowledge. 'It was very pleasing', he declaimed, 'and I was much gratified'.[10]

Threlkeld gave the prisoners a large hut. He planned to build them a boat so they could 'have a seine to fish [and] … send their produce salted to Sydney' to be disposed of through the missionary's agent. In return, they would be allowed to buy rations of flour, tea, sugar and clothing from Sydney, but no alcohol or tobacco. They were not to leave the mission without a pass authorising them to do so. Threlkeld noted that 'to all this they appeared cordially to agree', providing him and Langhorne with 'much gratification on the prospect of carrying into effect a plan long contemplated'.[11]

The missionaries' gratification was short lived. The men's feigned acquiescence to Threlkeld's proposal lulled the missionaries into a false sense of security that was necessary to allow their Aboriginal charges from Brisbane Water to escape during the night leaving most of their clothes behind. Threlkeld described his and Langhorne's 'sad mortification' the following morning when, on calling them to their morning lessons and instructions, the missionaries found 'every individual had disappeared!' Word later filtered back to Threlkeld that the former Aboriginal captives had returned to the Brisbane Water district.[12]

The Governor's hopes that their time spent in captivity would dissuade them from recidivism were in vain. In December 1839, Toby appeared at the Maitland Quarter Sessions with an Aboriginal co-defendant, Murphy, to face a charge of 'high-way robbery on the person of Thomas Cottrell, at Maitland, on the 21st of October last'. Four Aboriginal men were involved in the attack, only two of whom were recognised by Cottrell. After consulting with the judges and the Governor, the Chairman of the Quarter Sessions sentenced Murphy and Toby to ten years' transportation to Van Diemen's Land.[13]

Toby, 'recently released from Goat Island where he was undergoing punishment for a similar offence', told the court he 'perfectly understood the meaning of the indictment', indicating that he realised his actions contravened colonial law and could lead to prosecution and punishment. Not only was he willing to take such a risk on his own account, but he was also happy to be involved with three of his countrymen in committing a robbery. Rather than being sent to Van Diemen's Land, Toby and Murphy served time on Cockatoo Island, the Goat Island establishment having been relocated there.[14]

Another of the Aboriginal men, according to Threlkeld's account, reverted to what the missionary considered to be his former practices:

One Black of the number sentenced to work in irons at Goat Island had previously shot several females and chopped in pieces others with his tommyhawk. – On his return from confinement he joined his tribe [and] sat with them around a fire in the bush, seized a woman, was about to despatch her, when a black started up and cleft his skull with a hatchet, whilst another was buried in his heart.[15]

This tale bears a close resemblance to the stories about Musquito, who was said to have committed violent acts against both Aboriginal and white women. Such narratives take on the flavour of colonial myths, adding to a repertoire of accounts that served to justify colonisation on the basis of native inferiority.

After leaving Goat Island, Langhorne was to move to the Port Phillip District accompanied by two of the Aboriginal prisoners from Goat Island whose sentences were yet to expire. Langhorne was to establish an Aboriginal village at Port Phillip, a plan with which he was not particularly enamoured. He was well aware of the failure of similar initiatives and cautioned against forcing Aboriginal people 'all at once into an artificial mode of living'. English village life, Langhorne wrote to the Governor, was 'diametrically opposed' to the 'natural habits' of Aboriginal people. Langhorne did not lament the loss of his intended Aboriginal companions following their escape, telling Bourke 'I do not consider I have sustained any loss by their defection, it not being probable that they would have remained with me after the term of their legal sentence of imprisonment had expired'. He was, however, concerned to make appropriate arrangements for Purimal to be returned home.[16]

Langhorne wrote to the Colonial Secretary on 15 December 1836 stating that an Aboriginal man, Piper, was willing to accompany Purimal to Bathurst meaning Purimal could be repatriated 'without either trouble or expense'. Annotations on Langhorne's letter indicate his plan was initially approved, although it was proposed that Purimal be sent to William Watson, the missionary at Wellington Valley, rather than to Bathurst. Further enquiries were made into Piper's suitability to escort Purimal.[17]

Piper had recently accompanied the Deputy Surveyor Samuel Perry on an expedition, so Perry's opinion was sought. He wrote to the Colonial Secretary that 'altho' Piper is very honest I could not recommend him for the charge in question'. Alternative arrangements were put in place to return Purimal to Wellington Valley under civil guard. Watson later complained he had not been told what to do with Purimal, who arrived at his mission station in January 1837. He was at a loss to know whether the man was to be kept under restraint, or recaptured should he take to the bush.[18]

Two years after the Aboriginal convicts left Goat Island, the Conciliator of Aborigines in Van Diemen's Land, George Augustus Robinson, visited it on 15 September 1838. Robinson noted in his journal that 'the arrangement at Goat Island is very clean'. The Superintendent told him how the Aboriginal prisoners from Brisbane Water, while there, 'had learnt to cut stone well'. Robinson was interested in their progress because it provided evidence of Aboriginal capacity to take instruction. However, the men had also learnt to view their labour as punishment and later refused to exchange their newly learned skills for payment. On 3 September 1838, Robinson called on some Aboriginal prisoners at Sydney Gaol, a place he described as 'a dungeon' and 'a miserable hole'. While there, he saw the gallows on which two Aboriginal prisoners had been hanged. The week before his visit eight Aboriginal prisoners had been released from Sydney Gaol and sent to the Benevolent Asylum. When Robinson went to visit them, he found six had absconded while the remaining two 'had been taken out and sent on board of the *Prince George* revenue cutter by the Governor's orders to make sailors of them', a measure Robinson considered 'absurd and unjust'.[19]

6

Driving out the white fellows

During the early 1840s, disturbing news about Aboriginal attacks on settlers, stock and properties reached colonists almost daily in New South Wales. Conflict extended across the breadth and length of the colony. As Alexander Harris wrote on returning to England, 'the aggressions of the aborigines along the whole border of civilization grew worse and worse daily'. Local outbreaks of violence grew into 'an entire line of active hostility circumscribing the territory along its whole boundary'. Harris's description of the uprising was doubtless a key source used decades later by colonial journalist and historian Roderick Flanagan in writing his account of events because their works are strikingly similar. According to Flanagan, those in remote areas lived in constant fear of ambush. Stockkeepers' huts were stripped of their supplies. Thousands of head of stock were run off newly established stations. Some white women came under attack, and occasionally children were killed. Formerly friendly Aborigines sought to drive the encroaching settlers from their lands. Tribes from beyond the frontier travelled inland to take up arms against the white intruders. Such was the scale of hostilities that extended across the colony that it became known as the Rising of 1842–44.[1]

Settlers at the time had no doubt that they were coming under attack from organised groups of people, yet colonial historians later failed to concede Aborigines were capable of organising co-ordinated attacks. While Flanagan recognised these Aboriginal attacks bore the hallmarks of a large-scale military campaign, he and other colonists thought it simply would not have been possible for Aborigines to have organised themselves against the white intruders. Such blinkered views of Aboriginal societies were consistent with Social Darwinist thinking, which prevailed at the time. By the 1880s, European observers were cognisant of British philosopher and sociologist Herbert Spencer's notion that societies selectively retained those cultural traits most suited to their development. Aboriginal people, long since viewed by colonists as primitive children of nature, were considered far less advanced than the European societies within which such theories originated.

The Aboriginal uprising coincided with colonial intrusion into the Hunter Valley north of Sydney and the adjacent Liverpool Plains. Anxieties over the magnitude of the attacks and the Government's failure to curb them excited media interest. Newspaper reports of Aboriginal activity in the Hunter Valley throughout 1842 include accounts of hundreds of Aborigines attacking settlers and their properties adjacent to the McIntyre River, Aborigines driving off an entire herd of cattle from a station, as well as numerous other attacks on stock. According to the *Hunter River Gazette*, Aboriginal attacks in the Hunter Valley dated back to the earliest days of contact. Calling for a harder line to be taken against local Aborigines, the newspaper warned that if the Government did not do more to prevent attacks settlers were likely to take matters into their own hands leading to the 'utter extermination of the blacks'.

From correspondence received, the newspaper concluded that the spate of Aboriginal attacks across New South Wales in 1842 was on such a large scale and conducted so systematically that the men's strength in numbers could not be doubted. The Aboriginal attackers had sound knowledge of colonial weaknesses and the sparse numbers of settlers at the frontier were thought insufficient in number to cope with the organised Aboriginal onslaught. While settlers were left in no doubt that local Aborigines were waging war against them, captured Aborigines were not treated as prisoners of war. Instead, they were tried as criminals. The *Hunter River Gazette* therefore called for a stronger local police force to capture more Aborigines.[2]

Over the following months, large-scale attacks continued. Stations were targeted by large groups of Aboriginal men whose professed aim was to drive the white newcomers off their ancestral lands. Anxious absentee landlords read alarming letters from their property managers at the frontier. Some were sufficiently concerned that they forwarded these letters to their local newspapers. As well as sharing intelligence with other colonists in the area, they sought to pressure the colonial government to do more to assist them in repelling Aboriginal attacks.

One of these letters was written to absentee landlord C Doyle on 19 January 1843 by his son, who managed the family property at the Mooney district. Doyle sent the letter to the *Maitland Mercury* where it was published a fortnight later. It contained the alarming news that a large party of Aborigines had attacked Doyle's station. They took three horses and drove off the entire herd of 500 cattle. Earlier the men had taken another horse. The loss of these four horses cost Doyle the substantial sum of £129. One of Doyle's stockmen was killed in the raid. Another was wounded so severely it was thought he would not recover. Huts were destroyed in the attack. Six months' supplies were taken from the station. Doyle's son explained how Aboriginal warriors were 'coming opposite to the hut and daring the men to go out, saying they had killed all the horses, and would kill or drive all the white fellows off the Mooney, M'Intyre, and Barwin Rivers'. The younger Doyle added that Aboriginal men had driven away 1100 head of cattle from Messrs Eaton and Onus in the same district.[3]

Not everyone was willing to put their name publicly to their opinions. In January 1843, an anonymous correspondent from the Big River wrote to the *Maitland Mercury*. They were particularly anxious about an attack on a stockman nearby at Beddington's station.

The Aboriginal perpetrator was a 'civilized black'. The correspondent complained that the country was no longer peaceful and safe. Aboriginal men, in their opinion, were being allowed to go unpunished. The Government was doing little to protect settlers and squatters at the frontier. Left to fend for themselves, those in outlying areas risked being killed by a spear or by the gallows if they took matters into their own hands.

Readers of the *Maitland Mercury* learned how the formerly friendly Aborigines adjacent to the Namoi River had taken to killing cattle. One of the warriors had told the correspondent about an Aboriginal strategy to destroy all the horses to prevent the stockmen from being able to ride out to look after the cattle. The Big River correspondent speculated that 'if the blacks intend adopting this system of warfare it will be impossible that either ourselves or our men can move from our huts without the utmost danger, and of course, under such circumstances, our herds will fall an easy prey to them'.[4]

In April 1843 the *Maitland Mercury* demanded that the Government 'awaken from its lethargy, and shake off the effects of that dose of sickly sentimentality which has relaxed its energy' and do something about the 'series of determined, deliberate, and well concerted depredations committed by [the blacks]'. Asserting that 'this is our country by right of discovery and conquest', the editor described how settlers had been encouraged to leave an overburdened Britain and move to these distant shores. Their expectations, he wrote, were that their lives and properties would come under the full protection of British law. He wrote that:

> we have no wish to wage a war of extermination against the
> wandering tribes of this continent. We are willing to recognise
> the inhabitants as British subjects ... but we are not willing to
> grant them a licence to do evil with impunity; we are not satisfied
> that the slayer of a black man should be pursued with unfaltering

resolution, and that the blood of our own brethren should be spilled upon the earth, should cry aloud for judgment, and that our own government should turn a deaf ear to the cry.[5]

Across the frontier, colonisers considered themselves caught between two equally intractable enemies, the Government and Aborigines. They were as firm in their belief as to their inalienable rights to the land as the original inhabitants were in their determination to evict the unwelcome intruders from their traditional country.

The Aboriginal Rising involved hundreds of participants whose common goal was to drive the white intruders from their lands. Economic sabotage was a key strategy. Working together, large groups of Aboriginal men raided numerous stations and confiscated thousands of head of cattle. This goes well beyond taking a beast or two in compensation for loss of access to their lands or to make up for colonial depletion of kangaroo. Yet these events resulted in only a handful of Aboriginal arrests. As in the Brisbane Water war, the number of Aboriginal combatants captured and tried in the colonial law courts during the Rising was only a tiny fraction of those actually involved in this militant action.

The stories of those arrested around the Maitland area at the time and who appeared before the Circuit Court in September 1843 exemplify actions taken on a wider scale by Aboriginal groups throughout the colony. Tellingly, their actions are also consistent with Harris's and Flanagan's descriptions of widespread attacks on hutkeepers, shepherds and stock. In present-day Australia, such acts are described as having constituted frontier warfare.

The first serious incident that landed a cohort of Aboriginal men in Maitland Gaol happened in February 1843, about 20 miles from Maitland. The setting was *Stanhope* station, the property of brothers Robert and Helenus Scott. One of the brothers, Robert, was a former magistrate who had fallen from favour. He was removed from the bench in 1838 after his defence of the Myall Creek murderers. The then newly arrived Governor, George Gipps, was determined to make an example of those who unlawfully killed Aboriginal people. There was no place in his law courts for a man considered sympathetic to those who massacred the colony's original inhabitants.[6]

The main players in the incident at *Stanhope* were two Wonnarua men, Melville and Harry (or Long Harry); two free settlers, Anastasia Doyle and Mary Keough, who were sisters who had married shepherds; 9-month-old Anastasia Doyle and 3-month-old Michael Keough; 9-year-old Patrick Cavenagh, a visitor; and Edward Thompson, an assigned convict servant.[7]

Mary Keough understood Melville's and Harry's traditional country as being 'principally Lamb's Valley, Bolwara, Lower Patterson, & Wallaroba'. As seen through her eyes, both men were 'tall' and 'stout'. Harry was readily recognisable to locals because 'the left leg [is] much burnt & has lost the big toe & two small toes & the top joints of the two middle toes – his right foot is also much burnt'. Melville was about 5'10" tall, 'pockmarked, the left eye smallest' and had 'two gins one of them a half-caste'.[8]

On 11 February 1843, at around nine in the morning, 'a portion of the Paterson tribe headed by ... "Melville" and "Harry"' surrounded *Stanhope* station. Harry and Melville approached the shepherd's hut where the Keough and Doyle families and Thompson lived, and where the boy Cavenagh was visiting. Lighting their pipes, they asked after the absent shepherds. Thompson knew Harry and Melville. They had visited the hut before. In the course of conversation, Melville asked Thompson:

> whether he came to the colony as an immigrant, or a prisoner,
> and when he replied that he came as a prisoner they said it was
> well for him, as prisoners were obliged to come here against their
> will, but the immigrants came of their own accord, to rob the

black man of his land and gave him no food, and that they (the blacks) would pay them (the immigrants) off for it.[9]

This line of questioning indicates what might be termed a political awareness on Melville's part. He realised that the basis on which immigrants came to New South Wales varied. Some were compelled to come. Others chose to emigrate of their own accord to, as Melville saw it, 'take all land, and give nothing for it'.[10]

As Thompson talked with the men, it became clear to him that Melville knew a £5 reward was offered for his capture. He was suspected of killing the children of another colonial family and was, with Harry, also believed to have killed an Aborigine on Charles Boydell's nearby station. Tensions rose when Melville and Harry asked Thompson if he could lend them a musket 'to shoot wild ducks'. After walking a short distance from the hut to eat some bread, the men returned and told Thompson to give them everything he had in the hut. The watchman handed over his meagre supply of tobacco.[11]

According to Thompson, Melville 'expressed his determination to ravish the women'. He told the watchman 'white fellows have black gins, and now black fellows have white gins'. Melville may have been motivated by payback, retaliating for white men's unsanctioned liaisons with Aboriginal women. Thompson's immediate response was to distract Melville. Diverting the man's attention gave the women time to clamber out the hut's rear window and flee up a nearby hill. However, Thompson could only occupy Melville's attention briefly. As soon as Melville and Harry realised the women had gone, they started pursuing them. Doyle shouted that some stockmen were approaching and then hid herself and her baby behind the chimney of the hut. Melville searched fruitlessly for her.

Harry stayed with Keough, Thompson and the children, threatening to spear them if anyone moved. Melville searched the hut, taking all the blankets and other property. To intimidate the captives, he falsely claimed to have killed Doyle and her baby. Shortly afterwards, Melville took Keough into a nearby gully and 'ravished her'. He urged Harry to do likewise, but Harry declined. Melville killed the boy Patrick Cavenagh by beating him over the head with his waddy (club), and then struck the infant Michael Keough in his mother's arms until baby and mother fell to the ground. The men continued to beat them, allegedly shouting 'you bl...dy white b...s hang Black fellows now'. Afterwards, Thompson accompanied Doyle and her baby to a neighbour's property to report the events. On their return to the hut, they found the bodies of the two children. Mary Keough was almost lifeless. The woman eventually recovered sufficiently to provide a sworn statement detailing the day's events.[12]

Five days after the attack at *Stanhope* station, settler George Hobler saw a group of thirty to forty 'blacks, from the Glendon, Patrick's Plains, and Sugarloaf tribes' at the Hunter River. He thought they were after Harry and Melville who sometimes visited an Aboriginal camp on a small island in the middle of the river. As Hobler and his family watched, the Aborigines formed two parties and fired at the island using spears as well as five or six muskets. The Aboriginal group camping on the island fled to the opposite bank, and fought the intruders. The fight lasted about an hour, even spilling over into Hobler's garden. When it became apparent that neither Harry nor Melville was present, Jemmy, a man Hobler called 'chief of the divers', decided to go to Port Stephens to 'enlist that tribe in his cause' following which 'the whole matter should be settled with the spear and the waddie [waddy]'. Hobler's position as a bystander is one of many examples of Aboriginal and colonial lives unfolding in the same spatial and temporal zones but in completely separate 'places'.[13]

Almost a month elapsed following the attack at *Stanhope* station before Harry and Melville were finally arrested after an armed struggle on Hog Island in Paterson's River. Bobby, an Aboriginal man, alerted police to their probable whereabouts. The Chief Constable set out with a party of ticket-of-leave holders to capture the fugitives. They relied on Bobby's tracking skills to find them. After an armed confrontation lasting about an hour, Harry and Melville were taken captive. The editor of the *Maitland Mercury* described Melville as 'the most ferocious looking black I have ever seen in the country'.[14]

Despite Bobby's pivotal role in capturing Melville and Harry – local magistrates described him as 'the man mainly instrumental in their capture' – the Aboriginal tracker was not given the promised reward. According to magistrates Johnstone and Boydell, Bobby 'several times applied [for the reward] having partly acted as he did under the promise of something if successful'. The magistrates wrote to the Colonial Secretary asking him to bring the matter to the Governor's attention. Their letter was annotated 'I regret I have no funds out of which I can give him a reward'.[15]

Melville's and Harry's incarceration was just the start of a spate of Aboriginal arrests. The next taken into custody was a warrior with a withered leg, from which his descriptive Aboriginal name Therramitchee, meaning 'small leg', was derived. Therramitchee was well known to colonists around Cogo in the Hunter Valley. On 9 February 1837, he was one of nine or ten men who attacked a hut on Mr McLeod's farm at Cogo. The men pretended to need drinking water, then rushed into the hut and attacked the occupants. John Spokes was knocked to the ground. Two other men, John Pocock and another called Somerville, were attacked in their beds. After being hauled to the ground, they were hit with waddies and a boomerang. Both died of their wounds. A fourth man, Lennox, fought back. Spokes, who the Aboriginal men mistakenly thought was dead, managed to escape. He outran his pursuers and raised the alarm. By the time he and others returned to the scene, the hut had been sacked and only the men's beds remained. Therramitchee vanished from around Cogo following the attack. However, colonists in the area had long memories. Six years later he was rumoured to be at an Aboriginal camp on Major Innes's farm. Therramitchee's discovery resulted from information provided by 'some blacks of another tribe', providing another instance of some Aborigines finding it expedient to reveal the whereabouts of those sought by colonists. He was charged with the wilful murder of John Pocock.[16]

Further arrests followed. Using a similar modus operandi, about sixteen men broke into watchman Patrick Carroll's hut near the McLeay River, 107 miles from Port Macquarie, on 4 May 1843. Jackey Jackey, Fowler and Sorethighed Jemmy were among the intruders. Carroll shared the hut with some shepherds who, unfortunately for him, were out minding sheep at the time of the attack. When the men entered the hut, Carroll tried to appease them by offering them sugar, flour and tea. Jackey Jackey and Fowler hit Carroll with tomahawks. The man made a dash for freedom with four Aborigines, including Sorethighed Jemmy, following closely behind him. So-named because he had a large unhealed sore on his leg, Sorethighed Jemmy tried to strike Carroll on the head. As Carroll raised his hands protectively, the tomahawk slashed his hand and throat. Thinking quickly, he feigned death. Sometime later, Carroll's distraught dog stood over him, howling. He concluded, correctly, that his Aboriginal attackers had gone. With considerable effort, Carroll made it back to the hut. He later described graphically how having 'got a drink of water … more of it came out at the hole made by the tomahawk' than went into his stomach.

When the shepherds returned to the hut in the evening, they found Carroll in a very poor state. A surgeon, Henry John Madden, was called to attend to the man. He found the patient:

> in a very weak and exhausted state; he had a deep and incised
> wound on his neck, which nearly divided the windpipe; the gullet

was partially injured; he had also a wound on the right temple, which penetrated to the bone, and a contused wound on his hand. He was in a highly dangerous state; and so continued for nine days.

A full six weeks went by before the man recovered from his injuries. In the meantime, the 'outrage' was reported to the Commissioner of Crown Lands, Robert Massey Esq., on 6 May 1843.

Massey issued warrants for the arrests of Jackey Jackey, Fowler, Sorethighed Jemmy and another Aboriginal man named Pothooks. Two troopers were immediately sent to find them. Massey started out after the protagonists the following day. He was with trooper James Smith when on 30 May they found Fowler and Sorethighed Jemmy. Jackey Jackey was arrested three weeks later by a stockman, and joined Fowler and Sorethighed Jemmy in gaol. Jackey Jackey faced a charge of wounding Patrick Carroll with a tomahawk on the throat with intent to kill him. Fowler and Sorethighed Jemmy faced lesser charges of being present, aiding and abetting.[17]

Yet another Aboriginal man was lodged in Maitland Gaol in the same period. Tom (Kambago) was charged with spearing William Vant on 24 April 1843. Vant, a sherpherd, was employed by Mr David Archer at Durrundurra [today spelt Durrun Durra] near Moreton Bay. Just back from taking some lambs from his hut out to the ewes, Vant was stoking his fire as Tom's spear struck him below the shoulder blade. Another Aboriginal man allegedly tried to spear Vant in the bowels. The shepherd managed to grab the spear in his hand. When Vant told his assailants that he was not scared of them, the men ran off. Vant took five days to recover. Tom was charged with 'wounding William Vant in the back with a spear, with intent to kill him'.[18]

While awaiting trial, Harry, Melville, Therramitchee, Jackey Jackey, Fowler, Sorethighed Jemmy and Tom were housed in Maitland Gaol, a place with a reputation for being wretched. The gaol at Maitland was particularly crowded in mid-1843. As well as the Aboriginal prisoners, twenty-three other men were listed to appear before His Honour during the circuit. A further twenty-four men and two women were awaiting the Quarter Sessions; four men were to be moved to other stations; three men and six women were gaoled under sentences of hard labour; one male and one female were confined as debtors; four males and one female were being held in the cells; eleven males were under confinement; one male witness was housed in the gaol; and ten females were awaiting assignment. In total, 71 males and 20 females were in Maitland Gaol. The health of five male and three female prisoners deteriorated to such an extent that they had been transferred to the local hospital.[19]

7

The hanging judge

On Tuesday 12 September 1843 a party of Hunter Valley gentlemen rode in their carriages and gigs, and on horseback, to escort His Honor Mr Justice Stephen and his entourage into the town of Maitland. The gentlemen accompanied the Judge to his lodgings. In accordance with convention, Stephen attended divine service at St Peter's Church the following morning. The theatricalities marking the Judge's arrival were a forerunner to the main event. Stephen took his seat upon the bench at the Maitland Circuit Court at half-past eleven. He opened proceedings by reading Her Majesty's proclamation against vice and immorality. His presence in the courtroom so soon after attending divine service reinforced a symbolic link between church and state. It also imbued Stephen with moral authority derived from the Bible. Assuming a mantle of divine decree was pertinent to his practice as a puisne judge. In this role he was invested with the power to determine whether those who transgressed the laws of the land would live or die.[1]

The pomp and ceremony surrounding Stephen's arrival emulated the ritual surrounding the visits of judges to towns in England where assizes were held. With its elements of precedence and continuity, re-enacting this ritual created a visual allusion to the extension of the rule of law over the English colonies. As Stephen travelled across country to church and courtroom, he symbolised the transplantation of English justice into the Australian colonies. Indigenous systems of lore and law were overwritten in the process.[2]

Stephen told the court how pleased he was that of the thirty-nine prisoners listed for trial only eight of their number was 'of the class originally free'. Twenty-four were convicts or free by servitude, whilst the remaining seven defendants were 'of our benighted and unfortunate aboriginal or native population'. He addressed the jury in relation to the unusually distressing character of the crimes listed in the calendar:

> The crimes imputed to the seven aboriginals, I regret to say, are, if you shall believe the witnesses, of the most atrocious description; such indeed, as in two at least of the cases, should the unhappy men be found guilty, to preclude all expectation of hope or mercy in this world … It must be remembered that the prisoners labour under unusual and peculiar disadvantages; which you will do honor to yourselves in labouring to counteract, by even more than your ordinary care and caution.

The seven Aboriginal defendants Stephen referred to were Therramitchee, Tom, Jackey Jackey, Fowler, Sorethighed Jemmy, Harry and Melville.

In his opening address, the judge made it clear Aboriginal people belonged to a disadvantaged underclass. Yet he reaffirmed their status as British subjects. It was this that justified bringing them before the colonial law courts. In the courtroom, asserted Stephen, 'the same measure of justice and in the same scales' applied to all alike 'whatever the offender's colour'.[3]

Despite Stephen's rhetoric advocating impartiality, he already had a history of strong bias when it came to proposing how to treat Aborigines in the Australian penal colonies. Born in the West Indies on 20 August 1802, Stephen was educated in England where he read law. He set sail for Van Diemen's Land in 1824 where he took up the position of Solicitor General. Stephen's arrival in Van Diemen's

Land coincided with a marked increase in conflict between Aboriginal people and colonists known as 'the Black War' (1824–31). In 1830, Lieutenant Governor George Arthur approved a quasi-military operation, 'the Black Line', to round up all the remaining Aboriginal people in Van Diemen's Land and corral them down Tasman's Peninsula.[4]

At a public meeting held in Hobart Town on the eve of the Black Line, Solicitor General Stephen made an extraordinary statement regarding the island colony's original inhabitants. Prefacing his remarks by claiming that he was speaking as a private citizen, Stephen reasoned that as Aborigines were waging war upon the colonists:

> you are bound to put them down. I say that you are bound
> to do, in reference to the class of individuals who have been
> involuntarily sent here, and compelled to be in the most
> advanced position [convict stockmen in remote areas], where
> they are exposed to the hourly loss of their lives. I say ... that
> you are bound upon every principle of justice and humanity,
> to protect this particular class of individuals, and if you cannot
> do so without extermination, then I say boldly and broadly,
> exterminate![5]

It is remarkable that a man in Stephen's profession and position in colonial society was willing to go on the public record, albeit as a private citizen, advocating the extermination of Aboriginal people.

While Stephen was Solicitor General in Van Diemen's Land, an Aboriginal woman was murdered at Emu Bay while being pursued by some colonists. When Lieutenant Governor George Arthur sought Stephen's advice about whether to prosecute, the Solicitor General claimed that there was confusion over whether common law or martial law prevailed at the time. He opined a trial ought not to be held

90

because it could 'result in indiscriminate murders under Martial Law, or, if Common Law were held to run, colonists would hesitate before going out in Capture-Parties, when a death might very well bring them to the gallows'. The alleged murderers were never brought to trial.[6]

Stephen's opinions on how to treat Aboriginal people extended beyond Van Diemen's Land. In the mid-1840s, an Aboriginal prisoner Koort Kirrup was in Melbourne Gaol for sixteen months. He was charged with murdering station owner Donald McKenzie and his shepherd at the Portland Bay district in 1842. The man was unable to stand trial because of the lack of an interpreter. The Chief Protector of Aborigines for the Port Phillip District George Augustus Robinson and Assistant Protector William Thomas raised concerns in relation to Kirrup's lengthy incarceration. Colonial officials in Melbourne were also worried, as it was illegal to hold prisoners for lengthy periods without trial. Stephen proposed a solution to the dilemma: hang Koort Kirrup! Stephen showed no compunction in advocating the extermination of an Aboriginal man allegedly involved in attacking colonists. However, his advice was ignored and Kirrup was released from gaol.[7]

How then, would the Aboriginal inmates in Maitland Gaol fare under a colonial judge with a history of proposing extermination as a solution to colonists' 'Aboriginal problem'? At the time of the Aboriginal defendants' trials, the circuit courts were newly constituted in New South Wales. Circuit courts were expected to deliver considerable benefits to outlying regions. It would take far less time and money to access justice. Landowners would no longer have to send their servants to the cities to bear witness where they could be tempted by vice. Local juries could better appreciate local contexts. And punishments delivered locally were thought to have a great impact on local populations who could view the events rather than hearing about them days later.[8]

Most of these anticipated benefits did not apply to Her Majesty's Aboriginal subjects. Appearing before local juries in situations charged with emotional intensity and heightened by frontier conflict further disadvantaged Aboriginal defendants. When the seven Aboriginal defendants were put on trial in Maitland in September 1843, rumours were circulating that twelve or thirteen white men had been massacred by Aborigines. At the same time, an abundant harvest was on the verge of being reaped. With a heightened fear of potential losses of life and property, local settlers were unlikely to form an unbiased jury.

Therramitchee was the first Aboriginal defendant brought before Stephen, appearing on Thursday 14 September. He faced charges relating to the murder of John Pocock at Cogo. During the brief trial, the Attorney General told the court 'the same Creator who had written upon the heart of every white man "Thou shalt do no murder," had engraved the same commandment upon the heart of every human being, whether black or white'. He alluded to 'laws' that Aboriginal people had 'amongst themselves for the punishment of murderers', but did not elaborate what such punishments might entail. He encouraged the jury to deal with the case 'precisely in the manner as they would do if the prisoner at the bar was a white man', thus removing any possibility of Therramitchee's action being interpreted as an act of frontier warfare.

Like the Attorney General, defence barrister William Purefoy urged the jury not to allow 'any prejudice to exist in their minds on account of the colour or character of the prisoner, in consequence of the late outrages which have been committed by some of his countrymen'. He was asking the impossible. The jury comprised local people with firsthand knowledge of recent and ongoing frontier conflict. Some of the jury may have been involved in hunting for the alleged perpetrators, and could have been signatories to a petition to the Government in which demands were made for something to be done.

Reaching a guilty verdict in cases involving Aboriginal defendants provided colonists with a lawful means of dealing with what they saw as 'the Aboriginal problem'. The 100 per cent conviction rate of Aboriginal defendants at the September 1843 Maitland Circuit Court indicates local jurymen were more than happy to have local Aboriginal men capitally convicted.

In Therramitchee's case, there was just one material witness to the alleged murder six years earlier. Despite the victim Pocock surviving for thirty hours after the attack and possibly dying for want of proper medical attention, the jury returned a guilty verdict. Stephen sentenced Therramitchee to death. When the sentence was explained to him, Therramitchee shook his head and exclaimed 'bail me'.

Later on the day of Therramitchee's trial, Tom appeared to answer a charge of 'wounding William Vant in the back with a spear, with intent to kill him, on the 24th of April last, at Durrundurra'. Purefoy argued that under the statute *1 Victoria, c.85, s.2* Tom was entitled to be acquitted because the law required the wound to be shown to have been dangerous to life. The evidence before the court did not show that to have been so in this case. Stephen overruled Purefoy's objection, claiming that if the wound was inflicted by the prisoner with the intent to kill, regardless of whether the wound was dangerous to the victim's life, its infliction would constitute a capital offence. The jury took only a few minutes to return its guilty verdict. Tom was then sentenced to death. When asked if he had anything to say, he told the court through his interpreter that he 'did not do it – white people told lies'.

At ten the following morning, three more Aboriginal defendants were placed at the bar. Jackey Jackey was charged with 'wounding Patrick Carroll with a tomahawk on the throat, with intent to kill him, at the McLeay River, on the 4th May last'. Fowler and Sorethighed Jemmy faced charges of 'being present, aiding and abetting'. Patrick Carroll was the first witness. He positively identified the prisoners.

Jackey Jackey's right arm was bent and unable to be straightened. Sorethighed Jemmy had a large sore on his thigh. Their disfigured limbs were exhibited to the court as proof of their identities.

The court heard Carroll enjoyed a happy prior relationship with the defendants. Testimony was also given about the nature and circumstances of his injury and his recovery. Massey, the Commissioner of Crown Lands at the McLeay, was called on to testify about issuing warrants for the defendants' arrests. During his summing up, Stephen 'highly complimented' Massey 'on the promptitude which he had exhibited in the apprehension of the prisoners'. Such an observation from the judge could have left no room for doubt in the minds of the jurymen about the anticipated outcome. Unsurprisingly, the jury immediately returned a guilty verdict. When this was interpreted to the prisoners they all denied committing any offence. Stephen sentenced all three to death. His rationale was that hanging provided the 'most humane course which [sic] could be adopted both towards the blacks, and towards the unprotected stockmen and shepherds'. He pointed to the 'necessity of making examples of them'.[9]

Harry and Melville were next. They were charged with 'the wilful murder of Michael Keough, by beating him on the head, on the 4th February last, at Stanhope'. Despite rumours that one of the two had killed the Mulcahey children, and that Melville murdered an Aboriginal man at Charles Boydell's station, no further charges were laid. Speaking in good English, the defendants pleaded not guilty.[10]

The watchman Thompson was the first witness for the prosecution. He gave a detailed account of the conversations between him and the defendants, followed by a lengthy description of the attacks that followed. The sisters Keough and Doyle were called and corroborated Thompson's testimony. The appearance in court of the woman Keough startled the defendants. As a local, William Collins, later described:

While these rascals were on trial, they were driven into a terrible state of consternation when Mrs Keough entered the witness box to give her evidence. They ... had left her for dead by several heavy blows from a 'nulla nulla' ... their brutal weapons of warfare, and how she came to life again they could not make out. They would first look at her in a most frightened like manner, then at each other, and then 'gabber' together in their own 'gibberish', and thus they went on until she left the witness box.

Harry and Melville had not heard about the woman's survival. They must have been completely cut off from their local knowledge networks while on the run. Their reaction to her appearance shows how ill prepared they were for their trial. They had not been properly informed prior to the hearing about who would be called as witnesses for the prosecution.

After hearing the evidence, Melville strongly protested his innocence and cross-examined the witnesses. Melville claimed he had not been at *Stanhope* station on the day in question. He said he had 'never been in that part of the country; he did not know either of the women; and as for Harry he had fits, and could not go about at all'. Melville told the court that Harry's medical condition meant he was confined to camp where he relied on Melville to keep him fed on bush foods such as kangaroo and wallaby. Harry told the court that he was 'murry bad; not say much; had fit, and couldn't walk about'. He also protested his innocence.

In his closing address, Purefoy urged the jury to consider their verdict 'calmly and dispassionately' notwithstanding the 'atrocity of the crime'. Nevertheless, the jury immediately returned a 'guilty' verdict. In sentencing Melville and Harry to death Stephen described the act of which they had been found guilty as 'more the act of fiends than that of men'. He told them bluntly that they could not expect any mercy. As the condemned men were being removed from the courtroom, Melville retorted to Stephen that the judge was murdering him.[11]

In comparison with other defendants appearing before Stephen at the September 1843 Maitland Circuit Court, the punishments meted out to the Aboriginal defendants were harsher and more politically driven. Intended to dissuade other Aboriginal men from violent actions against colonists, the sentences reflected political and personal biases that were evident before, during and after the trials. Another element influencing the sentencing was undoubtedly the level of angst and outrage expressed by local colonists who were growing increasingly alarmed at the level of Aboriginal action against them.

Several weeks after their sentencing, the *Maitland Mercury* noted the order for the execution of Melville and Harry had been received by the local police magistrate, Edward Denny Day. The hangings were to be carried out at midday on Wednesday 18 October 1843 outside the walls of Maitland Gaol. The execution was to be staged only one day after the hanging at Newcastle of a white man convicted of killing a constable. This resulted in an administrative problem. Maitland did not have a drop of its own and had to rely on the apparatus being sent from Newcastle, but the local river steamer was scheduled to sail prior to the hanging of the white man. To overcome this hiccup, the local sheriff paid the steamer's operator £10 to delay sailing so that the required apparatus could be shipped up the river along with Melville and Harry. The prisoners were being held at Newcastle before being returned to Maitland for their execution. Hanging them near the locality of their offences was supposed to dissuade others in the area from committing similar offences.[12]

While in Newcastle Gaol, the various Aboriginal inmates under sentences of death were visited regularly by the Reverends Wilton, Campbell and Stewart, although the *Maitland Mercury* feared that 'the poor aborigines will obtain very little religious instruction for

the want of interpreters'. The men were said to be from a number
of different tribes. Melville was the only one known to speak some
English.

When the executions of Harry and Melville finally took place, a
large crowd gathered. Several Aboriginal people were present. The
local newspaper printed a detailed description of the theatrics that
included the requisite endorsement of colonial justice delivered by
the attending minister on the prisoners' behalf. He told the gathered
crowd that 'Melville and Harry acknowledge that the Governor had
done right in taking their lives, and die confessing the crime they
have committed'. The public spectacle of the hanged Aborigines was
recapitulated in the columns of the local newspaper:

> The clergymen then left the unhappy men, and in a few minutes
> the bolt was drawn and the drop fell. Harry struggled for a long
> time, and appeared to suffer a great deal. Melville being a heavier
> man died sooner, though it was some time before the quivering
> in his limbs subsided.

Avid attention was paid to the bodily signs of the hanging men to
ascertain to what extent the mantle of Christianity and therefore civilisation had been assumed by them. In accordance with the thinking
of the times, the movements of the bodies of the condemned revealed
to the onlookers the extent to which the prisoner enjoyed a clear conscience – a sign of repentance.[13]

A month after Melville and Harry were hanged, the *Maitland
Mercury* printed a brief article under the headline 'Black Fellow's
Notion of English Law' which read, in part, as follows:

> We have heard that a few days ago as a person who resides in
> East Maitland was out shooting in the bush … he came across
> two black fellows, one of whom said to him, 'Well, white fellow,

what news?' 'Oh, not much,' replied the other. 'B'lieve,' says the black, 'they hang black fellow in Maitland lately.' 'Oh, yes,' says the white. 'Did him kick much?' enquired the black. 'Oh, yes,' says the white, 'murry much, too much.' 'Then,' rejoined the blacks, attempting to lay hold of the man, 'come along, you b_ white b_, we hang you.' [14]

The white informant attributed his lucky escape to being armed. Melville's and Harry's executions did more to mollify those who had petitioned the Government for action – and to reinforce the rule of law in their eyes – than it did to persuade local Aboriginal people to refrain from taking militant actions against colonists.

The week after Melville and Harry were hanged in Maitland, Therramitchee was executed in front of the gaol at Port Macquarie. The prisoner spoke English quite well. He was later said to have paid avid attention to the Reverend John Cross's consoling words. A military guard attended the execution, as did all the prisoners from the barracks and the ironed convict gang. Despite the best efforts of the local policeman, Aboriginal people would not view the hanging. They were too frightened, and only one Aborigine who frequently came into the settlement was coerced into watching. Nevertheless, the colonial authorities hoped that the public spectacle of Therramitchee's execution would deter Port Macquarie Aborigines from committing further acts against the settlers in the area. [15]

The death sentences imposed on the remaining four Aboriginal prisoners were commuted to transportation. Tom, Jackey Jackey, Sorethighed Jemmy and Fowler were shipped from Newcastle Gaol to Port Jackson where they arrived at the penal station on Cockatoo Island on 1 November 1843. They laboured there until 17 April the following year. The men were then sent to Darlinghurst Gaol in Sydney before being boarded onto the *Governor Phillip* and sent to the harsh penal station at Norfolk Island. [16]

Despite their apparent reputations as dangerous convicts, the men's life sentences were reduced substantially to two years. Jackey Jackey's fate after his confinement at Norfolk Island is unclear. Sore-thighed Jemmy pined so much for his kin and country that Norfolk Island Commandant John Price arranged his free passage home.[17]

Fowler and Tom spent two years labouring on Norfolk Island before arriving in Hobart on the *Lady Franklin* on 19 June 1846. They joined a work gang at Darlington probation station on Maria Island. Less than a month later, they were back in the Prisoners' Barracks in Hobart. Soon afterwards, they were repatriated to New South Wales on the brig *Louisa*. After a brief stay at Hyde Park Barracks, where they received rations, Fowler and Tom were sent home. On 28 September 1846, the Principal Superintendent of Convicts was informed by the Colonial Secretary's Office that approval was granted for their return to Port Macquarie and Moreton Bay respectively 'at an expense not exceeding two pounds fifteen shillings, to be defrayed out of Colonial Funds'.[18]

In the meantime, Harry and Bownas were among a number of other Aborigines tried at the Maitland Circuit Court. In their case, the presiding judge was Chief Justice Roger Therry. These Aboriginal defendants appeared before him on Wednesday 12 March 1846 charged with 'assaulting, with intent to rob, one Peter Davis, at Congarina, on the 28th May last'. On being found guilty, Harry, 'a most dangerous character', got fifteen years' transportation. Bownas, who had 'been useful at various times to the police', received a lighter sentence of twelve months in Newcastle Gaol.[19] Harry arrived in Van Diemen's Land on the *Louisa* on 26 April 1846. He laboured for 21 months in a convict gang before being assigned to private individuals as a servant. Harry obtained a ticket of leave on 26 January 1848, but contravened its provisions and was sentenced to nine months' hard labour. He absconded on 28 July 1853, but was eventually recaptured. On 24 January 1854 he was sentenced to eighteen months' hard labour. After several stays in hospital, Harry died at Impression Bay on 15 January 1856.[20]

Because of their allegedly low intelligence and lack of religious precepts, Therry considered Aboriginal defendants as 'objects of great commiseration', particularly when condemned to death. Like his fellow judges, Therry advocated equality of all before the law but admitted that Aboriginal men 'suffer[ed] loss of life for offences for which the white man only suffers transportation or hard labour on the roads'.[21]

Harry and Bownas, like other Aboriginal defendants before the colonial law courts, stood indicted as members of an Aboriginal 'race' that colonists, and indeed the presiding judges, intended to subdue by punishing the few as an example to their many countrymen. The marked disparity between the sentences meted out to Aboriginal prisoners and to others is not fully explained through recourse to the differences in magnitude of the charges faced. Take, for example, Michael Kelly, the sole non-Aboriginal defendant at Stephen's September 1843 Circuit Court who faced a murder charge. His trial, which related to the death of a man during election riots, lasted ten hours. Stephen was at pains to point out to the jury the distinction between murder and manslaughter. After retiring for ten minutes, the jury found Kelly was guilty of the lesser charge of manslaughter and Kelly avoided the death penalty. He was sentenced instead to seven years' transportation.[22]

The only prisoners to hang following the September 1843 Maitland Circuit Court hearings were Melville, Harry and Therramitchee. Local jurymen may have taken only a matter of minutes to hand down their guilty verdicts in the cases involving the seven Aboriginal defendants at the September 1843 Maitland Circuit Court, but Stephen was almost indecently hasty in donning his black cap to pronounce death sentences upon them. The 'hanging judge' seems an appropriate epithet by which to remember him.

8

Exemplary punishments at Port Phillip

On Friday 9 October 1840, a large group of 'Goulburn blacks' arrived in Melbourne. They planned on joining their Waverong allies to avenge a spearing by some Watowerong. This need not have directly concerned colonists yet the latter were unsettled. Such was the level of disquiet that the Superintendent of the Port Phillip District, Charles La Trobe, called a meeting to plan an attack on the Aboriginal camp. Chief Protector of Aborigines George Augustus Robinson attended the meeting, as did Major Samuel Lettsom of the 80th Regiment. Against Robinson's advice, the military decided to attack the Aboriginal camp.[1]

Early the following morning, the camp was surrounded by soldiers and police. The uniformed men rounded up 300 people and shifted them to a stockade at the prison barracks. An eyewitness was 'shocked at the cruelty of the military and police'. Another witness said that women, the old, and the infirm were 'goaded with bayonets by the soldiers and hit with the but [sic] end of their muskets or cut by the sabres of the native police'. La Trobe told the Chief Protector that his officials 'were drafting out the worst characters'. Thirty-five men and boys were later 'chained by the leg, two together, and lodged in gaol'.[2]

The Aboriginal prisoners thought that 'they should all die'. The local commissariat officer was heard to comment, 'what is to be done with them? I think the best way would be to hang them all!' Such views were shared by some of the white prisoners in Melbourne Gaol who, when Robinson visited, 'made use of very sinistrous and approbious [sic] language as I went passed them blooddy [sic] blacks wished them all hung'.[3]

Over time, a number of the men were released from custody. Eventually those remaining in gaol were tried for sheep stealing. Robinson noted the Aboriginal and English names of the ten defendants in his journal as: Nan.der.mile (Mr John), Lo.gir.ma.koon (Jaggy Jaggy), Pine.jin.goon or My.tit (Napoleon), Coro.in.you.lit or Un.mo.ware.in (William), Mor.er.mal.loke or Yar.mer.bo.pe (William), Pee.beep (Mr Malcolm), Tar.roke.nun.nin (Harry), Larm.bid.er.ruc (Billey), Wile.gurn (Mr Murray) and War.wo.rong (Mr Murray).[4]

The men, dressed in 'check shirts, fustian trousers, and jackets', appeared before the Resident Judge on Wednesday 6 January 1841. The 'totally unfit and incompetent' interpreters failed to communicate the nature of the evidence to the Aboriginal defendants, leading the Chief Protector to denounce the trial as 'a farce ... got through with indecent haste'. After a few minutes, the jury decided only War-worong was not guilty. The rest were sentenced to ten years' transportation.[5]

Governor George Gipps recommended to La Trobe that the men be imprisoned in Sydney if found guilty. They could join the 'few Blacks' Gipps had already sent to Cockatoo Island. So less than a week after sentencing, the Aboriginal convicts were put on board the cutter *Victoria* to be taken out to the brig *Vesper* to sail for Sydney. However, the men's destinies lay elsewhere. Thirteen white male convicts and one female convict were in the hold of the *Victoria*. The nine Aboriginal convicts remained on deck, still wearing leg irons but with their handcuffs removed. The newspaper report stated that 'on their way down the river the people on board the cutter amused themselves by terrifying the blacks, telling them that they would be hanged on their arrival at Sydney'. When the vessel tacked near land the ironed Aboriginal men leapt overboard. The guards opened fire and 'two were seen to sink to rise no more'.[6]

Tarrokenunnin was wounded during the escape. Robinson later visited him in Melbourne Gaol where he told the Chief Protector 'white men told the natives they were going to Sydney to be hung, natives plenty frightened and jump overboard. All natives dead in water'. Tarrokenunnin was released from Melbourne Gaol later in the year. In September 1841 he visited Robinson along with 'Bullert, a Sydney native'. He assured the Chief Protector 'all the Goulburn blacks were saved when they escaped the Victoria cutter'.[7]

Gipps privately reprimanded La Trobe for instigating an inquiry. Gipps thought 'in matters of this sort where there has been a loss of life, the less the Ex. Govt. interferes the better'. La Trobe agreed, but was concerned about Aboriginal cases because of the 'ignorance & indecision' on the part of the Protectors of Aborigines and the 'indisposition' of the local magistracy to become involved owing to blurred lines of responsibility. The propensity of various colonial officials to shift the blame was highlighted during La Trobe's inquiry. Nobody wanted to take responsibility for the debacle.[8]

Questions over how much responsibility the colonial judiciary ought to assume over cases involving Aboriginal people were raised in Melbourne several years later. This time, the concerns were over whether and to what extent colonial law ought to be applied to cases solely involving Aborigines.

Towards the end of 1843 Little Tommy, an Aboriginal man from the Port Fairy area of the Port Phillip District, accompanied a wool dray to Melbourne. Little Tommy arranged to work his way back home by helping a Merri River settler, James Cosgrove, and his wife to drive their bullock team. Farm owners such as the Cosgroves often relied on labour from Aboriginal people because white labour was scarce and expensive. Little Tommy joined the Cosgroves at the Wardy Yallock inn (near Cressy) and travelled with them as far as Manifold's station by Lake Colac. On 20 or 21 January 1844, a group of twelve to fourteen Koenghegulluc warriors began following Cosgroves' dray. These men were bound by customary law to retaliate against Little Tommy's tribe for the death of their kinsman Eurodap (*alias* Tom Brown). The Cosgroves' servant Bill, a 'Sydney native from Yass Plains', told the settlers the men intended to kill Little Tommy. The quick-thinking Cosgroves put Little Tommy on a mule to give him a chance to outrun the attackers. However, the unfortunate man could not ride. He was soon overtaken by the Koenghegulluc and killed. The warriors used a combination of traditional and colonial military technologies. As well as being speared eight times, Little Tommy was shot in the head. This later gave rise to confusion over who delivered the fatal wound.[9]

Perhaps because Little Tommy was with the Cosgroves, the colonial authorities took an interest in his death. The authorities sought the alleged perpetrators, and news of Jacky Jacky's subsequent arrest travelled as far as Melbourne. The following extract from Robinson's personal journal provides a rare insight into the informal networks through which news relating to Aboriginal prisoners travelled:

> On Wednesday 3 April, met Mr and Mrs Manifold in Cashman shop, said a Black belonging to the Jarcoorte at their station was in custody at Geelong – charged with murder of a Black from Port Fairy at Mr Manifold's – this Black boy killed at Manifold's was in revenge for the murder of Eurodap Tom Brown – Charley the Jarcoort who travelled with me was subsequently killed by the Port Phillip Natives in retaliation.[10]

For the first half-century of British colonisation the authorities chose not to intervene legally in matters solely involving Aboriginal people.

In the 1830s, a series of landmark cases were heard in the Supreme Court in Sydney that resulted in the colonial judiciary deciding it had the authority to intervene in internecine conflict. So despite Little Tommy's death having occurred in a tribal context, legal proceedings were instituted against Jacky Jacky.[11]

In a significant departure from the usual practice, at the preliminary hearing in Geelong evidence was admitted from an Aboriginal witness. Bill, the Cosgroves' servant, made his mark on his sworn deposition and was permitted to take the following oath: 'I know that it is wicked to tell a lie, I will tell the truth'. According to Bill, the Koenghegulluc men asked him 'what blackfellow' they had with them, and declared 'we kill him directly'. Bill told the court that he recognised Jacky Jacky as one of the men who had speared Little Tommy and that another man, Long Bill, shot Little Tommy. On the basis of the sworn statements provided by Cosgrove and Bill, the Geelong Bench committed Jacky Jacky to stand trial at the Court of the Resident Judge in Melbourne.[12]

Jacky Jacky appeared before Judge Jeffcott on Tuesday 23 April 1844. When he was brought to the bar, it was found the Assistant Protector who was supposed to act as an interpreter was absent. The Standing Counsel for Aborigines, Redmond Barry, told the court he thought Jacky Jacky could speak English, but had since been informed otherwise. After some debate about the irregularities in Jacky Jacky being questioned without an interpreter present, it was suggested that Billy, another Aborigine in the courtroom, could act as an interpreter as he:

> could talk English a little; he believed there was a God; bad man went up into the sky. Upon further consideration – it was good man who went up into the sky, and a bad man must go down to the devil.

Following his confused regurgitation of Christian scripture, Billy was passed over as a suitable interpreter. Anxious to dispel 'an impression' that 'Aborigines are not liable to the same punishment, and are under a different protection from British subjects', Jeffcott reprimanded the Crown Prosecutor for failing to procure an appropriate interpreter. The 'impossibility of communicating between the prisoner and the jury' saw Aboriginal prisoners stood down, according to Jeffcott, rather than any desire on the part of the law to differentiate between Aboriginal offenders and settlers. Jacky Jacky was remanded in custody.[13]

On Wednesday 15 May, Jacky Jacky reappeared in the Court of the Resident Judge and was indicted for 'the wilful murder of an aboriginal boy named Little Tommy, by wounding with a spear at Wardy Yallock, on the 22nd January last'. He faced a second count of 'aiding and abetting' Long Bill in committing the murder. When instructed to plead, he told the court 'another one black fellow killed him'. This statement was taken as a plea of 'not guilty' and was considered sufficient proof of Jacky Jacky's capacity to understand the proceedings for the trial to proceed.

The Reverend Francis Tuckfield, a former miner and fisherman turned Methodist missionary, was the sworn interpreter. Redmond Barry acted as defence counsel. Despite Jacky Jacky's plea, the jury found him guilty as charged but recommended mercy 'on the ground of his ignorance of the habits of civilized life'. Jeffcott donned the black cap and sentenced Jacky Jacky to death, but undertook to 'forward the recommendation of the jury to the Governor'. Jacky Jacky's sentence was commuted to transportation for life to Van Diemen's Land.[14]

Jacky Jacky was about 30 years old when he arrived in Hobart Town on the *Flying Fish* on 27 January 1845. His convict record states: 'Transported for wilful murder on one Tommy an Aboriginal Native stated this offence killing a black boy on Mr Manifold's

Estate. States it was not him that did it. Alic did it'. Reverend Tuck-field also identified Blind-Eyed Alic as the organiser of the attack.[15]

Jacky Jacky may have been considered dangerous, because he was transferred to Norfolk Island. In 1825, the then Governor of New South Wales, Sir Thomas Brisbane, told Lieutenant Governor George Arthur 'to forward here [Sydney] for the purpose of being sent to that [Norfolk] Island, such desperate characters as he considered dangerous or insecure in Van Diemen's Land'. Jacky Jacky's transfer also complied with Gipps' February 1844 proposal that the 'worst of the singly convicted' convicts from New South Wales be sent to Norfolk Island. Such was the harshness of the punishment, Jacky Jacky died in custody at Norfolk Island just eight months later.[16]

Another intriguing example of Aboriginal use of colonial and traditional technology is evident further west in the Port Phillip District in a series of events that played out near the Grampians. This case, too, resulted in an Aboriginal man being transported to Norfolk Island and Van Diemen's Land for acts of frontier warfare construed as crimes against the colonists.

Between 1838 and 1840 the lands adjacent to the Grampians occupied by Djab Wurrung and Jardwadjali underwent a 'squatting invasion'. The white intrusion resulted in extensive violence. Between thirty and forty men of the Konongwootong gundidj clan of Jardwadjali were killed by the Whyte brothers in March 1840, and the Darkogang gundidj clan was virtually destroyed by 1841. Both Djab Wurrung and Jardwadjali engaged in what was later described by a settler who lived in the area between 1841 and 1842 as 'guerrilla warfare'. Nearby Mt Arapiles – a natural fortress – provided an ideal base from which to launch Aboriginal attacks.[17]

Jardwadjali and Djab Wurrung actively resisted white encroachment primarily through depriving the squatters of large numbers of their stock and flocks. They were also astute observers of colonial

practices. As early as 1840, they were adopting new practices, particularly in relation to animal management. Blending their traditional
practices with methods adapted from observing squatters, Djab Wurrung constructed a bush fence to enclose sheep taken from a local
station. In a similar way to which kangaroo were dealt with, they
broke the sheep's legs to prevent them straying. Most of these animal
thefts led to the perpetrators being tracked down. When individuals
involved could not be found, 'the whole clan would be punished in a
later reprisal'.[18]

In June 1845, La Trobe was petitioned by stockholders in the
Wimmera for protection against Aborigines. Without it, they feared
being run off the land and financially ruined. Local stockholders and
business partners Messrs Baillie and Hamilton had lost about 800
sheep and lambs, while others were also affected. The petitioners
described the impossibilities of recovering their animals. The mallee
scrub was 'almost impenetrable'. Any sheep, if relocated, often had
broken legs. In response, La Trobe sent native and border police to
the region including Henry Dana and his men, who were stationed
near Mt Arapiles.[19]

News of the unrest at the Wimmera spread as far north as
Maitland. The *Maitland Mercury* reprinted a report in which it was
claimed colonists' servants were leaving them 'fearing to risk their
lives longer in such a dangerous vicinity'. Not 'love or money' could
procure replacements. As the paper explained, some Aboriginal
people were inventive in addressing the scarcity:

> In our advertising columns will be found an announcement, as
> novel as it is pleasing, that the aborigines of the Lake Colac tribe
> are ready to undertake the charge of cattle, on terms, in addition
> to shepherding the flock of sheep already in their possession.[20]

Perhaps news of Aboriginal involvement in similar roles with the

Australian Agricultural Company had travelled along the extensive Aboriginal trade network that criss-crossed the continent.

When Henry Dana and the native police went to the Wimmera in 1845, the contingent was drawn from the force instituted in 1842. Mooted in the Bigge Report, the possibility of investing Aboriginal men as native constables became an actuality in the Port Phillip District. This model of law enforcement went through three distinct phases with Aboriginal Police Corps being instituted in 1837, 1839 and 1842. The native police came to be a devastatingly effective instrument used by the colonial authorities against other Aboriginal people.[21]

In July 1845, Dana wrote to La Trobe about an armed encounter between his men and some Jardwadjali of the Choorite balug clan. The events leading up to this encounter, told from the perspective of settler Thomas Baillie, were detailed in a sworn statement enclosed with Dana's letter. Baillie and his business partner Hamilton occupied land near a lake about 15 miles from Mt Arapiles. On Thursday 10 July 1845, while Baillie and his shepherd were attending the sheep 'several Natives rushed from the Forest and took away the whole flock'. The station owner and his shepherd pursued them, recovering some sheep.

Hamilton fetched Dana and his native police who tracked the missing animals. After travelling 30 miles, they 'came up with a number of sheep with their legs broken'. They found 200 sheep 'in a bush yard' and some Aborigines nearby. In the fracas that followed, Dana explained how 'the Ringleader of the party was cut down after a long resistance, by Yupton a corporal of the native police and made a prisoner of; he is badly wounded. I have ordered him to be marched to Melbourne as soon as his wounds will permit'. The 'ringleader' was Yanem Goona, also known as Yanengoneh ('spring from the earth') or Old Man Billy Billy. Dana justified opening fire, killing at least three Choorite balug men and wounding others, by claiming he and his men were at risk, but may have exaggerated the danger. Robinson, the Chief Protector of Aborigines, claimed the native police openly boasted they 'were not going to take prisoners but to shoot as many of the blacks as they could'. A history of retributive killings is evident in a newspaper report on the loss of Baillie's and Hamilton's sheep that stated 'the tribe who committed this serious depredation is the same which Messrs Powlett and Dana at different times thinned of its fair proportions in a skirmish with the black rascals'.[22]

Goona's committal hearing in August 1845 included a conversation between the prisoner and the bench, which highlights the farcical nature of the proceedings. A local newspaper reported how the prisoner 'who is almost grey with age, noticed little that took place'. Apparently he barely understood English. When the man was asked what he had to say in his defence, Goona replied 'borack!' The bench tried again, asking whether he could 'say anything why we should not commit you to take your trial?' Goona said 'borack!' He was then informed 'it is our duty to commit you to take your trial', to which Goona answered 'yes!' He was returned to gaol to await 'another legal farce relative to his capacity to comprehend the nature of the proceedings, and understand the details of the evidence'.[23]

Goona was charged in the Court of the Resident Judge on 17 October 1845 with 'having on the 10th of July last, stolen fifty wethers, fifty ewes, and fifty lambs, the property of Mr. Bailey [sic] and another, of Colkennett, in the District of Port Phillip'. Richard Buckett, who lived near Goona's clan, was the interpreter. During the trial, Redmond Barry raised the issue of acquainting the prisoner with his right to challenge the jury. Mr Justice Therry responded that it could not be supposed that any of the gentlemen who had to try the case could have any personal feeling against the prisoner, who was an entire stranger to them, he being 'nothing more than a wild man of the woods', an attitude the judge held towards Aboriginal people throughout his life.

Baillie and Dana appeared as witnesses for the prosecution. No defence witnesses were called. The Crown Prosecutor produced a licence demonstrating that Baillie and Hamilton had depastured stock in the Wimmera. Because he failed to show how Baillie and Hamilton were connected with the licence, Therry directed the jury to acquit Yanem Goona as 'there had not been sufficient evidence adduced to bear out the information'. The interpreter explained the situation to the prisoner.[24]

Yanem Goona appeared in court the following day on a new sheep stealing charge. This time, the jury returned a guilty verdict even though none of the witnesses positively identified the prisoner as being personally involved in committing the crime. Controversially, Therry found 'that if this black was a member of the community where the sheep were found altho [sic] he had no hand in the actual stealing or killing, yet as a member of that community was equally guilty'. As various officials made accusations against each other in relation to the previous day's botched trial, Goona was sentenced to ten years' transportation to 'Old Man Cruel' (as Robinson put it) or Van Diemen's Land.[25]

Goona arrived in Van Diemen's Land on 29 December 1845 where he was described as an illiterate 'pagan' labourer. Measuring 5'5" in height, his hair and whiskers were 'greyish'. He left behind a wife and two children. Required to serve a three-year period of probation, he was sent to Norfolk Island. A visitor there described how 'whenever he mentioned the Grampians [Yanem Goona] invariably cried from the thought of home'. This behaviour is typical of a particular illness 'validated within Aboriginal culture' that involves 'longing for, crying for, or being sick for country' and is akin to clinical depression. The underlying cause of this illness in Aboriginal people is 'removal from their country, place of dreaming, or spirit for extended periods of time'.[26]

Less than two years later, an ailing Goona was returned to Van

Diemen's Land where he arrived on 18 August 1847. He was sent down Tasman's Peninsula to the Salt Water Creek Probation Station, which was primarily an agricultural station. Over the following year, Goona's health continued to decline. He was moved to nearby Impression Bay, a substantial convict station that doubled as an invalid depot, where he died on 31 October 1848.[27]

9

Sentences to 'instil terror'

As the frontier continued to expand across the Port Phillip District in the 1840s, dozens of Aboriginal men were taken into custody following violent confrontations with settlers. These encounters often took place at the far reaches of 'civilization', at shepherds' huts and isolated stations, and on squatters' runs. Given the vast distances between many of these locales and the Melbourne law court, judges were keen to be seen to be dealing sufficiently harshly with those Aborigines who appeared before them to dissuade outlying settlers from taking matters into their own hands.

Many of the conflicts arose through competition over land and resources. One such incident transpired on Monday 19 October 1845. At sunrise, Koombra Kowan Kunniam and four other 'blackfellows' forced their way into the Brazels' small wooden house near Geelong. Kunniam, who Margaret Brazel later identified in court, was armed with a gun. One of the others took it from him, fired it into the air, and then returned the gun to Kunniam. The men took some salt beef worth 2 shillings before pointing at one of the Brazel children and stating 'plenty of fat!'. The worried mother thought this meant they intended to eat one of her children. It seems more likely the men were justifying taking the salt beef by indicating the child was well enough fed so taking food would not cause undue hardship to the family. Brazel was so convinced of the men's cannibalistic intentions that she cooeed loudly to attract help, causing the intruders to flee. Dennys, the settler on whose farm the Brazels built their hut, later captured Kunniam. On a subsequent visit to the hut since vacated by the Brazels, the property owner noticed the door had been broken. The hut was burned down some time later, an act that Dennys attributed to Aborigines.

Following these incidents, Koombra Kowan Kunniam *alias* Cornigobernock was arrested on the grounds that 'he did on the 19th day of October last, feloniously break and enter the dwelling house of Mr. D. Brazel, situated on the Murrabool River in the Geelong district, and steal therefrom 10lbs. of beef, value 2s.'.

When Kunniam appeared before the Resident Judge in Melbourne on 21 January 1846, Assistant Protector William Thomas interpreted. Redmond Barry was defence counsel. Mr Justice Therry was happy to concur with Barry's argument that as 'the property was not properly described as laid down in 7 Carrington v. Payne, King v. Rawlins' the case must be considered solely in terms of larceny. 'This', said Therry, 'would be a safer course'. The jury returned a guilty verdict, and Kunniam was remanded in custody to await sentencing. On being informed of the outcome of his trial, Kunniam exclaimed 'Borack!' 'Borack!', which translates as 'no, not so!' The following week he was sentenced to seven years' transportation.[1]

Four months later, Kunniam arrived in Van Diemen's Land on the *Flying Fish*. Kunniam, who was allocated the convict number 625, was about 25 years old and stood 5'5¾" tall. He had a black complexion, large head, black curly hair that was cut close to his head, no whiskers, a round visage and a low forehead. His forehead was dominated by bushy eyebrows that overhung his black eyes. He had a large nose and mouth, thick lips and a small chin. Described as being a 'pagan' who could 'neither read nor write', his trade was listed as 'labourer'.

Kunniam was assigned to a gang at Southport to serve one year's hard labour. He returned to the Prisoners' Barracks in Hobart on 19 June 1847. Three months later Kunniam was admitted briefly to hospital, but within several days he was sent to Jerusalem (present-day Colebrook), north of Hobart, to join a road gang. On 14 April 1848, Kunniam was admitted to hospital for a longer stay. On 17 November 1848 he was well enough to be sent to the Launceston Hiring Depot and was sent into service with a settler, Mr Buesnel of Patersons Plains. However, his health continued to fail and just four years into his seven-year sentence he was admitted to hospital for a third time. Koombra Kowan Kunniam died at Impression Bay at Tasman's Peninsula. He left behind a widow, Tooturook, who later lived at the native police headquarters, Narre Narre Warren, presumably as the wife or concubine of one of the men stationed there.[2]

Warrigal (variant spelling Warrigle) Jemmy was brought before the recently appointed Resident Judge William à Beckett and a civil jury in the Court of the Resident Judge on Saturday 17 October 1846. He faced five charges relating to an incident almost three months earlier at the Lower Loddon. These charges were 'unlawfully, maliciously, and feloniously wounding John Forrester, with a spear with intent to murder him, at the Lower Loddon, on the 28th July, with intent to maim, disfigure and disable and to do grievous bodily harm'.[3]

Warrigal Jemmy had earned a notorious reputation among early colonists at the Lower Loddon, some of whom had, in turn, earned an equally notorious reputation among local Aboriginal people. In a letter dated 29 September 1853 to La Trobe, settler AM Campbell claimed he had 'cultivated a friendly feeling with the natives'. Despite this cordial relationship, when Campbell was away in Melbourne local Aborigines 'enticed' his Aboriginal servant Jack away from the station and killed him. Campbell also received a less than friendly visit to his hut from 'seven strange blacks'. On going to a nearby river, Campbell turned and saw:

one of the natives (Warrigal Jemmy, afterwards transported for life) following me a few yards behind, with my own axe uplifted and clasped in both hands. I fixed my eye upon his, walked deliberately up to him, and gently took hold of the axe, which he quietly relinquished.

Campbell walked back to his hut with Warrigal Jemmy, 'conversing with him, as if he had done nothing to excite my suspicion'. He later explained that he had not spoken about this incident until about two years after the event. Men he described as 'the natives of this place' told Campbell they thought Warrigal Jemmy had intended to kill him on impulse.[4]

The squatter on whose station Warrigal Jemmy committed the offence for which he was later arrested was James Cooper (variant spelling Cowper). Cooper took up land near the junction of the Loddon and Murray Rivers in 1845, naming his station *Boramboot*. However, he did not appoint 'an experienced overseer', in the absence of which Cooper's shepherds took liberties with local Aboriginal women. They encouraged Aborigines to visit their huts by providing food. Once they established relations with the women, the shepherds stopped giving food to the men. Aboriginal men then helped themselves to sheep in payment for the women's services.

Fearful of local Aboriginal men, Cooper's shepherds were armed at all times. A spate of violent incidents took place, including an incident in October 1845 when blows were exchanged between one of Cooper's shepherds and some Aboriginal men who had attacked a sheep. The shepherd, William Britton, shot the men's dog. Several days later, on 8 October 1845, Britton and another shepherd did not return with their flocks in the evening. Britton's body was found 'naked with spear wounds, opened, and his entrails taken out, and beaten about his face and head apparently with a tomahawk, and his ears cut off'. The second shepherd's body was later found in a similar condition.

William Dana and his Native Police were sent to 'pacify' the area. On 1 February 1846, they killed several Aborigines and wounded many more after opening fire on about 200 people. Chief Protector Robinson was sent to investigate, while Henry Dana went to reinforce his brother William's contingent. Robinson and the local Protector, Parker, were unable to obtain any further information from Aborigines or squatters. William Dana, the only white man present at the February incident, informed Robinson that his party was 'attacked by the natives whilst patrolling the banks of the river'. They fired, and when some Aborigines were shot the rest disappeared 'among the reeds'.[5]

In August 1846 another party of Border Police was sent to the troubled district. They located and arrested Warrigal Jemmy who was armed at the time with a carbine and some pistols. The events that led to criminal charges being laid against him were detailed in four witness statements, including one provided by the shepherd John Forrester.[6]

On 28 July 1846, Forrester was tending sheep at the Lower Loddon when he was 'startled by feeling a spear thrown which passed through the tail of my coat'. The surprised shepherd was confronted by a number of men including Warrigal Jemmy, who threw a second spear at him. The spear, after striking the lock of the shepherd's gun, entered his vest and shirt. As the point of the spear had broken off, the weapon simply grazed his body. Forrester later said in court that, because he was afraid of being killed, he decided not to use his gun. Another spear was aimed at him, following which the 'blacks rushed the sheep' and took forty from the flock of 1900 sheep.[7]

Warrigal Jemmy was brought before the District Bench and remanded in custody, pending further evidence from the station where the alleged incident had taken place. According to Robinson, a native policeman acted as Warrigal Jemmy's interpreter during the initial examination of the prisoner. On Monday 12 October 1846 he was committed to stand trial in the Court of the Resident Judge.

Warrigal Jemmy was tried before Resident Judge William à Beckett and a jury of twelve male settlers on Saturday 17 October 1846. The Crown Prosecutor, assisted by Sydney Stephen, mounted the case for the prosecution. On being asked to plead, Warrigal Jemmy told the court 'borac me do it; nother black fellow'. Denying the charge and suggesting that another Aboriginal man had perpetrated the alleged crimes implies that Warrigal Jemmy understood his situation sufficiently to cast doubt on whether he had been correctly identified as the offender. The interpreter, Assistant Protector Parker, nevertheless informed the court of the impossibility of conveying to the prisoner his right of challenge. It was agreed that Redmond Barry could exercise that right on Warrigal Jemmy's behalf. The jury was sworn without anyone being challenged and, after hearing the evidence, they found the prisoner guilty on the last four counts against him. Warrigal Jemmy was sentenced to life transportation to Van Diemen's Land.[8]

On the day he was sentenced, 17 October 1846, an indent was prepared at the Port Phillip District stating that Warrigal Jemmy's native place was the 'Loddon River'. Described as a 'labourer', his year of birth was estimated to be 1820, making him 26 years old. He was 5'9" tall with a black complexion and hair and brown eyes. The prisoner had fourteen scars across his shoulders. It is likely that these scars were cicatrices formed during initiation ceremonies to mark his transition to manhood. His charge, conviction and sentence were recorded on the indent, as was his status as 'an aboriginal black native of the District of Port Phillip'. This indent was the legal instrument that enabled Warrigal Jemmy's labour to be transferred officially from the Port Phillip District of New South Wales to Van Diemen's Land.[9]

Although sentence had been passed on Warrigal Jemmy, and despite the indent having been prepared, it was not immediately apparent whether it would be carried into effect. Like any sentence passed in the colonial law courts, appeal could be made to the Executive Council. A letter seeking mitigation of the sentence was written by the Assistant Protector stationed at the Loddon River, Edward Parker, on 12 December 1846. Identifying the prisoner as 'Warrengil [sic] Jemmy otherwise Keetnurnin', Parker asked the Chief Protector that he be allowed to submit a statement to the Executive Government. He pointed out that the prisoner was 'convicted on the evidence of one man'. Parker called into question the witness's ability to correctly identify Warrigal Jemmy because the man had been speared from behind.

The Assistant Protector informed the Executive Government about the 'intense prejudice and strongly hostile feeling existing on certain stations on the Murray against the natives'. He suggested such hostility could result in prosecution witnesses being easily swayed into not being 'very scrupulous' when it came to 'swearing to the identity of a black'. Such an attitude, according to Parker, would be bound to earn an employee favour with their employer or provide an opportunity to 'gratify revenge' against local Aborigines. Parker described Mr Cooper's station as having 'been particularly in a disorderly state ... the men being of bad character, and under no proper control'.

The Assistant Protector advocated 'commuting the prisoner's sentence to imprisonment for a limited time', prophesying that 'transportation for life in the case of the prisoner is in effect a sentence of early death'. Parker thought that the prisoner's 'return after two or three years' imprisonment to his country and people 'would ... as he is a man of remarkable quickness and intelligence be productive of much good, in the warning it would afford to the other natives'.[10]

Robinson endorsed Parker's request that Warrigal Jemmy's sentence be commuted to 'a limited period' and forwarded the letter to Acting Superintendent William Lonsdale. Lonsdale sought the

Resident Judge's opinion and received a scathing response from à Beckett. He justified the sentence he'd imposed, stipulating that 'it is sufficient to say that it is a sentence which I, in my discretion, believed to be my duty to pass'. He intended the sentence to be exemplary and denied that it could be considered 'severe', stating:

> Warringel [sic] Jemmy was one of a Tribe of 50 whose manifest design in assembling together, at the time of the attack by the prisoner was spoliation and murder, and for this tribe to learn that their captured comrade had been punished only with temporary confinement, would I think, be but an encouragement to them to carry their design into effect at some future period.

In the same letter, à Beckett elaborated his views on the difficulties of bringing Aboriginal men to justice:

> Reports are from time to time authenticated of the most wanton attacks on the flocks and herds of the squatters, and of the mutilation and murder of those charged with their care, but in hardly one instance out of a hundred, have the offenders been brought to justice. The difficulty of identity, of capture, of detention and safe conduct for hundreds of miles, the expense and inconvenience of bringing witnesses the same distance, and finally the probability of the prisoner's discharge ... from the want of an Interpreter – All this goes far to render the law but a nominal protection for the settlers against the incursion of the blacks, and operates upon the blacks themselves, who are quite intelligent enough to be aware of these obstructions to their punishment, as an incentive and encouragement to persevere, when once commenced, in their career of pillage and murder.

The Resident Judge reasoned such circumstances tempted the 'distantly located' colonist to 'take the law into his own hands'. He saw it as much a matter of policy as it was of law that once an Aboriginal prisoner was successfully tried and convicted, he ought to be given a sentence that would 'instil terror' into those who lived 'in daily fear of encountering similar evidence'. Exemplary sentencing could also persuade colonists to seek redress through the law courts.[11]

On 8 January 1847, Acting Superintendent Lonsdale forwarded these letters to Sydney. He told the Colonial Secretary the remarks he solicited from à Beckett in response to Parker's letter fully addressed the concerns raised. He added that he 'considered Mr. Parker has attempted to advocate the cause of the Blackman in a very unjustifiable and inconsiderate manner'. The Colonial Secretary concurred with the judge, finding that 'the allegations of Mr. Parker do not appear to be supported by the facts of the case'. Mitigating the sentence 'would be offering an inducement to the white people to take summary revenge in every case of aggression from the blacks'. Despite Parker's concerted efforts, the original life sentence stood.[12]

In the meantime, a plan was floated to have the prisoner retained in Melbourne and trained as an interpreter. However, this fell through and Warrigal Jemmy arrived in Van Diemen's Land on board the *Flying Fish* on 10 May 1847. When his details were taken, the colonial scribe annotated 'Roman Catholic' on his record. Almost all other Aboriginal convicts were considered pagans (the other notable exception was Billy Roberts *alias* Samboy or Jimboy, a 'Protestant'). The 'stout made' Warrigal Jemmy was required to do three years' hard labour. He was initially stationed at Lymington south-east of Hobart.[13]

Prior to Warrigal Jemmy's arrival, Billy Roberts (an Aboriginal convict sentenced to transportation for life in the Supreme Court in Sydney for assaulting 'one Fanny Hasselton, by striking her on the head with a tomahawk') was sent to Lymington to serve thirty months' hard labour. On arriving from Sydney on 18 April 1847 on board the *Waterlily*, Roberts was recorded as being 5'9" tall, aged about 30, with a 'black' complexion, a 'large, long' head, 'black woolly' hair and 'bushy black' eyebrows. He had lost a front tooth in his upper jaw (probably through initiation rites), and carried scars in the centre of the forehead, over his right eyebrow and on his right cheek-bone. Roberts was in ill health. On 22 April 1847, just four days after arriving in Van Diemen's Land, he was admitted to the Hobart Colonial Hospital.[14]

Warrigal Jemmy and Billy Roberts may have heard about each other before both were sent to the hiring depot at Parsons Pass near Buckland in April and May 1848 respectively. About ninety convicts were retained at this depot, with a local landholder paying sixpence per convict per day to have the men labour to clear his steep, forested land. Less than a month after Roberts' arrival at Parsons Pass, the two Aboriginal convicts and another man, Thomas Jones (tried at the Salop Assizes in England on 18 March 1842), absconded from their work gang. Roberts had already been disciplined for 'breaking out of barracks at night' almost a year earlier and had committed several other offences. Jones' conduct record lists offences ranging from using profane language to making false statements to avoid work. Unlike his fellow absconders, Warrigal Jemmy committed no offences prior to absconding.[15]

The Convict Department advertised in the *Hobart Town Gazette* a reward of '£2, or such lesser sum as may be determined upon by the convicting Magistrate' for each of the three. Less than two weeks later, Warrigal Jemmy was lodged in Longford Gaol. He was transferred to the Prisoners' Barracks in Launceston before being sent to the Port Arthur penal station in August 1848. Founded in 1828 at Stewarts Bay down Tasman's Peninsula to take advantage of its proximity to numerous stands of useful timber, Port Arthur expanded to become the largest penal establishment in the colony. It was used as a place of secondary punishment for those men who transgressed once within the confines of the convict system. On his arrival, Warrigal Jemmy was made to labour in chains and given a diet restricted to bread and water for having absconded from Parsons Pass.[16]

Warrigal Jemmy escaped briefly from Port Arthur but was apprehended by 20 February 1849. In 1852 and 1853, he was hired out to G McSheen of Liverpool Street, PB and H Cooley of Macquarie Street, and McRobie of Macquarie Street, all resident in Hobart. He eventually got a ticket of leave on 19 May 1854, and was granted a conditional pardon on 12 June 1855. Just six days later, Warrigal Jemmy was admitted to the Hobart Colonial Hospital where he died, aged about 35, on 30 June 1855.[17]

Following the escape from Parsons Pass, Roberts' apprehension was gazetted on 19 September 1848. He, too, was sent to Port Arthur in August 1848 where he was later sentenced to four days' solitary confinement for using threatening language. A number of other offences were recorded against him, including an attempt to strike an overseer. Following an assault on a fellow prisoner in February 1850, Roberts served thirty days' solitary confinement. He was transferred to Norfolk Island the following month and died there on 23 July 1850 at about 34 years of age.[18]

Jacky Jacky, Yanem Goona, Koombra Kowan Kunniam, Warrigal Jemmy and Billy Roberts all unwittingly fulfilled Parker's prophecy that transporting Aboriginal men was tantamount to delivering a sentence of early death. It is unlikely that news of their deaths was given to their families or to the Aboriginal Protectors. In his 1848 Annual Report, Robinson asked 'whether or not it would be desirable for the Government to be informed respecting the Aborigines already transported, in order to mark the effect of the punishment that the same might be made known ... to the tribes generally, and especially to their connections and friends'. He explained how when asked by the men's relatives for information, he 'was unable to afford the slightest information respecting their relations not even whether they were living or dead'.[19]

10

Aboriginal deaths in custody

Rocky triangular-shaped Cockatoo Island is a 'natural hulk' near Sydney 'just where Port Jackson narrows into the creek called Parramatta River, and about a quarter of a mile from either shore'. When in March 1839 Governor George Gipps found the Norfolk Island penal station was overcrowded, Cockatoo Island was an obvious location for a new convict establishment. It was 'surrounded ... by deep water, and yet under the very eye of Authority'. Sixty convicts from Norfolk Island were first to arrive. They laboured to dig a well and quarried stone for 'the erection of the New Circular Wharf' at Sydney. Gipps predicted the sandstone island 'may be ultimately made to supply this material to Sydney in the same way that the Penitentiary at Sing Sing supplies Building Stone to New York'. Soon after its inception in 1839, Cockatoo Island became 'the most important convict prison in the colony'.[1]

Many Aboriginal men transported in the 1840s and 50s ended up at Cockatoo Island where they laboured alongside 300 or so other convicts. Most of their fellow convicts had committed offences within New South Wales or were 'regular incurables, doubly and trebly convicted' transferred from Norfolk Island. Before long, Cockatoo Island suffered from a bad reputation. As colonial adventurer Godfrey Mundy explained:

> Cockatoo, like ... [Norfolk Island] may be considered as a
> college for rogues, of which New South Wales and Van Diemen's

Land are merely preparatory schools. The members must have matriculated, graduated, and become professors, in order to be entered on the books. A 'little go' in vice will scarcely entitle to residence![2]

For Aboriginal convicts, Cockatoo Island had a further claim to infamy. The mortality rate was higher than at Goat Island. Being sent to Cockatoo Island truly gave Aboriginal convicts cause to expect 'death in its most horrible form'. The majority of Aboriginal convicts transported to Cockatoo Island died shortly afterwards, some on the island itself but many at the General Hospital in nearby Sydney.[3]

In 1839, the first Aboriginal convicts arrived at Cockatoo Island. The five men – Sandy, Billy, Jemmy, Cooper and King Jackey – were defendants in *R v Sandy and Others 1839*. The men were suspected of murder following the suspicious disappearance of two convict shepherds although the charge was later downgraded to robbery. The defendants were indicted for 'stealing one waistcoat, the property of the Queen, two carbines, three pistols, seven blankets, one waistcoat, a quantity of gunpowder, six bullets, and a quantity of flour, the property of John Browne, John Hector and Edward Trimmer, from their dwelling-house at the new station, between the Gwydir and Namoi Rivers, on the 16th March'.

The 'new' station at which the alleged crime occurred was established that very same month because the co-owners found it 'necessary … from the great increase of their sheep and cattle' to supplement their original landholding on the Liverpool Plains. The hut housing the convict shepherds and their overseer was built adjacent to a creek where 'fifty or sixty blacks' usually camped, a group that belonged to a larger contingent of about 500 to 600 people. The events that led to charges being brought against the five Aboriginal defendants occurred as their land was being usurped.

Sandy, Billy, Jemmy, Cooper and King Jackey were taken into custody in late March by the Commissioner of Crown Lands, who 'decoyed' the prisoners into his tent. Given that William Mayne, in his capacity as Commissioner, was also a 'partial protector' of Aborigines, his actions call into question his capacity to act in either office. Mayne was nevertheless credited with restoring peace to the newly 'settled' area between the Gwydir and Namoi Rivers that had been in 'open war'. He was lauded by Chief Justice Dowling, who presided over the Supreme Court hearing on 16 August 1839, for bringing the Aboriginal defendants before the court, a rare event, according to the judge, despite there being not infrequent reports of 'many acts of outrages committed' by Aborigines.

The defendants spent five months awaiting trial because of the lack of an interpreter. Despite his incomplete knowledge of the men's language, eventually John Haggard or Haggart, a servant, filled the role. Sandy, Billy, Jemmy, Cooper and King Jackey pleaded 'not guilty'. Responding to a question about whether they preferred a civil or military jury, they said they 'did not like soldiers'. A civil jury was sworn, as was Haggard. Doubt was expressed as to the interpreter's capacity to fulfil his role. Dowling told the Attorney General to deal with the Aboriginal defendants 'the same as with a deaf and dumb man' and reminded the jury to deal with the prisoners 'exactly if they were white men placed in the same unfortunate condition'.

The case against the defendants was complicated by rumours about the murder of the convict shepherds whose hut the men allegedly robbed. On the grounds that the alleged murders 'could scarcely be separated' from the robbery of the shepherds' hut, details were provided to the court. On returning to his hut on 17 March 1839 after obtaining fresh supplies, Alexander Taylor suspected something was amiss. A search uncovered the remains of a man, but as these were not in a fit condition to be identified positively no murder charges could be laid. The court was provided with a vivid account of the grisly find:

> the bones found about forty rod from the hut were naked, putrid,
> and broken to pieces; the skull had several wounds on it, and a
> hole in the forehead, evidently done with a spear; the bones were
> quite green and apparently now stripped of the flesh; the thigh
> bones were broken and the marrow taken out.

The Attorney General made it clear to the jury that the sole reason
the defendants stood before the court indicted with robbery rather
than murder was because the remains could not be positively identified. This, he said, was 'the reason why the prisoners had not been
put on their trial for a more serious offence'. The description of the
remains with its references to a spear wound and bone marrow being
taken left no doubt that Aboriginal men, probably those at the bar,
were responsible.

Although the court was told that it was impossible to tell whether
the remains belonged to a white or black man, the spectre of cannibalism was raised through the description of flesh being stripped
from the bones and marrow removed. It was insinuated the remains
were indeed those of an unfortunate convict shepherd, with the jury
further unsettled by the news that no trace was found of the second
shepherd. The Attorney General observed how the defendants had
previously been on good terms with the white men and were 'treated
with confidence'. They had also 'shewed that they were not inferior
in intelligence to many white men'. Treachery was implied to the
packed court. After becoming privy to this information, the jury were
directed 'against allowing any out-of-doors observations which might
have reached their ears, to influence them in the consideration of the
case'. The charge, they were reminded, was 'simply that of robbery,
unconnected with that of murder about which much had been said,
and stated in evidence, from which it could scarcely be separated'.[4]

Because of the impossibility of the court receiving Aboriginal evidence, nobody could attest to the defendants' claims to have received the stolen property from two other Aboriginal men. The six-hour trial ended with the jury retiring for half an hour, and returning a guilty verdict. The defendants were sentenced to ten years' transportation to Cockatoo Island. They seemed 'greatly depressed', exhibiting countenances that displayed 'a most woebegone and wretched expression, as if expecting death in its most horrid form'. On having it explained that they 'would be sent across the sea for ten summers', the men 'brightened up'. The Attorney General expressed the hope that their punishment 'when it is made known to their tribe, will have a salutary effect'.[5]

Sandy, Billy, Jemmy, Cooper and King Jackey were transported to Cockatoo Island on 3 October 1839. Their sentences were halved to five years. The Aboriginal convicts probably laboured hewing stone. They may have been involved in digging silos, twenty of which were constructed at the island. These 'excavations in the solid sandstone rock [were] shaped like a large bottle', each with the capacity to hold 'up to 5,000 bushels' of wheat. Any convicts considered insufficiently productive during their working day were denied meals and left in the silos until their rate of work increased. The harsh regime at the penal institution took an extraordinarily high toll on its Aboriginal inmates. Within two months of their arrival on Cockatoo Island all five Aboriginal convicts were dead.[6]

While most Aboriginal convicts transported to Cockatoo Island died within a very short time of arrival, some survived a little longer. In 1840, Murphy, Toby and Tallboy *alias* Jackey arrived at the station to serve sentences of transportation ranging from three years to life. The experience of one of these men, Murphy, was most unusual because he survived the harsh conditions at the establishment long enough to be released from custody when his sentence expired on 11 February

1843. He was sent to Hyde Park Barracks then transferred back to Maitland. Perhaps his prior experience at Goat Island better enabled him to cope than other Aboriginal convicts. Toby, who arrived at Cockatoo Island with Murphy on 11 February 1840, was less fortunate. He died on 3 December 1841, just over halfway through his three-year sentence.[7]

Murphy's convict experiences did not deter him from recidivism. He was arrested in 1846 for larceny and sent back to Cockatoo Island as a 'rogue and vagabond'. This labelling marks a significant shift in the way Aboriginal people in outlying townships were policed, excluded from mainstream society, and sent into captivity. Around the time Murphy was arrested, complaints proliferated in Maitland from white residents concerned about 'pilfering and other annoyances perpetrated by the aborigines'. One such annoyance related to the conduct of Aboriginal people in town:

> We have been frequently disgusted at the number of naked
> blacks strolling about the streets of Maitland, and we are glad
> to find that this outrage upon public decency has at length been
> taken notice of by the proper authorities. Orders have this week
> been issued to the constables to apprehend such of the blacks as
> are found in a state of nudity in the streets of the town, and place
> them in the lockup, afterwards to be dealt with by the bench of
> magistrates.

These instructions were issued to the local police in October 1843, and three years later were extended to provide for the arrest of 'all aborigines who may be found loitering around the premises of any townsfolk'. By October 1846, Aboriginal people were effectively excluded from the township itself. Any Aborigines on the streets of Maitland were likely to be arrested and brought before a bench that had avowed to deal 'rigorously with them under the Vagrant Act'.[8]

Murphy was arrested on 28 October 1846 after being found taking bottles from the back of a local pub. He appeared at the Maitland Quarter Sessions on Monday 12 October 1846. Described in the *Maitland Mercury* as 'one of the native denizens of the soil, who rejoices in the Milesian cognomen of Murphy', he had shaken his waddy at the publican who disturbed him before being apprehended later the same day. When Murphy was brought before the Police Bench, he was sentenced under the *Vagrant Act* to six months' imprisonment with hard labour.

Murphy 'received his sentence with the utmost resignation', having already served time in local lockups, Newcastle Gaol, and on Cockatoo Island. The *Maitland Mercury* suggested Murphy had 'no doubt discovered that the beef and bread of those establishments are better than the scanty and precarious diet of the bush'. This remark taken in the context of the overall disparaging tone of the article about his arrest is indicative of the attitude that shaped the writer's perceptions. The foods of civilised life and the predictability of their availability were naturalised as a superior prospect when seen through Aboriginal eyes than the uncertainty of subsistence in the bush.[9]

Murphy evidently survived his 1846 sentence of hard labour, but cumulatively his imprisonment took a toll on his health. On Wednesday 1 July 1852, he was arrested and brought before the Police Bench charged with 'stealing a bundle'. He got twelve months' hard labour and was sent to Parramatta Gaol. On 13 May 1853, the Visiting Justice of the Gaol wrote to the Colonial Secretary about Murphy's health. In the Medical Officer's opinion, his health was such that 'further confinement would be attended with danger'. An annotation in the margin of the letter made it clear that Murphy was to 'be discharged when well enough' but he never recovered sufficiently to be released.[10]

The *Hunter River Gazette* used a similarly disparaging tone when, in addition to its regular report on the state of Newcastle Gaol, it mentioned that among the prisoners was 'His Grace the black Duke of Wellington, who is to be tried on a charge of injuring Her Majesty's white lieges'. The Duke of Wellington appeared at the Maitland Assizes on Friday 11 March 1842 as did another Aboriginal defendant, Fryingpan, charged with spearing cattle. Because the interpreter was unable to arrive in time for their cases to be heard, both defendants were remanded in custody.[11]

Wellington was indicted at the September 1842 Maitland Circuit Court 'for killing a cow, the property of Mr. William Scott, of Richmond'. Scott's overseer, George Bull, told the court it had been policy in the district to 'conciliate the natives' through allowing them to kill the occasional bullock to indulge their fondness for beef. While this initially met with some success, tensions rose to the point that Bull considered the 800 Aborigines in the region to be at 'open warfare with the settlers'. In the month preceding Wellington's trial, Aboriginal men killed two male colonists, while another two barely escaped with their lives. The occasional slaughter of a beast for Aboriginal consumption had been replaced by wholesale economic sabotage:

> lately they had killed beasts from mere wantonness, in some
> instances only cutting out the tongues, and making no use
> whatever of the carcases. Whole flocks had been treated in this
> manner … [T]hey had also slaughtered several hundreds of
> bullocks and a flock of maiden ewes, consisting of 497, all but 13.

Bull explained how a lookout was stationed near the stockmen's huts as an attack was carried out. The man would be punished by being 'exposed to have a number of spears thrown at him by all his fellows' if any lack of vigilance led to his companions being spotted.

Chief Justice Dowling was interested to know whether Aboriginal people 'had any conception of right to property'. Bull assured Dowling the men knew exactly what they were about when they attacked the colonists' stock and flocks. Dowling then sentenced Wellington to ten years' transportation. This was an unusually severe punishment for killing one cow despite the obvious context of ongoing frontier conflict. When asked to say why he ought not to be punished, Wellington 'merely grinned in the judge's face, and denied the charge'. As Dowling handed down his sentence, the defendant 'laughed outright, as if he considered it all a very fine joke'. While Wellington may have displayed a defiant attitude towards colonists at the frontier and in the courtroom, his spirit was broken in confinement. He arrived on Cockatoo Island on 15 October 1842 to serve a reduced sentence of three years but died at the General Hospital on 31 May 1843, after serving just six months.[12]

Fryingpan's case was delayed until the March Assizes where he also faced a charge of 'killing a cow'. The farm overseer Bull was the sole witness. He came across Fryingpan and five or six of his companions cutting up a freshly slaughtered cow, one of seven killed that day. Fryingpan and his cohort were portrayed as 'treacherous savages'. Bull said they hailed him with the word 'coolon' to imply friendship, only to throw spears at him once within range. The overseer brandished his gun at the men, chasing them away. Although the alleged event took place almost four years earlier, on 20 August 1839, Bull claimed to be certain of Fryingpan's identity. The defendant was sentenced to ten years' transportation, later reduced to three years. Fryingpan arrived on Cockatoo Island on 17 April 1843 where he died in custody on 9 March 1844.[13]

Tallboy *alias* Jackey arrived on Cockatoo Island on 11 September 1840 under a life sentence for being an accessory to the murder of a stockkeeper, Frederick Harrington, formerly employed by the late Reverend Samuel Marsden. Tallboy appeared in the Supreme Court of New South Wales before Mr Justice Stephen on 12 August 1840 charged with murdering Harrington 'by inflicting several deadly wounds on his head, by striking him with a tomahawk' and with being an accessory to the murder. The station where the alleged crime was committed, a run belonging to Mr James Walker on the Liverpool Plains, was at Myall Creek. In opening the case, Crown Prosecutor Roger Therry pointed out to the jury that:

> The present was only one of many outrages that had been committed on the whites by the aborigines in that distant part of the colony ... [I]t was a well-known fact that not only the property of the settlers in the distant parts of the colony had been assailed by them, carried of [sic], and wantonly destroyed, but a number of whites had from time to time fallen victim to the savage fury of the blacks. It was only twelve months since, not less than seven white men had been tried for, convicted, and executed for having been concerned in an outrage on the blacks.[14]

Therry was alluding to the cases *R v Kilmeister (No. 1) 1838* and *R v Kilmeister and Others (No. 2) 1838* that followed the Myall Creek Massacre in which he had assisted the Attorney General. The massacre involved the particularly brutal murder of around thirty Aboriginal people (mostly women and children) by twelve armed stockmen on 10 June 1838. The first trial ended with all eleven defendants being acquitted. After the second trial, public outrage over the hangings of seven men for killing Aboriginal people led to the Government never retrying the remaining four prisoners. Such strength of sentiment must have been almost impossible to set aside when Tallboy appeared before the Supreme Court less than a year later, charged with murdering a white man from the same area.[15]

Alexander Harris, 'the ne'er-do-well son of a respectable English family' who temporarily took refuge in New South Wales to avoid a court martial, was in the colony at the time of the massacre. He later described how:

> From this time forward (*i.e.* from the execution of the seven stockmen) the mischief increased. The blacks were driven out of huts where hitherto they had always found countenance and kindness. They in retaliation either did, or incited the wilder blacks to do, violence to the settler's property and to his men's lives. Then again, in return, the men and many of the masters shot them, with no more compunction than they would so many bush-dogs, in the secrecy of the bush, and left them there.[16]

Because of the secrecy with which colonists began to 'dispose' of Aborigines following the hangings, it became of paramount importance that the law courts were seen to be dealing effectively with Aboriginal offenders. The Myall Creek Massacre not only provided a turning point in Aboriginal and settler relations at the frontier, it was also instrumental in changing the way colonial judges dealt with Aboriginal defendants. Following the hangings of six white men and one 'mulatto', Aboriginal defendants were dealt with much more harshly than previously.

In summing up in Tallboy's case, Stephen cautioned the jury 'against being led awry by anything that had fallen from Mr Therry about seven white men having been executed for an outrage, of which it had been stated they had been guilty against the blacks'. He stressed that there 'was but one law for the black man as well as the white'. However, Stephen also stressed that 'laws should be strictly enforced' in punishing Aboriginal people when they committed outrages against whites, because any failure to do so could result in white people, 'by not knowing justice was done', becoming 'influenced by a spirit of revenge' and then committing crimes against Aborigines. On 12 August 1840, Stephen sentenced Tallboy to hang because he had been found guilty of the lesser charge of aiding and abetting. Tallboy denied any guilt and said 'he did not know what it was that *bit* the black men to make them kill the whites'.[17]

Tallboy's sentence was commuted to transportation for life. He was sent to Cockatoo Island. In November 1841 the Colonial Office wrote to the Principal Superintendent of Convicts to say 'the Secretary of State has signified Her Majesty's Pleasure of a Pardon being granted to the Prisoner [Tallboy, or Jackey at Cockatoo Island] on condition of being confined for life at Cockatoo Island'. The news came too late for Tallboy who had died on 28 November 1840 in the General Hospital.[18]

In the month Tallboy died, Billy *alias* Neville's Billy, appeared before Dowling in the Supreme Court in Sydney charged with 'killing a white man named John Dillon at Ullabalong, by spearing him, on 29th of February last'. William Jones, an umbrella maker from Sussex Street, Sydney, was the interpreter. A former convict, Jones had previously lived for about eight years near the Castlereagh River where he learned some of Billy's language. When the charge was put to him, Billy pleaded not guilty and alleged it was other Aboriginal men who killed Dillon.

In opening the case, the Attorney General acknowledged that Aborigines were 'at a disadvantage' in court, particularly as they could not call other Aborigines as witnesses. He said that it 'also frequently happened in cases of aggression by Aborigines, that the first offence was given by the whites, by their carrying off the gins of these blacks and otherwise annoying them'. He was, however, satisfied that this had not been the case in relation to Dillon. The victim was known to have been kind to Aborigines, and gave Billy bread and milk on the morning of the spearing. Billy also was the recipient of another 'particular kindness' when Jackey Neville, a settler living near Bathurst, gave him some clothing following which the prisoner had become known as Neville's Billy.

The two prosecution witnesses were Border Police, the first being William Jackson. Jackson told the court he heard from the dying Dillon's own lips that Neville's Billy was the person who speared him. Dillon, a free man 'on friendly terms' with local Aborigines, attributed the attack to his being unable to meet further Aboriginal demands for bread and milk after feeding Billy. Following Dillon's death, Jackson and another border policeman, William Power, rode out for ten days with six or seven stockmen unsuccessfully seeking the fugitive. Eventually a 'tame black' called Old Ben offered to 'bring him in', following which Billy acknowledged ownership of the alleged murder weapon. When asked 'what for you tumble down Waddy Monday?' (the nickname given Dillon by local Aboriginal people because of his wooden leg), Billy said to the border police he was told to do it by several other men.

In evidence, Power said Billy spoke English 'pretty well'. He claimed Billy had previously seen several men being hanged in Bathurst and had inquired whether he was to be dealt with in the same way. This information was presented as further evidence of the defendant's guilt, but also reveals some knowledge on Billy's part about how white justice worked in the colony. In any case, Billy refuted Power's claims, stating that the border policeman 'told lies of him'. This closed the case for the prosecution, following which the court-appointed defence counsel, Mr Broadhurst, spoke of 'the strong feeling which was known to exist in the Colony against the blacks' and urged the jury to 'try the case dispassionately and without prejudice'.

In summing up, Dowling pointed out to the jury some of the disadvantages faced by Aboriginal defendants. Reminding the jurymen of their status as 'intelligent, British subjects', he told them they were:

called on to administer justice to a savage, who was ignorant of the language, laws, and customs of civilized life; and called on them to mark the situation in which the prisoner and the judges were placed in such trials; by a fiction of law he was amenable to British law. He was accused of the murder of a British subject, a white man, one of a race of men who had seized on his native land; he was by fiction of law, a British subject, and as such was entitled to be tried by his peers, his equals; were the jury his equals? Did they know his language, his habits, or his customs? [The defendant] was not in a situation to conduct his own defence – he could not even instruct his counsel; he might have witnesses, but they … not being christians, would not be admitted to give evidence … it was in fact a one-sided trial.

Dowling instructed the jurors to pay attention solely to the evidence. He suggested the evidence was inconsistent with that usually tendered to support cases involving murder because it 'depended entirely on the frail memory of two illiterate men' whose testimonies showed some discrepancies. Although they were provided with grounds on which they could dismiss the case, the jury nevertheless returned a guilty verdict.

On 7 November 1840, Billy appeared before Dowling for sentencing. Dowling called Billy 'one of the wild children of the woods' who had been 'moved and seduced by the instigation of the devil' to murder Dillon. While acknowledging the prisoner's ignorance of God and Christian laws, he held Billy accountable for his actions because they were 'contrary to the law of nature' and sentenced the prisoner to death.[19]

Gipps exercised the royal prerogative of mercy and in a letter dated 19 November 1841, the Principal Superintendent of Convicts was notified that Billy was to be granted 'a conditional pardon' and was to be 'confined for three years on Cockatoo Island in Port Jackson'. Neville's Billy arrived on Cockatoo Island on 13 February 1841. Having narrowly escaped the hangman's noose, Billy's imprisonment led to his death at the General Hospital just two months later.[20]

A case involving an Aboriginal defendant, Darby, was also set

One of the first aboriginal convicts, Bull Dog was transported to Norfolk Island in 1805.

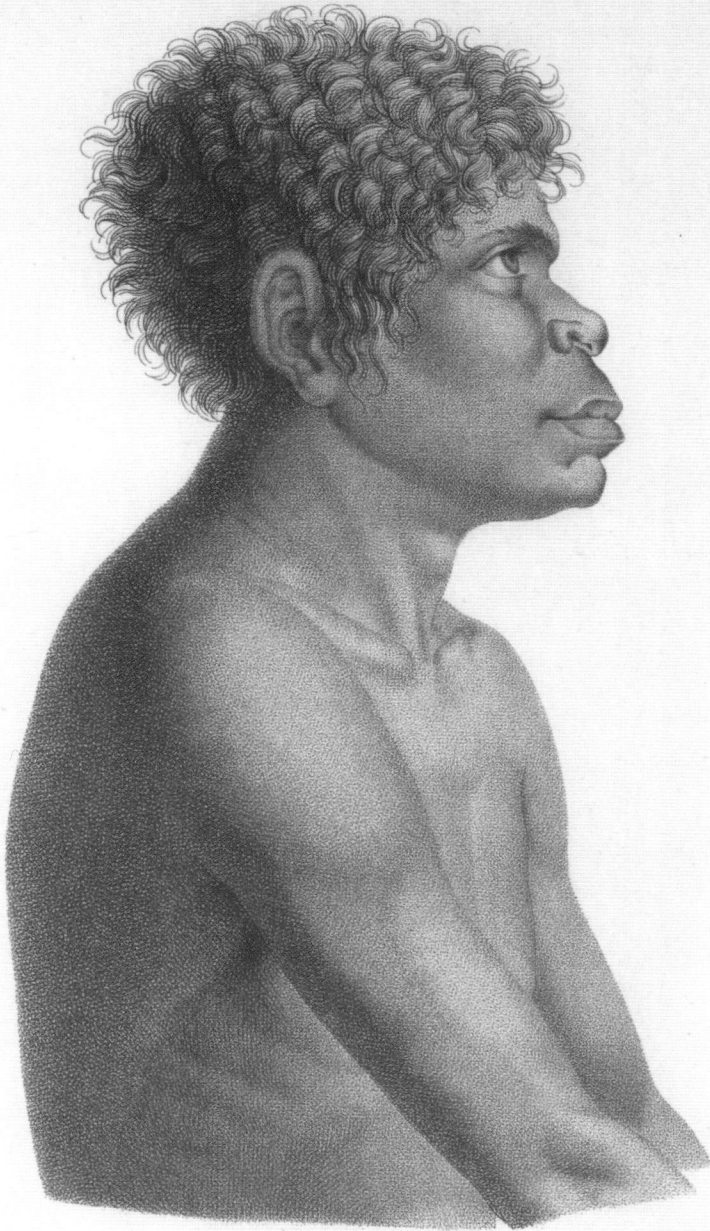

N. Petit del.   *J. Milbert direx.*   *B. Roger sculp.*

NOUVELLE-HOLLANDE : N.^{LLE} GALLES DU SUD.

OUROU-MARÉ, *dit* BULL-DOG *par les Anglais, Jeune guerrier de la Tribu des* GWÉA-GAL.

De l'Imprimerie de Langlois.

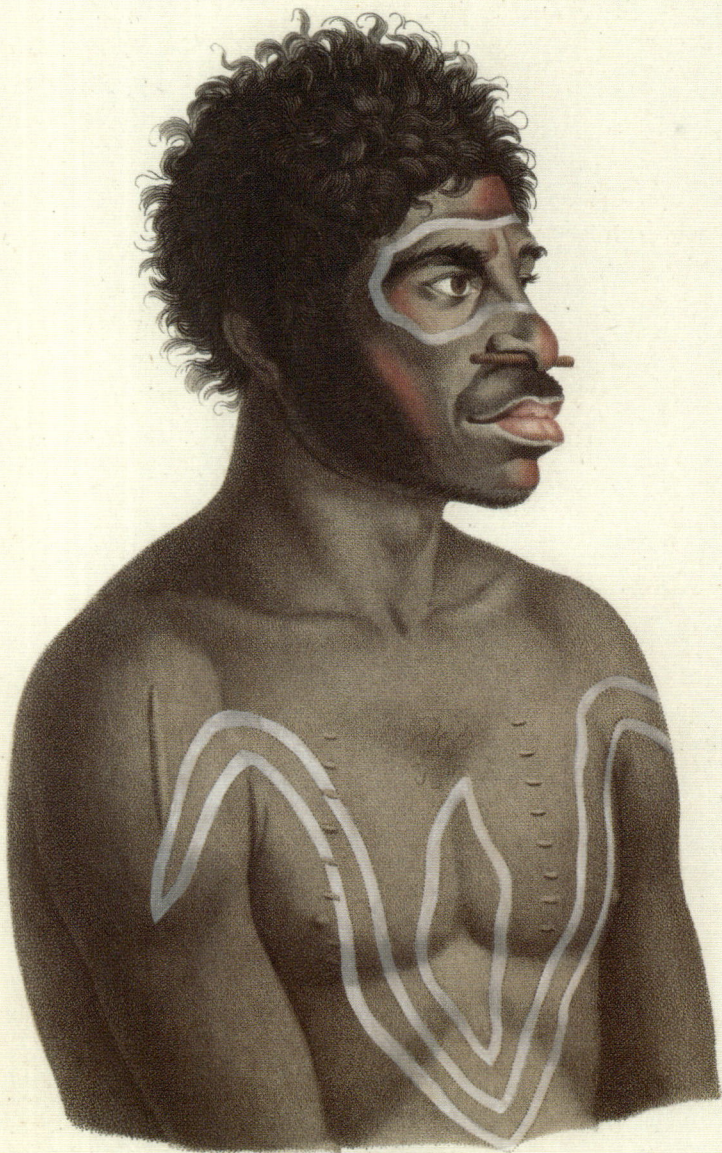

N. Petit del.   J. Milbert direx.   B. Roger sculp.

NOUVELLE-HOLLANDE.

Y-ERRAN-GOU-LA-GA.

De l'Imprimerie de Langlois.

Above Aboriginal native police under the command of white sergeants were used in the Port Phillip district to capture other aborigines.

Left Transported to Norfolk Island with Bull Dog, Musquito was hanged in Hobart in 1825.

Full credits for all illustrations in this section are on pages ix–x.

Above John Skinner Prout's depiction of the convict-built penal station at Port Arthur, Tasmania, 1846.

Right A convict's conduct record, like Yanem Goona's, provides details about their sentence, physical appearance, location, punishments, rewards and eventual outcome.

588	Yanem Goona				Transported for killing sheep with intent to steal the carcass. Gets his offence								
	Tried Melbourne Sep. 7th Oct. 1845		Millwar		Sheep Stealing. Married.								
	Emb.d	Arr.d 29 Oct 1845			a native of P.P. do not understand English								
	Pagan	cannot read or write												

Trade	Height	Age	Compltn	Head	Hair	Whiskers	Visage	Forehead	Eyebrows	Eyes	Nose	Mouth	Chin	N. Place
Labourer	5/5	60	a mean of colour	round	English	D.o	large	High	Black	Black	Flat	Wide	Round	N.S.W.

Remarks An aboriginal native of Melbourne

Period of Probation three years
Station of Gang Rofsett Island 14/8 etc. PP3 18 etc. etc. S.W.R. Impression Bay
Class

Offences & Sentences   Remarks

Arrived P. Lady Franklin 1846 & ordered to PPB to complete 4/P.P. then to be reported [to] Hobart

Died in Hospital at Imp. Bay
31st Oct.r 1848.

Hyde Park Barracks, Sydney, home to Khoi Captain David Stuurman in the late 1820s, and to aboriginal convicts in transit.

Museum Africa, Johannesburg. MA1954-568

Above 'Hottentot Convict' is one of many Khoi images by Cape Colony artist Charles Davidson Bell.

Right top Indents from the *William Glen Anderson*, on which Khoisan men were transported to Van Diemen's Land, are among the many convict records in the Tasmanian archives.

Right bottom Joseph Boulcott's farm in New Zealand's Hutt Valley was fortified to create a stockade where redcoats and Māori clashed on 2 April 1846.

Above William Duke visited Hohepa Te Umuroa at the Hobart Penitentiary and painted his portrait.

Right Hohepa Te Umuroa and his companions signed their portraits by John Skinner Prout at the Hobart Penitentiary.

*Hohepa
(Tei murata)
New Z*

In the Penitentiary
Hobarton
Nov

Ko mete

NEW ZEALAND

IN THE PENITENTIARY
HOBARTON
Nov 16.

Te Kumete

Te Waretiti

TE·WAREITEA· NEW ZE...

IN THE PENITENTIARY HOBAR...
NOV. 17.

Ko pi ta ma
te ka ni   NEW ZEALAND

IN THE PENITENTIARY   HOBOR
NOV 17. 4?

Te Rahui

Matiu Tikiahi

TOKOTOAI METAU TINANA
— ohoa —
HOHEPA TE UMAROA
WANGANUI NUITIRENI
I MATE HURAE 19
— 1847 —

Here lie the Remains
of
HOHEPA TE UMUROA
of Wanganui
NEW ZEALAND
died July 19

Most unusually for a convict, Hohepa Te Umuroa's grave site at Darlington on Maria Island is marked with an elaborate headstone.

against a backdrop of sporadic frontier conflict. When Philip Gidley King, in his capacity as a Justice of the Peace, wrote to the Colonial Secretary to advise him of Darby's 'atrocious conduct' in relation to the alleged rape of Elizabeth Lindsay, he mentioned how 'the blacks in this vicinity' had 'become more daring' after their 'late repulse of the Mounted Police at the Manning River'.

King complained of 'pilfering' by Aboriginal people, suggesting they would 'repeat their brutal practices until murder ensues, unless some active measures are taken to prevent it'. He informed the Colonial Secretary a £10 reward was posted for Darby's capture and asked that a further reward be offered. In response to this request, the mounted police were ordered to seek Darby. In addition, a reward of £26 or a conditional pardon was posted for the man's capture.[21]

Darby appeared before Mr Justice Dickinson in the Maitland Circuit Court on 11 September 1848. Having heard the prosecution witness's testimony, Mr Purefoy who had undertaken 'to watch the evidence on behalf of the prisoner' called into question her ability to 'identify a black whom she said she had never spoken to before, nor had seen by himself' but only as part of a group on a few previous occasions. The judge told the jury Elizabeth Hinton (*nee* Lindsay) may have been mistaken in regard to the prisoner's identity but affirmed she gave her evidence 'very clearly and in a very becoming manner'. Following the 'guilty' verdict, the judge advised the court that prisoners found guilty of rape were no longer subject to the death penalty and handed down a sentence of 'death recorded'. Dickinson explained he 'did not think the prisoner's education and opportunities could have fitted him for an early death'. The judge also 'thought the example of such a being losing his life was more likely to excite commiseration and pity than to act as a warning'. Dickinson's views exhibit a shift away from earlier judicial and administrative thinking that rationalised Aboriginal hangings on the basis that staging such events might provide an effective deterrent.[22]

Darby was remanded in custody in Newcastle Gaol. The gaoler wrote to the High Sheriff in Sydney on 16 November 1848 to inquire what he was supposed to do with the prisoner. A few weeks later, Darby was transported to Cockatoo Island where he arrived on 6 December 1848 to serve fifteen years on a road gang. The following year, on 12 May 1849, the Visiting Magistrate to Cockatoo Island, HHS Browne JP, wrote to the Native Police Office to state that Darby had died on Cockatoo Island the previous afternoon 'of natural causes' after having 'been an inmate of the hospital for some time'. There were no suspicious circumstances, so arrangements were made for the internment of Darby's body.[23]

11

A less destructive alternative

Near the end of 1850, the Native Police Office wrote to the Colonial Secretary about the death of Jemmy, another Aboriginal convict at Cockatoo Island. Penned by Visiting Magistrate HHS Browne JP, the short note said Jemmy had 'been a patient in the hospital for some weeks' and 'died from natural causes'. Browne's letter became the catalyst for an official investigation into the extent of Aboriginal deaths in custody on Cockatoo Island. In the margins of the letter, the Colonial Secretary wrote an instruction to a public servant to 'ask for a return of the number of Aboriginal Natives that have died on the Island during the last five years specifying the cause of death and of year'.[1]

Browne provided the Colonial Secretary with a return prepared by Superintendent Charles Ormsby at Cockatoo Island dated 16 December 1850. Ormsby's return revealed that of the nineteen Aboriginal convicts transported to the island between 1 January 1839 and 16 December 1850, twelve died on Cockatoo Island or in hospital in Sydney. Four convicts – Fowler, Sorethighed (variant spelling Southighed) Jemmy, Jackey Jackey and Tom (whose cases were discussed in chapter 6) – were sent to Darlinghurst Gaol pending a transfer to Norfolk Island. Billy Roberts *alias* Samboy or Jimboy (mentioned in chapter 9) was transferred to Van Diemen's Land. Another man, Murphy (who later died in custody as discussed in the previous chapter), completed his sentence, while Tom (introduced in chapter 5) remained on Cockatoo Island at the time.

While Aboriginal deaths in custody were not a new phenomenon, the concentration of such a proportionately large cohort of
Aboriginal convicts on one penal island was out of the ordinary
in New South Wales. This was the compelling factor that raised
administrative awareness about, and concerns for, the men's plight.
The statistics provided by Ormsby were sufficiently shocking for the
Colonial Secretary to issue immediate instructions for a board to be
assembled to 'consider some alternative which would be less destruc-
tive to the lives of these people than ... confinement on Cockatoo
Island appears to be'.[2]

The authorities' concern was no doubt exacerbated by the dis-
proportionately high number of deaths among Aboriginal convicts
when compared with their colonial counterparts. Aboriginal convicts
at Cockatoo Island were, for example, almost ten times more likely to
die within the first year of their sentence than non-Aboriginal male
convicts shipped to Van Diemen's Land between 1840 and 1844.[3]

By the time the authorities were notified of Jemmy's death, there
was no doubt in the minds of those overseeing Aboriginal convicts
that confinement was very dangerous to their health. In submitting
Ormsby's return, Browne wrote it was 'quite conclusive that the confinement of Aboriginal Blacks in the ordinary Penal Establishments
seriously affects their Health and Constitution and leads ultimately
to disease and death'. He noted that as it was customary to remove
seriously ill prisoners to the General Hospital, few of the Aboriginal
convicts died on Cockatoo Island itself yet their subsequent deaths
were the outcome of being held in captivity there.[4]

In February 1851, the Medical Adviser to the Government Dr
Patrick Hill wrote to the Colonial Secretary in relation to 'mortality
amongst the Aborigines at Cockatoo Island'. He enclosed a letter
from Browne reporting two further deaths along with a letter from
Dr O'Brien, the Visiting Surgeon to Cockatoo Island. Hill told the
Colonial Secretary he had met with Browne and O'Brien 'to consider

the subject of the mortality amongst the Aboriginal natives who have been confined on Cockatoo Island during the past five years for criminal offences'. The three shared the opinion that the high mortality rate was not predicated on any factors specific to Cockatoo Island such as climate. Instead, the deaths resulted from 'the fact of their having been confined'. They suggested the deaths probably would have occurred 'in any other locality' given that it 'is a well known fact that savages do not bear captivity but pine and die in any situation' of incarceration.

The men concluded that shifting Aboriginal prisoners from Cockatoo Island to other sites of incarceration 'would be useless' in terms of ameliorating the high death rate. Instead, they recommended that these prisoners ought to be divided into two distinct classes of men and treated differently:

> In cases where the offence has been of a grave and serious
> character and where the liberation of the culprit would tend
> to endanger society, we believe the evil must be submitted to,
> in minor cases it might be a consideration for the Executive
> whether a mitigation of sentence might not be granted when the
> health is observed to break down.[5]

The likely deaths in custody of Aboriginal men convicted of more serious offences were seen as an unfortunate but unavoidable evil. Under the framework proposed by Hill, Browne and O'Brien, only those considered to present a lesser threat to society might be considered for early release.

The Colonial Secretary directed the Visiting Surgeon 'to watch carefully the state of any Aboriginal prisoner who may be sentenced to Cockatoo Island or any of the other gaols in the colony'. In cases where 'longer confinement is likely to endanger their lives', the Visiting Surgeon was to be instructed to 'immediately report their cases'.

On 25 March 1851, he approved an official circular drafted four days earlier by the Medical Adviser who then forwarded it to 'the visiting surgeons at the gaols of Sydney, Parramatta, Goulburn, Bathurst, Maitland, and Brisbane'. It read:

> The attention of the Government having been drawn to the mortality which has been found to prevail amongst Aborigines of this Colony when confined for any length of time in gaols or other places of imprisonment, I am instructed by His Excellency the Governor to request that you will watch carefully the state of health of any Aborigines who may be imprisoned in ____ Gaol, and that you will immediately report, through the Visiting Justice, the case of any Aboriginal Native whose life you may consider to be endangered by longer confinement in order that the necessary steps may be taken for his liberation if the circumstances of the case may seem to justify such a step.

The official circular did not draw the distinction made in Hill's initial recommendation, but nevertheless hinted at this where it referred obliquely to whether 'the circumstances of the case' could be seen as justifying liberating an Aboriginal man otherwise likely to die in custody. Culpability and the capacity for reformation was predicated along racial lines – a person's perceived biological make-up being inextricably tied in the colonial mind to character traits that were considered to be innate and possibly immutable.[6] This point is elucidated particularly well in official correspondence relating to a case involving an Aboriginal man known as Peter.

Aged about 20 in 1851, Peter was described by the Reverend Thomas Sharpe of Bathurst as a 'very quiet' person 'who appears very wishful to have his soul saved'. Peter was in custody under sentence of execution handed down during the Bathurst Circuit Court for rape and assault. The minister's words were reproduced in a letter written by the missionary William Watson from the Apsley Aboriginal Mission petitioning the Governor and Executive Council to consider mitigating Peter's sentence. The missionary presented personal details relating to the death of the prisoner's parents and brother as well as more general comments about such cases in the hope of saving Peter's life. Watson suggested it would be more instructive and inhibiting to local Aboriginal people if 'some other severe punishment' were substituted as 'they would have a living evidence before them of the painful consequences of crime'.[7]

While Watson attributed Peter's predicament to his personal circumstances and the bad influence of the worst characters among the colonists, Mr Justice Therry took a different perspective. In a report to the Governor, he naturalised Peter's situation by recourse to colonial discourses about Aboriginal inferiority, stating that 'unquestionably ... even the most intelligent of the Aboriginal Natives are removed from even the most uneducated persons of the British race [by] ... many degrees of intelligence'. Referring to what he saw as their 'defective intelligence', Therry asserted Aborigines were 'persons who reflect very little, and who carry facts in their minds but for a short time'. He agreed with Watson that commuting Peter's death sentence to some other punishment would be instructive to other Aborigines, although he was 'at a loss to suggest' a suitable alternative.[8]

The Executive Council considered Peter's case on 4 March 1851. 'After mature deliberation', the Council decided the sentence of death would be carried out 'in Bathurst on Friday the fourth day of April'. This proved difficult to arrange. In a letter dated 11 March 1851, the Colonial Architect Edmund Blacket wrote that he had 'experienced very much difficulty' in having the gallows built because the workmen were throwing 'many ... obstructions ... in the way of its construction'. Blacket anticipated further problems in relation to 'its conveyance and erection at Bathurst', so proposed hiring men from

Sydney to perform the task.[9]

Following representations from a lawyer, the Executive Council ordered a stay on execution for a fortnight to allow the case to be brought before the Supreme Court. Therry and his fellow judges found no merit in the legal arguments put to them, but noted the rescheduled execution was to take place on Good Friday and could not be carried out on that date. Accordingly, the Executive Council decided Peter would 'be pardoned on condition of his being kept to hard labour on the roads or other public works for the term of fifteen years, and for the first three years of the said term to hard labour in irons' at Cockatoo Island. Within three months of his arrival on Cockatoo Island, Peter was dead. Suffering from 'inflammation of the lungs and liver', he was moved to the island's hospital on 16 July 1851 where he died on 2 August 1851.[10]

Despite convict transportation to New South Wales ending in 1841, and in the face of mounting evidence of the extraordinarily high death toll among Aboriginal convicts, Aboriginal men continued to be sent to Cockatoo Island well into the 1850s. Their mortality rate remained high. However, following official recognition of the issue of Aboriginal deaths in custody, persons charged with the care of Aboriginal prisoners were subjected to increased scrutiny. For example, when the Visiting Magistrate to Cockatoo Island reported that Joseph Milay died in the hospital on the island on 6 May 1853, questions were immediately raised as to whether there had not been 'some general rule applicable to the care of Aboriginal criminals'? A 'special report' was requested to explain why the instructions issued in the March 1851 circular appeared not to have been adhered to in Milay's case.[11]

In response, the Superintendent of Cockatoo Island claimed the only official correspondence held in his files about such matters was a letter dated 7 January 1851 in which the Colonial Secretary announced the establishment of a board of enquiry, a point confirmed in a letter from George West, the Visiting Surgeon to Cockatoo Island. In an annotation on West's letter, the point was made that the 28 March 1851 circular had been sent to the Visiting Surgeons at the respective gaols and the then Medical Adviser Hill. The Governor considered that as the Visiting Surgeon to Darling-hurst Gaol was one and the same person as the Visiting Surgeon to Cockatoo Island, the man ought to have been 'aware of the Instructions as applying equally to all Aboriginal Prisoners wherever the place of their imprisonment might be'. West later explained how the circular was 'immediately upon its receipt placed amongst the official letters in the Gaol Hospital' where it had since been relocated and brought to the attention of the relevant medical personnel. Deaths of Aboriginal convicts were no longer going to pass unnoticed and unremarked, with the colonial authorities from the Governor down raising questions about such incidents and apportioning blame to more minor officials.[12]

Increased vigilance and concern for the wellbeing of Aboriginal prisoners occasionally led to anomalous decisions. Two men, Peter and Stupid Tommy, were tried at Goulburn on 21 December 1854 and sentenced to three years on a road gang. They were sent to Cockatoo Island. They later requested tickets of leave so they could live in the district of Bong Bong. Stupid Tommy was eligible to gain this indulgence but was retained on Cockatoo Island so as not to separate the two Aboriginal prisoners. Presumably this outcome was predicated on the basis of concerns for Peter's wellbeing. Questions were raised about the conduct of both prisoners because it was recognised that the Crown was 'acting illegally by retaining a man who ought to be free'. Following this, both received tickets of leave.[13]

By 1858, the Visiting Surgeon was writing to the Colonial Secretary to inform him of the ill health of an Aboriginal convict, Billy Morgan, rather than waiting for death to eventuate. According to West, Morgan had pleurisy, a condition he was previously hospitalised for on four occasions. Enquiries revealed that the man arrived on Cockatoo Island on 7 June 1856 after being found guilty of murder. He had been sentenced at the Bathurst Circuit Court on 22 March 1856 to fifteen years on a road gang. Morgan's conduct on Cockatoo Island was 'good'. On 22 May 1858, West wrote to the Visiting Magistrate to Cockatoo Island to inform him that Morgan had again been admitted to hospital 'laboring under a similar attack of the lungs'. The Visiting Surgeon thought Morgan's 'life will be endangered by longer confinement on the Island'. His report was sent to the Colonial Secretary, with the Visiting Magistrate's suggestion that Morgan would have to be kept in hospital because 'were he to be let out his death could be certain'. This level of official care and concern for the wellbeing of an Aboriginal convict was unheard of prior to the 1850s.[14]

As the frontier extended across Queensland, Basket, Billy, John Bull, Du Key, Michie, Tommy (also known as King Kabed) and Duk were sentenced to transportation after court appearances in Brisbane in the mid-1850s. Circuit court judges continued sentencing Aboriginal men to transportation, including Harry Brown or Browne (also known as Yarry) sentenced at Maitland for rape, and John Keating (also known as Tommy) convicted at Bathurst and given two years with hard labour for assault with intent to commit rape. Similarly, Paddy was convicted in the Supreme Court in Sydney of assaulting 8-year-old Eliza Kennywell at Lismore Station for which he was sentenced to 'three years' hard labour on the roads or other public works of the colony'. All eventually received tickets of leave, with Keating getting his Certificate of Freedom. As late as 1865, Jackey got five years at the Mudgee Quarter Sessions for assault with intent while John Peacock was given five years at the same Quarter Sessions for horse stealing. Both were issued with Certificates of Freedom in 1869. So many Aboriginal men surviving within the convict system in the Australian penal colonies long enough to gain tickets of leave or freedom was unprecedented. Their survival suggests the conditions under which they were kept to hard labour were ameliorated sufficiently to preserve their health.[15]

- II -
THE CAPE COLONY

12

From the 'Cockatoo of Cape Town' to Sydney

Established by the Dutch East India Company (Vereenigde Oost-Indische Compagnie or VOC) in 1652, the Cape Colony was ideally located as a supply replenishing depot between Europe and the East and provided somewhere for invalided sailors or soldiers to rest and recuperate. For the next century and a half the Colony was left to its own devices and 'rambled away from the beaches far into the interior'. Dutch farmers, formally known as Boers but now referred to as Afrikaners, encroached on lands used by the coastal-dwelling Khoi cattle herders and the San or Bushmen hunter-gatherers who lived inland. Afrikaners also impinged on the boundaries of Xhosa territory. Their intrusion was met with resistance. Unlike the slave population, the indigenous Khoisan retained their freedom; however, as more of their lands and resources were taken over by the colonists, many became bondsmen working under contract as farm labourers. Others took on roles as soldiers, or sought refuge at missions, or joined the Xhosa in taking up arms against colonists.[1]

Near the end of the eighteenth century, the British came to appreciate the Cape Colony's strategic location and resources and, in 1795, seized it for their own use. When the British took over administration of the Cape Colony, they inherited a complex population. The Dutch had imported slaves into the Colony from as early as 1653, sourcing labour from Mozambique to Singapore and places in-between. Some of these slaves intermarried with the indigenous Khoisan (a collective term for the indigenous Khoi or 'Hottentot' and San or 'Bushmen'), forming a population referred to as 'Bastard-Hottentots'. Some Khoisan and European relationships resulted in a 'Bastard' population, while a variety of other terms were used to describe various other racial admixtures. Because of their prior claims to, and connections with, the land, the British were concerned about the potential for the Khoisan and Xhosa to form an alliance against them.[2]

Tensions between the Xhosa and the Dutch and, later, the British led to a series of nine frontier wars at the Eastern Cape spanning the century from 1779 to 1879. During the initial British occupation at the Cape from 1795 to 1803, three frontier wars were fought between the Dutch and Xhosa, all of which ended in stalemates. During these wars, numerous Khoi farm servants absconded from their colonial masters to join the Xhosa forces, sometimes taking guns and horses with them. This was a double blow for the farmers. With a growing shortage of slave labour in rural areas over the period leading up to the prohibition of the slave trade at the Cape in 1807, Khoi labour was becoming increasingly important to the rural economy. As part of a truce, and to entice insubordinate Khoi back to the land, the British proposed that those who laid down their arms could receive land grants. However, before the British could implement their proposal, the Cape was ceded back to the Dutch in 1802 under the Treaty of Amiens.

The Batavian Government was less inclined than the British to endorse Khoi autonomy. One of its priorities was to have the Khoi labourers who had deserted their positions on farms return to the land. A system of contracts was introduced in 1803 which favoured Boer masters more than their servants. Yet the new Governor, Lieutenant General Jan Willem Janssens, honoured the British proposal to award land at the Klein River, a tributary of the Gamtoos River, to

Khoi chieftain or 'Captain' Klaas Stuurman. Stuurman was considered one of the most important 'rebel' Captains.[3]

The role of Captain was in part a product of colonial circumstances, but its roots are to be found in long-established tradition. During the early period of European contact, the Dutch colonisers gave recognition to the chiefs of large tribes comprising a number of clans. Over time, these larger social entities disintegrated leaving clans, led by Captains, as the most significant social unit. Dutch East India Company officials maximised their influence by installing Captains of their own, bestowing a staff of office upon their chosen leaders and ensuring that the role became hereditary, usually passing from father to son.[4]

In his dealings with the Batavians, Stuurman was persistent in his claims for land. He also exhibited a willingness to negotiate with them at a time when not all Captains were so inclined. This saw him occupy 'a position of some importance in relation to the government's main goal of detaching Khoi from Xhosa and re-establishing peace'. Stuurman's persistence paid off and his followers settled on their allotted land. Significantly, this small enclave within the eastern district of the Cape Colony was the last freehold land in the Colony to be held by Khoi. Before he could join them on the land, Stuurman was killed in battle, leaving one of his brothers, David, to take over his position.[5]

South African historian Vertrees Malherbe identified a key incident of mistreatment in David Stuurman's early working life that probably influenced him to abandon his role as a farm labourer in favour of joining the Xhosa. It relates to punishment received at the behest of his master, the Afrikaner Johannes Vermaak, for whom Stuurman laboured. Vermaak took his servant to the Field Cornet Hendrik de Bruyn's place insisting that Stuurman be shot. After negotiating, Vermaak settled for Stuurman being 'tied to a wagon and beaten with sjamboks'. This method of punishing Khoi was described in a Sydney newspaper: 'beating and cutting with thongs of the hide of the sea-cow (hippopotamus) or rhinoceros are only gentle punishments, though those sort of whips, which they call "sjamboks", are most horrid instruments, being touch pliant and heavy almost as lead'. Harsher punishments reported to be in use at the Cape included 'firing small shot into the legs and thighs of a Hottentot' and even 'roasting alive … in extreme cases'. Following the whipping he received, Stuurman's suffering was compounded through being 'salted and left in the burning sun, for some hours'.

Stuurman and Vermaak remained on bad terms. When the farmer died, a number of his Khoi servants abandoned the Widow Vermaak and the farm. Their desertion upset some of the Afrikaners who allegedly murdered Magerman, one of Stuurman's companions, as the Khoi were en route to Algoa Bay. Stuurman joined his brothers in their rebellion against the colonists, a war that cost not only Klaas's life but also that of another Stuurman brother, Andries. After the war, when David Stuurman's followers had settled on their land grant in 1804, missionaries based at Bethelsdorp began to minister to the nascent community, treating it as an outstation of the London Missionary Society mission.

By 1809, the fragile accommodation between the small Khoi settlement and the surrounding Afrikaners was breaking down. Xhosa were impinging on the region, and the old distrust about alliances between Khoi and Xhosa loomed large in the colonists' minds. Suspicions were aroused when the missionary Van der Kemp visited the village and found the males to be absent and the women to have abandoned Christianity. Most of the cattle had been eaten. These disturbing signs led to the colonists destroying the Khoi village, using the pretext that Stuurman had refused to hand over several Khoi who allegedly deserted their Afrikaner masters. Some Khoi escaped the Afrikaner action to join the nearby Xhosa, most were pressed into service with local farmers, and several were sent to attend school.

The Afrikaners also took four prisoners – David Stuurman, his brother Bootsman, Cupido Michiel and Cobus Wildschut. The men were sent to Cape Town, and were accompanied by three of David Stuurman's wives and seven of their children. Initially, the entire party was put into prison on the grounds that they had engaged in 'suspicious conduct, living in a Kraal near the boundaries of the Colony'. Rather than appearing before the Court of Justice, it appears that an Executive decision was taken to have the men removed to Robben Island, eloquently referred to within the Australian penal colonies as 'the Cockatoo of Cape Town'. The documentation authorising Stuurman's removal to the prison island on 11 September 1809 described a different crime: 'disobedience to the Field Cornet'. His three male companions were removed to Robben Island the following month for the same alleged crime. In the interim, four of the Stuurman children died in custody.[6]

At the end of 1809, a group of prisoners escaped from Robben Island probably using a whale boat to reach the mainland. The escapees included both Stuurman brothers and their two companions. After splitting up to help avoid detection, Bootsman Stuurman was recaptured. However, David Stuurman, Michiel and Wildschut, managed to rejoin the Xhosa. A long stand-off ensued, during which time Governor Cuyler tried to entice Stuurman to surrender but to no avail. Stuurman lived among the Xhosa throughout the fourth and fifth frontier wars and was not recaptured until near the end of 1819 after being at large for a decade.

Stuurman was returned to Robben Island at the end of December 1819. Following another escape in August 1820, Stuurman was recaptured and sentenced to be transported for life to New South Wales. After being forced to watch as some of his surviving fellow escapees (some died during the attempt) were flogged, branded or hanged, Stuurman was returned temporarily to Robben Island until room could be found on a convict transport to convey him to the

Australian penal colonies. Under the Dutch, it had been possible for Cape Colony officials to banish miscreants. But under the English, the option of transporting convicts to the Australian penal colonies became a possibility. As early as 1815, Governor Somerset at the Cape requested permission from London to have people transported from the Colony to New South Wales. In response, the Admiralty instructed convict transports to stop at the Cape.[7]

Cape Colony courts found transportation a particularly attractive option in dealing with its various non-European populations. Sending Khoisan, slaves and others across the ocean with little hope of ever returning home provided a much more exemplary punishment than simply shipping them to Robben Island, in sight of Table Bay. Even a sentence to seven years' transportation to the Australian penal colonies effectively became a life sentence. The few Australian Aboriginal convicts who survived incarceration were repatriated when their sentence expired, but Khoisan were simply left to their own devices.

Overcrowding and illness on convict transports meant that it could be a long wait between sentencing and the sentence of transportation actually being carried into effect. Stuurman remained at the Cape following his 2 September 1820 trial through to February 1823 when the *Brampton* arrived at Table Bay. The transport had sufficient room to take on board convicts from the Cape.[8]

Another of the fourteen convicts loaded onto the *Brampton* with Stuurman was also described as a 'Hottentot', Jantje Piet, convicted for murder. Piet was to have been executed on 29 April 1820, but the Governor of Port Elizabeth, Sir Rufane Donkin, 'did not think it decorous' to carry the sentence into effect because this was the day on which the accession to the throne of King George IV was proclaimed at the Cape of Good Hope. Instead, Donkin granted the man a respite and wrote to Earl Bathurst, Secretary for War and the Colonies, for consent to have Piet's sentence commuted to transportation for life to New South Wales.[9]

On 28 July 1822, the *Brampton* sailed from London under the command of Master Sam Moore, a violent and abusive man, and with Surgeon Superintendent Morgan Price on board. Its cargo was to comprise Irish men under sentences ranging from seven years to life, as well as several free settlers. Most were from the labouring classes, with occupations ranging from errand boy, shearer and ploughman to brogue maker, music dancing master and linen weaver. Some were known to be rebels. Many had already spent a considerable time in gaol prior to departing from the Cove of Cork on 8 November 1822. The convicts were guarded by a detachment of the Third Regiment (Buffs) during the voyage.[10]

The few historians who have researched the transportation of Khoi convicts to the Australian penal colonies considered David Stuurman and Jantje Piet to be the first shipped to New South Wales. However, as the two waited on Robben Island for their forced passage to Sydney, another Khoi convict was already labouring for the Government of New South Wales on the public works. Sometime towards the end of January 1829, the 4'9¾" tall 'Hottentot convict' Hendrik Wessels absconded from his work gang. His unauthorised absence was advertised in *The Australian* newspaper on 30 January 1829, with readers instructed 'in the case of apprehension, he is to be delivered over to the proper authorities'. There do not appear to be any extant records within Australia explaining how Wessels arrived in New South Wales or what might have befallen him between his escape and death.[11]

The month after Wessels' escape in Sydney, in February 1823 Stuurman and Piet were put on board the *Brampton* along with twelve other convicts from the Cape to sail for Sydney. Two months later, on 20 April 1829, the convict transport arrived at Port Jackson. The indent prepared on board the vessel records that Stuurman and Piet were both tried at the Cape of Good Hope and were under sentence of transportation for life. In both cases, their 'native place' was listed as 'Cape'. Stuurman, standing at 5'3", was by far the shorter of the two; Piet was 5'10". Both men's complexions and hair are described as 'black', as are Stuurman's eyes. Piet's eyes were dark brown. The taller man was aged 40, whereas no age is recorded for Stuurman. Along with the soldiers, tailor and butcher who joined the *Brampton* at the Cape, Piet's 'calling' is listed as 'waggon driver'. Stuurman's is simply 'Hottentot'.[12]

A week after their arrival at Port Jackson the convicts from the *Brampton* were disembarked on Monday 28 April. The Governor, Sir Thomas Brisbane, travelled into Sydney from nearby Parramatta and inspected the newly arrived men. He was reportedly 'pleased at their healthy appearance', and the convicts were then 'distributed through-out the Colony' and put to labour. Piet's ability to control a team of oxen hauling a wagon meant his labour would be a valuable com-modity in the Australian penal colonies, just as it was at the Cape. In Van Diemen's Land, readers of the *Hobart Town Courier* were encouraged to 'congratulate' themselves on their 'condition' because the comparative costs of farming were much lower than at the Cape. Comparing the price of oxen, in 1829 a good working beast cost a Cape farmer the equivalent of £45 whereas the price in Van Diemen's Land had fallen from £20 in 1824 to just £7. Moreover, farmers at the Cape required on average five wagons and 150 'trained oxen' to work their land and haul their crop to market. Costs were involved, too, in acquiring an experienced wagon driver who (in 1829) could cost anywhere between £70 and £80.[13]

Piet's immediate destination is not apparent. However, in muster records compiled two years after his arrival in New South Wales, his details are accompanied by the remark 'vide Jan or Jaen Paap'. Paap, who had been tried at the Cape on 15 August 1820, was another of the Cape convicts who arrived on the *Brampton* with Piet and Stuur-man. He was described as a 'mulatto', and was a tall man, standing at about 5'11". Paap's age was given as 40 years in 1823, and his usual occupation was 'tailor'. By 1825, Paap, whose original sentence was for only three years' transportation, had a ticket of leave and was able to pursue his own business opportunities. It was not uncommon within the convict system for friends, acquaintances or spouses to have people close or at least known to them assigned as convict servants. It is therefore quite possible that Piet was in the tailor's employ, perhaps as a delivery driver.[14]

The 1825 muster records that Stuurman was labouring in Sydney as part of a Government gang constructing much-needed public works. A census of the colony's population taken in 1828 shows his location as Hyde Park Barracks, an elaborate brick building erected in Macquarie Street, Sydney, in 1819 to house convict men and boys. While Stuurman was in New South Wales, he was far from being forgotten by his relatives and supporters at the Cape. The Scottish poet and abolitionist Thomas Pringle, sometimes referred to as the 'Father of South African Poetry', took up Stuurman's case after hearing details from the missionaries at Bethelsdorp. After returning to England, Pringle published an article about 'the circumstances that attended the extinction of the last independent kraal ... of free Hottentots' that also exposed Stuurman's plight. Sir Richard Bourke, who was Acting Governor at the Cape from 1826 until 1828, read the article and, according to Pringle, 'immediately wrote to the Governor of New South Wales'. This intervention probably facilitated Stuurman being awarded his ticket of leave on 24 March 1829, at which point he had served only half of the required twelve years of a life sentence.[15]

Stuurman's ticket of leave records details of his trial date and convict transport as well as providing personal details intended to identify him. His year of birth is given as 1773, with his 'native place' being '50 miles from Cape Town'. His height is listed as 5'3¼" and his complexion 'copper colour'. Stuurman's once 'black' hair was now

159

'black to grey and woolly', his eyes 'brown encircled in blue', and he had a distinctive feature: he was 'lame of the right leg'. By the time he had earned his ticket of leave, Stuurman had become a 'labourer'.[16]

In the meantime, in 1827, New South Wales Attorney General Saxe Bannister began an eighteen month visit to the Cape. 'Devoted' as he was 'to the welfare of … coloured inhabitants and convicts in the Empire', Bannister met some of Stuurman's surviving children at Bethelsdorp. He later wrote about Stuurman's case, decrying the way in which 'the British functionary' Landdrost Cuyler who prosecuted Stuurman and oversaw the forfeiture of the prisoner's land had apparently obtained it for himself. Cuyler then 'held the Stuurman children in "abject servitude", whilst David Stuurman is pining, if alive, in New South Wales'. Bannister facilitated a petition from the Stuurman children to the Cape Governor Sir Lowry Cole to request the return of their father. The case, thought Bannister, was 'as much deserving mercy, as those of the Scottish Jacobites'.[17]

Bourke returned to England near the end of 1828, where he sought and gained consent for Stuurman to be returned to his country and family provided that the Cape Government did not object. Several years later, in December 1831, Bourke relocated his family to Sydney and took up a new appointment as Governor of the colony of New South Wales. He was thus able to inquire firsthand into Stuurman's circumstances. Rather than being the bearer of good news to the unfortunate convict, Bourke found instead that Stuurman had died the previous year, on 20 February 1830, at the General Hospital near Hyde Park Barracks in Sydney. He conveyed the sad news to Stuurman's family and friends. There appears to be no extant records regarding any burial, but given that cadavers were often donated for dissection during this period it is possible that this, too, was Stuurman's fate.[18]

Despite his relatively short enforced sojourn in New South Wales, Stuurman lived on in people's memories and was later portrayed as a patriot and hero of the Khoi resistance. London-born, Melbourne-based journalist and writer Marcus Clarke, best known for his novel *For the Term of His Natural Life* (1874), published a lengthy article, 'Stuurman – Brothers, Patriots, and Hottentots' in the *Sydney Morning Herald* on 6 May 1879. Clarke railed against the Dutch, describing the condition of Khoisan at the Cape under Dutch rule as 'something to shudder at', and recounted examples of Boer mistreatment of indigenous people. His account of Stuurman's life at the Cape relies on key sources such as Pringle. Unfortunately, he had nothing to add to the little that is known about Stuurman's experiences within captivity in New South Wales.[19]

In 1900, an author using the nom de plume 'Erin-go-bragh' wrote a piece for *The Queenslander* newspaper's Children's Corner on Lessons in Modern Geography titled 'The Last Hottentot Chief'. Like Clarke's earlier work, it concentrated on how terribly the Dutch had treated the Khoisan, which is hardly surprising given Australia's involvement in the South African (Boer) War at the time. The column also celebrated Klaas and David Stuurman as men who occupied 'a foremost position' when the English gave the Cape Colony back to the Dutch. It was also said, though, to be shameful that the English had later, on their return to the Cape, outlawed David Stuurman to New South Wales. With regard to Stuurman's term in the Australian penal colonies, the writer concentrated on Bourke's role in trying to obtain his release and repatriation. The only observation about Stuurman himself was that his conduct within the convict system 'had always been good'. 'Erin-go-bragh' concluded the article by reminding readers of the bronze statue commemorating Bourke that stands at the entrance to the Domain in Sydney, remarking with reference to his efforts to secure Stuurman's release that 'it was almost deserved for this one kind action alone'.[20]

Another mention of Stuurman four years later (in 1904) in the *West Gippsland Gazette* was far less empathetic. Written in the context of a 'Hottentot' uprising in German-controlled parts of South-West Africa, the unnamed author described 'Hottentots' unflatteringly as 'a curious wizened, yellow-faced tribe' who were 'lazy, careless and of light but active build'. Briefly tracing the evolution of the Cape military regiments comprised almost wholly of Khoisan, the writer also mentioned 'the last of their chiefs' who was 'deposed and sentenced to penal servitude for life in chains' in 1810. Brief mention is made of Stuurman's subsequent escape and recapture and his transportation to New South Wales where he died in 1830. Stuurman is not, however, mentioned by name. The article concluded by reassuring readers that the 75 000 'Hottentots' at the Cape were unlikely to rise up against the British administration there.[21]

13

Indicted for the crime of theft

Following Commissioner Bigge's reports on the Australian penal colonies, he was asked to undertake similar investigations at the Cape Colony, Mauritius and Ceylon (Sri Lanka). Bigge set sail for the Cape in February 1823 with fellow Commissioner of Eastern Enquiry Major William Colebrook, arriving there in July. At the Cape, they reviewed the administration of the Colony, paying particular attention to judicial, religious and financial matters. The British were particularly keen to investigate how and to what extent English law could be introduced, to emancipate government slaves, and to improve on the integration of Khoisan into colonial society.[1]

Initial recommendations from Bigge and Colebrook led to the Colonial Office drawing up a Charter of Justice under which the Cape Supreme Court was established in 1827. In a reformed judicial system that mirrored arrangements being implemented in New South Wales, the Supreme Court would hear all major civil and criminal cases and was given appellant jurisdiction over the lesser courts. Putting an English framework around the Roman-Dutch legal system they had inherited was one of Britain's first steps towards modifying the Colony's laws to conform to English jurisprudence. The notion of equality under the law was one of the precepts behind the abolition of district courts comprising the *landdrost* and his board or *heemraden*. These institutions inherited from the Dutch were considered incapable of impartiality when it came to trying non-European defendants.[2]

The British advocated ideals such as equality under the law, but in reality the newly instituted Supreme Court of the Cape of Good Hope did not practise what its London-based masters preached. The personalities of the four judges who sat upon its bench informed practices that ranged from infighting and nepotism to stubbornness and inefficiency. Senior puisne judge William Menzies particularly favoured measures to deal more harshly with crimes committed by non-Europeans and is remembered as having 'carped when required to go on circuit to hear cases involving the Khoikhoi'. Contrary to British aspirations towards equality before the law, the Supreme Court on occasion used transportation 'as a major deterrent to prevent the colony's non-Europeans from committing petty crimes against person and property'. For example, Chief Justice Sir John Wylde, former Deputy Judge Advocate in New South Wales (1816– 25), sentenced Clara, a Khoisan or slave, to be transported to New South Wales for stealing her mistress's comb. Another Khoisan, Jacob, suspected of stealing a sheep, was sentenced to be transported to New South Wales 'for the term of his natural life'. No evidence has survived to indicate that either Clara or Jacob ever arrived in the Australian penal colonies.[3]

The new judicial system saw the Supreme Court judges travelling on circuit. Circuit courts were held just twice a year in each of the three judicial districts (western, eastern and midland). No two circuits were held at the same time because at least three of the four Supreme Court judges were required in Cape Town to form a quorum. Judges on circuit had to fit in travel between court sittings. The journey from Cape Town via wagon to Swellendam, George, Uitenhage, Graham's Town, Somerset, Cradock, Colesberg, Beaufort, Patats River, Worcester and back to Cape Town took 312 hours. Judges sometimes spent up to ten hours per day either at the bench or in the saddle. Senior puisne judge William Menzies observed in 1828 that he regularly rode between 60 and 70 miles per day, was sometimes required to travel through the night, and was often compelled to sleep in his wagon. Following his death while on circuit in 1850, Menzies' demise was attributed at least in part to the rigorous requirements of the system under which he laboured.[4]

In 1831, it was Sir William Westbrooke Burton's lot to travel the arduous circuit. Burton, the son of a solicitor, began his career as a naval midshipman in 1807 before eventually being called to the bar in November 1824. Just three years later he accepted the position of second puisne judge at the new Cape Supreme Court, where his appointment was welcomed by Acting Governor Sir Richard Bourke. In a letter to Menzies penned while on an earlier circuit, Burton wrote that he 'cannot beli[eve] that there is any colony where the Puisne Judges have so arduous a duty as the Circuit imposes upon them here'. He particularly regretted having to leave his wife, Margaret, behind in Cape Town during his ten-week ordeal.[5]

During Burton's 1831 circuit, he sentenced six Khoisan men to transportation. At Somerset on 23 March 1831 three men aged from 25 to 50 were found guilty of cattle stealing. Klaas Loman and Arnoldus Jantje, whose crimes 'were aggravated by being before convicted of the same crime of theft', were sentenced to transportation for life. Willem Pokbaas, with no prior convictions, received a lesser sentence of seven years' transportation. The men were probably working together to rob Afrikaner farmers and may well have been supplying stolen beasts to Mandoor Wildschut, an elderly San also on trial at Somerset. Wildschut, who at age 60 stood 5'4" tall, faced charges of receiving stolen oxen. He was twice acquitted, but on his third appearance on 25 March 1831 was found guilty and sentenced to be transported for life. Adrian Van Wyk, aged 55, was tried during the same circuit and was sentenced to life transportation for 'stabbing a woman'. Willem Hartzenberg, aged 23, appeared before Burton after being charged with breaking into a cellar. He had already served five years for a similar offence. On this occasion, his misdemeanor saw him also sentenced to transportation for life.[6]

As death sentences or sentences to transportation required executive fiat, Burton had to justify these sentencing decisions. He reasoned that as Pokbaas was relatively old, inflicting corporal punishment or subjecting him to hard labour would be too cruel. Yet he was reluctant to impose too light a punishment given the serious nature of Pokbaas's offence. Wildschut, too, ignited Burton's compassion on the grounds of his age. But his crime also could not be ignored. According to the judge, Wildschut was 'represented to me as the captain of a very mischievous and dangerous band of bushmen'. Van Wyk's sentence to transportation was based on his being given the benefit of the doubt in a case that could otherwise have resulted in hanging for murder. The remaining three men – Loman, Jantje and Hartzenberg – were all repeat offenders whose previous punishments failed to curb their recidivism.[7]

The sentenced men were held at Robben Island pending the arrival of a convict transport. It was not long before they caught their last glimpse of their homeland. The 389 ton, newly built convict transport *William Glen Anderson* departed Portsmouth on 1 June 1831 and arrived at Table Bay in mid-September with room on board. The transport was on its way to Van Diemen's Land. Captain Smith, the master of the vessel, died en route, leaving James Fawthrup to take command. He was assisted in overseeing the 177 male and two female prisoners by Surgeon Superintendent Charles Inches. The guard was drawn from the 4th Regiment, and comprised one man each at the ranks of major, lieutenant, sergeant and corporal, and twenty-seven rank and file soldiers.[8]

The indent prepared on board the *William Glen Anderson* prior to its convict cargo being unloaded at Hobart states that all six Khoisan prisoners on board were tried at the 'Cape of Good Hope'. It records their heights as ranging from 5'2", Klaas Loman being the shortest in stature, to 5'9¼" for Willem Hartzenberg. Scant personal details are recorded, but the few remarks listed beside the names of the Khoisan convicts reveal poignant details. Jantje and Hartzenberg left wives behind at the Cape. Loman had 'no relations'. Wildschut is described as 'an old Bushman whose language cannot be understood'. His occupation was left blank, while the other Khoisan were said to be labourers. As the *William Glen Anderson* prepared to sail for Batavia, the prisoners offloaded in Van Diemen's Land were being accommodated within the convict system. The six Khoisan, all described as 'mulatto' in the convict description records, were dealt with in accordance with their capacity in terms of labour and the perceived risks in housing them.[9]

Mandoor Wildschut, described in papers assigning convict servants to their colonial masters as a 'wild man not to be understood', was sent to the penal station at Port Arthur to join the invalid gang. He died there on 5 January 1834. Willem Pokbaas, a 'cripple', also joined the Port Arthur invalid gang and worked in the office. Both he and Wildschut were earmarked for the probation station at Maria Island, although neither was transferred there. Instead, Pokbaas was sent to Launceston on 11 September 1835 to work in Commissary George Hill's office. After completing his seven-year sentence, Pokbaas had no way of returning home. He became reliant on 'the alms of the charitable', and spent his nights sleeping rough behind the lime kilns at Veteran's Row in Launceston. A decade later, the local newspaper reported 'a man of colour, named William Pockless' had been found dead. His death was ruled by the coroner as instantaneous following 'the bursting of an aneurism of the aorta'.[10]

The remaining four Khoisan were assigned as servants to various colonial masters. Adrian Van Wyk served Lieutenant William Gunn, 'a man of distinguished courage, gigantic stature and strength, and a most untiring energy'. The 6'7½" tall Gunn had retired to Van Diemen's Land following a career with the East India Company. He farmed near Sorell, 15 miles from Hobart, and enjoyed a distinguished career capturing bushrangers, albeit at the cost of an arm. The Lieutenant and a contingent of soldiers were pursuing Matthew Brady and his gang when the bushrangers turned the tables on their pursuers, locking them in Sorell gaol for the night along with a group of Hobart Town dignitaries in the vicinity for a dinner party. In the fracas, Gunn was shot. He was recompensed with a government pension of £70 per annum and appointed to superintend the Hobart Town Prisoners' Barracks.[11]

Gunn was not at all happy with the conduct of his newly assigned servant. On 22 April 1833, he reported Van Wyk's conduct as 'turbulent and disorderly'. Three days later, the servant was found drunk. Van Wyk was punished with three days in the cells then sent to join a road party. After being found with 'turnips in his pockets' that he could not account for on 26 June 1834, he was given three days' solitary confinement on bread and water. The following month, Van Wyk was charged with 'neglect of duty and refusing to work'. His health was suffering in exile, and on 18 July 1834 he was transferred to the invalid road party at Green Point (now Bridgewater). Several months later, in September, he was sentenced to three lashes, one for each hour's absence from his road party.

While under sentence, Van Wyk lived at various locations in Van Diemen's Land, including New Norfolk, a small inland town west of Hobart. Such mobility was typical in the lives of convict labourers who moved from place to place as one job ended and another began. Van Wyk received his ticket of leave on 24 February 1840, although his offending continued. As well as being absent from a muster, he received a 5 shilling fine for getting drunk. His conditional pardon followed on 17 May 1843, with word being received from the Secretary of State on 7 April 1848 that Her Majesty approved the pardon. While he was not allowed to return to the Cape, Van Wyk was given the comparative freedom of being allowed to live anywhere within the Australian colonies or New Zealand.[12]

When the *William Glen Anderson* discharged its human cargo, Dr Thomas Gorringe was also seeking a servant. The surgeon lived with his family at Green Ponds (now Kempton). Land Commissioner Roderic O'Connor took a dim view of the medico's rural venture, lambasting him for 'farming miserably' and being 'nearly insolvent'. Nevertheless, Gorringe took Klaas Loman into service. By February 1833, Gorringe had asked the Government to take Loman back owing to the servant's 'general idleness'. Trouble brewed at the next household that hired Loman. He received a month's imprisonment with hard labour for using bad language and 'beating one of his fellow servants repeatedly'. On his release, he was reassigned to the Bayly household but fared no better. On 25 July 1835, Loman was admonished for severely neglecting his duties.

A high point in Loman's convict career came in August 1835 when he caught a prisoner who absconded from the Grass Tree Hill road party. However, shortly afterwards Loman received twenty-five lashes for refusing to work. This pattern repeated, and earned him a week in prison on a diet of bread and water in December 1835 for 'insolence and neglect of duties'. Most of the rest of Loman's captive life was spent doing hard labour, initially on a road gang but later in chains at Port Arthur where he was sentenced, in May 1839, for a year after 'stealing one opossum skin rug of the value of 20 shillings the property of Mr McKenzie'. He also worked on the town surveyor's chain gang, but was found drunk and given a further month's hard labour. The bench recommended a transfer to the New Town Bay hulk gang. His ticket of leave was issued on 6 January 1842, but Loman continued to be found 'drunk and disorderly' and served further time in solitary confinement. His drunkenness was compounded in August 1842 by an assault on a constable, which earned Loman twelve months' hard labour in chains. He died shortly thereafter while still in custody.[13]

Willem Hartzenberg, also known as William Moses, was hired

by William Pike who owned Park Farm at Jericho. In August 1832, Pike complained that Hartzenberg disobeyed his orders and abandoned his employment on 21 August, not returning until the following evening. For this offence, Hartzenberg was given fourteen days on the tread-wheel. This involved holding a bar and trudging up and down stairs with other convicts whose combined manpower turned a large wheel to generate power. Their overseer ensured each man maintained silence. Afterwards, Hartzenberg was assigned to the road gang at Constitution Hill, a particularly steep section of the highway connecting Hobart and Launceston. This was heavy work, so being put on short rations for a fortnight in December 1832 after being found gambling would have taken its toll.

On 14 January 1833, Hartzenberg absconded from the Constitution Hill road gang but was caught the following day. He was transferred to the Bridgewater chain gang for six months' punishment, before being reassigned. Things went badly. After assaulting his master, Hartzenberg was sent to do hard labour with the Melton Mowbray road party. He continued to accrue punishments, being whipped one hundred times for trying to break out of gaol and later being sent to Port Arthur. His transfer was inevitable because Hartzenberg declared in front of a magistrate that he would kill Howell Howell [sic], the local constable at Bothwell. Howell, a convict from England who arrived on the *Andromeda* in 1827 under a life sentence, was dismissed the following year and also sent to Port Arthur for trying to induce a convict to escape from a road party so that he could 'capture' them and obtain a reward. Perhaps he had similarly tried to advantage himself at Hartzenberg's expense.

The constables escorting Hartzenberg to Port Arthur got as far as Austin's Ferry, 65 miles from the penal station, when their prisoner made a bid for freedom. It cost him another fifty stripes. On 5 November 1834, a further one hundred lashes was ordered. This time, he had got as far as Wedge Bay, about nine and a half miles from Port Arthur, before being caught. While at large, he took a tinderbox and knife from a messenger he had stopped on the road. For this, Hartzenberg got fourteen days' solitary confinement on top of the whipping. Fault continued to be found with him. He received fifty more lashes in December 1834 for 'making use of insolent and threatening language to the overseer and refusing to work'. For having a pipe and tobacco, Hartzenberg spent another ten days in solitary confinement in January 1835. Later, he absconded from another convict work gang, this time at Grass Tree Hill, and was sent back to Port Arthur, a place he seemed unable to avoid.[14]

By the mid-1830s, the space set aside in the register to record Hartzenberg's misdemeanours was full. A new page in a different register also filled rapidly. Between 1835 and 1845, Hartzenberg was sentenced on seven occasions to solitary confinement on a diet of bread and water for an overall total of thirty days for offences ranging from taking thread from the tailor's shop and 'privately working on Sunday', to trying to steal biscuits and destroying his government blanket. He did more than five and a half years' hard labour at Port Arthur, mostly in chains, for eleven offences ranging from using a pipe and tobacco to trying to break out of Brighton Gaol while en route to Port Arthur. His return to the penal station from Green Ponds road gang resulted from another of his numerous, but unsuccessful, attempts to abscond. An earlier attempt resulted in fifty lashes in February 1838, the last of the whippings Hartzenberg received in custody. Of the numerous charges brought against him, Hartzenberg was only acquitted of one, letting men fish while he was in charge of a boat.

Despite his blotted record, Hartzenberg progressed through the classes in the convict system, attaining second class on 8 September 1846 and third class on 16 December 1847. When he was returned to Port Arthur on 10 February 1869, Hartzenberg was classified as a class-four prisoner or ticket-of-leave man. Outside the convict system, he sustained himself through working as a gardener. His record was not entirely clean; on 27 August 1862 he was found guilty of breaking and entering someone's home in Richmond. However, the offence that triggered his return to Port Arthur in 1869 was not theft. This offence, being 'idle and disorderly', derived from the potential for him to engage in criminal activity. This earned Hartzenberg a six-month sentence to imprisonment and hard labour.

In July 1869, he was transferred to the pauper depot at Port Arthur. Like Pokbaas, he had become an impoverished old man with no means of returning home. At the time, the Tasmanian Government was in the process of having Port Arthur wound down. The local press became critical of the practice of shipping 'old men' to the penal station as conflicting accounts emerged over the state of things down the peninsula. One story claimed 'that the heads of departments instead of living together in brotherly good feeling ... thereby showing example to the inmates and contributing to their comfort, maintain a cat and dog life in which the superior authority of the Commandant gives him the power ... of being annoying and irritating'. The *Mercury* claimed insufficient resources were set aside for the adequate care of paupers at Port Arthur, predicting that 'the Dead Island of the establishment ... [was] in all probability destined to be the final resting place of not a few of them'.[15] When Hartzenberg died in 1875 he may have joined approximately 1000 others, including officials, their families, soldiers, seamen and convicts, on the Isle of the Dead.

When Arnoldus Jantje arrived in Van Diemen's Land he was assigned to W Yeoland. Jantje's first offence was recorded on 5 November 1832 as 'gross insubordination', which earned him three months' hard labour on the Launceston chain gang. His conduct as a convict was marred by drunkenness, a repeated offence that saw him admonished and receiving punishments ranging from sleeping in a cell and being put into solitary confinement to doing three days on a tread-wheel on a diet restricted to bread and water. On 22 January 1841, Jantje was found guilty of 'gross misconduct in ill-using a cow, the property of his master, which died from the ill treatment'. He had to do another three months' hard labour. On completion of this, he received his ticket of leave but continued to accrue fines, mostly for drunkenness but also for failing to attend the 1842 muster. Nevertheless, in January 1846 Jantje's conditional pardon was approved on the grounds that he had 'held a Ticket of Leave very much beyond the ordinary time and there being no serious offence on record against him'. This was not, however, the end of Jantje's convict career, which recommenced when he met up with Scipio Africanus.[16]

In June 1837, Scipio Africanus disembarked in Sydney from the former slaver, the *Schah* schooner, after leaving behind his parents, brother and sister at the Cape. He lived at a Mr Stewart's place in Sydney, working as a groom. This arrangement did not last long. On the night of Thursday 7 September, Africanus caused a 'tremendous hubbub' when he sneaked into a fowl-house in Pitt Street. The birds caused such a commotion that Mrs Savage and a retinue of servants rushed down the yard to see what was amiss. The astonished woman saw 'a dark ball in one corner from which projected something very much resembling the paw of a bear, in the claws of which was her pet bantam cock'. She told the servants to remove the intruder, and 'after a little poking, out rolled a Hottentot, in full feather, cognominated Scipio Africanus'. When questioned, Africanus 'simply shook his head', so he was handed over to the local police. On being admitted to Sydney Gaol, his age was recorded as ten years and his height as 5'4".

At the Sydney Quarter Sessions on 13 October 1837, Africanus was found guilty of horse stealing and taking two fowls from a Mrs Lowitt in Sydney. He was sentenced to seven years' transportation and shipped to Van Diemen's Land on the *Marian Watson*, arriving in Hobart on 30 October 1837. Perhaps it was the youth's short stature that led to Africanus being listed as only 10 years old at Sydney Gaol, because after he was questioned in Van Diemen's Land his age was recorded as nineteen. Africanus's life in captivity was characterised by numerous attempts to abscond. He was punished through being whipped, put in solitary confinement on a diet of bread and water, and being given hard labour in chains. After labouring in the Campbell Town chain gang then on the road party in 1839, he was transferred to Port Arthur for 'being an incorrigible runaway'.

At Port Arthur, Africanus continued to accrue offences. Among other punishments, he was reprimanded for 'washing his shirt during divine service', and given six months' hard labour in chains for 'having pork improperly in his possession'. His numerous illicit bids for freedom had the opposite outcome from that which he hoped, as his sentence was extended rather than truncated. Africanus did not receive his ticket of leave until 6 August 1847, having served three years on top of his original sentence. As a ticket-of-leave man, he continued to upset the authorities. He pretended to Constable Flannery that he was a free man when the policeman found him drunk on 5 August 1848. He also failed to report to the Police Office when required and was warned against continuing to consort with 'another man of colour named Jonkiss'. This man was undoubtedly Arnoldus Jantje, whose name was originally recorded in the convict records as Jantjes. The two Khoisan were living rough in the bush, and were suspected by the District Constable of 'gaining their living by sheep stealing and kangarooing, without a License'. When the police let Africanus go, he gave his word that he would go and live at a Mr McCrae's at the Eastern Marshes. However, after seven days in the cells he rejoined Jantje in the bush.

The following month, September 1848, Africanus again attracted unwanted attention. He was found being 'out after hours' and given three months' hard labour as well as being prohibited from living in Hobart. Reverting to his earlier pattern of behaviour, Africanus absconded from the Spring Hill road party in November 1848 and was punished with eighteen months' hard labour in chains to be served at Norfolk Island. In October 1849, he absconded from Norfolk Island and a £2 reward was offered for his capture. Finally, on 19 August 1850, Africanus received his Certificate of Freedom.[17]

Following Africanus's release, he and Jantje met up again. Less than a year later, both were back in court, appearing at the Richmond Quarter Sessions on 21 July 1851 charged with stealing a clothesline and other articles (trousers and a waistcoat) from Michael Fagan. Both got six months' imprisonment with hard labour at Richmond Gaol. At the end of August, they were sent to join the gang working at Cascades on the outskirts of Hobart. Just before Christmas, on 23 December 1851, Jantje was transferred to the Prisoners' Barracks then released 'to freedom'.[18]

Jantje's original convict conduct record states that he was at Cascades on 23 June 1876. As another impoverished and displaced Khoisan, he was probably admitted to the Cascades Pauper and Invalid Establishment and Reformatory. In a newspaper article published the following month, the Cascades establishment was described as 'semi-benevolent' and 'semi-penal', a likely destination for a destitute, elderly former convict.[19]

Africanus did not enjoy his freedom for long. On 19 April 1852, he appeared at the Richmond Quarter Sessions where he received a sentence to transportation for life. He was sent to Port Arthur and resumed his old pattern of absconding. In his final attempt at throwing off the constraints of the convict system, Africanus drowned in January 1853 when his canoe overturned near Tasman Island, just off the tip of the peninsula where Port Arthur stands.[20]

Throughout the 1830s, the civil court continued to use transportation of Khoisan from the Cape to the Australian penal colonies to instil in those left behind the fear of being sent over the sea forever. Unusually for indigenous convicts, the next prisoner to arrive from the Cape was female. Mina Magerman was shipped to New South Wales on board the *Diana* in 1833 after being convicted of 'culpable homicide'. The 5' tall, 27-year-old woman, recorded in the convict records as being from 'Cafferland', was tried on 15 April 1830. She was sentenced to seven years' transportation. Given the seriousness of the crime, her sentence seems remarkably light, so mitigating circumstances can reasonably be assumed. Magerman's occupation is given as 'servant', so she may have been sent into service when she arrived in New South Wales.[21]

By the mid-1830s, the population of the colony of New South Wales, including Port Phillip, numbered 25 254 male convicts and 23 121 free males over the age of twelve compared with a mere 2577 female convicts and only 11 973 free females over the age of twelve. This gender imbalance made women sought-after commodities, as servants, wives and child bearers. While still within the constraints of the convict system, Magerman married William Stephens, a black American convict who arrived in New South Wales on the *Atlas* in 1819 after being sentenced to seven years' transportation. Her marriage to Stephens was recorded on her Certificate of Freedom, issued on 3 May 1838, just five years after her arrival in the colony.[22]

Magerman's marriage did not last. In the closing months of 1859, Sydney was rocked by an event dubbed 'the Durand's Alley tragedy' by the media. At a house in the alley, an Irishwoman, Margaret Wallace, was assaulted in October 1859, lingering for a month before dying in hospital. The late Wallace, 'a drunken dissolute character', was said to give the appearance of being sixty although she was only forty. An investigation into her death saw charges brought against a 'man of colour' known as Joe. During the inquest, it was revealed that she 'had for some years been living with an African black, known by the sobriquet "Black Jack"'. This was none other than Stephens, the one-time husband of Magerman. After receiving his ticket of leave, Stephens lived in Sydney where he worked as a bricklayer's labourer until his 'legs gave way', following which he collected bottles (and reputedly ran a brothel) for a living. Despite frequent quarrels, Wallace and Stephens cohabited for five years prior to the woman's death. His marriage to Magerman was not mentioned during the coronial inquiry.[23]

Back at the Cape, in the mid-1830s tensions were rising. The imminent emancipation of the slaves and the prospect of a sixth war with the Xhosa fuelled colonial insecurities. It was in this general climate that Chief Justice Wylde rode the circuit in late 1834 during which he sentenced thirteen Khoisan men to transportation. All of the sentences were approved by the Governor. As with the cohort conveyed on the *William Glen Anderson*, those under sentence were indicted for theft.[24]

Nine Khoisan were transported to New South Wales on the *Eden* in 1836. Jan Aaron and Africaander Speelman appeared before Wylde at Graham's Town on 14 October 1834 charged with office breaking. Aaron, who had previous form, received a life sentence, although by 1837 he held a ticket of leave. Speelman got seven years. The following day, Hermanus Baardman, Kleinboy Adam and Williem Marthinus were found guilty of robbing a wagon and sentenced to transportation for the term of their natural lives, to be kept at hard labour at Robben Island while awaiting passage to the Australian penal colonies. Adam received his ticket of leave in New South Wales in 1837. Willem Hans, also called Carolus, appeared before Wylde at Somerset on 27 October 1834 charged with theft. Hans had a history of similar offences. The Chief Justice sentenced him to life transportation. Another Jan Aaron, also known as Jan Bastaard, received a life sentence from Wylde the following day for housebreaking and outhouse breaking with intent to steal, and theft. He, too, had prior convictions. Despite his life sentence, he also received a ticket of leave in 1837. Wylde was at Graaff-Reinet by 3 November where he sentenced Matthys Jantje to seven years' transportation for theft. These eight were joined on the *Eden* by Paul Tygervalley who was sentenced on 26 April 1836 to transportation for life for cellar breaking.[25]

Two other Khoisan were transported to New South Wales in 1836. Cobus Zeeland, a Lutheran with no education employed as a groom and labourer, arrived on the *Lady Nugent*. He was under a sentence to seven years' transportation imposed at Swellendam on 23 September 1834 after stealing a goat. Zeeland received a ticket of leave two years later, in 1836. It was not his first offence. Jan Windvogel who, like Zeeland, was single was transported to New South Wales for life. The 25-year-old, 4'10½" tall stockman with a short, cocked nose and injured fingers was found guilty of burglary and theft when he appeared before the Graham's Town Circuit Court on 5 April 1836. He had already served a seven-year sentence at Graham's Town for a prior conviction before boarding the *Earl Grey* for New South Wales. Both eventually received tickets of leave, with Zeeland later becoming eligible for a Certificate of Freedom.[26]

In May 1837, the Secretary of State for War and the Colonies Lord Glenelg distributed a circular stating that His Majesty's Government had resolved to put an end to the practice of shipping 'negro' convicts to the Australian penal colonies. The circular was sent to the Cape, where the judiciary was encouraged to confine prisoners locally and generally opt to make use of Robben Island instead. This resolution did not, however, prevent the transportation of court-martialled Khoisan soldiers to the Australian penal colonies in the early 1840s.[27]

14

Mutiny and desertion

Towards the end of the Dutch East India Company's governance at the Cape, Europe was on the brink of war. The threat of widespread conflict following the French Revolution prompted the VOC to shore up its defences in the colony. It formed the Corps van Pandoeren (Corps of Pandours), a regiment of Khoisan and coloured soldiers under the command of white officers. The regiment was retained by the British when they took over the colony in 1795, and was renamed the Cape Regiment. Several name changes followed as administration alternated between the British and the Dutch. From 1817 until 1827, it was called the Cape Corps of Cavalry and Infantry. After the infantry section was disbanded in 1827, the remainder of the regiment became known as the Cape Mounted Rifles. This locally raised regiment continued to operate into the 1850s, participating in several frontier wars.[1]

In the days of the VOC, the Corps initially functioned as 'a counterweight to the suspect free burgher population'. When war broke out in Europe in 1803, numerous indigenous soldiers were recruited into the Cape Corps. When the British arrived at the Cape in 1806 they recruited yet more Khoisan into the military. While the indigenous soldiers formed a fighting force loyal to their Dutch and British masters, those men who were married did not appreciate being separated from their homes and families. The Afrikaner farmers also bore some resentment towards the colonial administrations that drafted the men. Their indigenous labour supply was depleted,

179

they were required to provide the military recruits with weaponry, and the force being amassed could potentially be used against them. However, following the brief resumption of Dutch administration at the Cape in 1803, the Corps was envisaged as being useful against 'rebel' Khoisan and Xhosa or potential European foes rather than against farmers.[2]

In the early 1840s, eleven Khoisan soldiers arrived in the Australian penal colonies following courts martial. The majority took part in a mutiny at Fraser's Camp, located between Graham's Town and Trompetter's Drift at the Fish River, on the night of 19 February 1838. The mutineers, under the command of Ensign Fraser, were on their way back to their headquarters at Graham's Town from Fort Peddie to where Fraser had marched a relief party to replace disaffected soldiers. During the night, some of the disaffected men fired on the officers, killing Ensign Thomas Crowe and wounding Ensign Fraser. Fortunately for the latter, the Khoisan soldiers stationed at Fraser's Camp came to their defence and prevented further bloodshed. Five of the mutineers were taken into custody. Sixteen others fled into the bush. The soldiers' insubordination alarmed colonists, who were concerned over how widespread the disaffection had become. Worried colonists feared that disaffected Khoisan soldiers might join forces with the Xhosa against them. The strength of such concerns led to ample resources being provided to ensure the mutineers were rapidly apprehended and brought to trial.[3]

Private Piet Lynx, a 20-year-old, 5'1¾" tall Khoisan soldier, was considered a ringleader at the Fraser's Camp mutiny. His court martial was held in Graham's Town on 2 April 1838 and comprised fourteen military officers presided over by Lieutenant Colonel Grieve of the 75th. The officers 'swore upon the Holy Evangelists' in front of Lynx, then three charges were put to the disgraced soldier. He stood accused of taking part in the mutiny at Fraser's Camp during which several muskets loaded with powder and ball were fired at the officers 'while peacefully assembled in Quarters', killing Crowe. The second charge pertained to having an intent to kill some of the officers 'and other peaceable subjects of Her Majesty', while the third count related to the soldiers deserting following the mutiny.

Lynx, who was illiterate and not fluent in English, was provided with a sworn interpreter, Frederick Rex. After hearing the charges against him, Lynx pleaded 'not guilty'. The Corp's senior officer Lieutenant Colonel Henry Somerset, in the role of prosecutor, called the witnesses. Fraser appeared first, confirming that the sergeant and twenty rank and file soldiers were all present following tattoo roll call. Afterwards, he and his companions, Crowe and O'Reilly, were playing a rubber of whist with Mr and Mrs Cope when they were fired upon sometime between nine and ten in the evening. The besieged officers were joined in the Commissariat Store by loyal Cape Corps soldiers, while a small cohort ventured out to arrest several of the mutineers.

Ensign John O'Reilly was called next. He confirmed Fraser's account, and informed the court martial that on taking a roll call immediately after the fracas he found twenty-two soldiers were absent, Lynx being one of them. A military messenger riding into Fraser's Camp the following day with a reply from Trompetter's Drift to a message sent by O'Reilly reported seeing Lynx and eleven other mutineers on the road. Lynx, the messenger said, appeared to be one of their leaders, along with Stephanus Windvogel, and had tried to coerce him to join their mutiny.

Evidence corroborating Fraser's account was heard from Thomas Cope from the Commissariat Department, and Sergeants Henry Woodhouse and Caesar Caesar [sic] of the Cape Corps. Woodhouse named the sentry Kevitt (Kieweit) Stuurman as one of the soldiers who fired upon him. Stuurman was later transported to the Australian penal colonies for his role in the mutiny.

Private Jacob Human was then called. One of the mutineers, he avoided prosecution by turning Queen's evidence. Human described how, after roll call, Windvogel asked him whether he would shoot at the English. The private claimed he initially refused, but acquiesced after Windvogel cocked his gun at him. They were joined by Lynx and went to the Commissariat Store. Several more soldiers, including Cobus Kivido and Hendrick Uithaalder (also transported to the Australian penal colonies), joined them. Windvogel fired the first shots, followed by Lynx. The ringleaders coerced the others to fire upon the English officers and the Commissariat and his wife. Afterwards, Windvogel and Lynx urged their mutinous companions to join with the Xhosa to attack the military posts at Committee's Drift, Fraser's Camp and Fort Peddie. Human claimed that as the mutineers set off, he went his own way, discarding his boots and trousers before reporting the men's misdeeds to Somerset.

Next, the messenger referred to by O'Reilly, Private Jacob Speelman, was called. When he met the mutineers on the road, they asked him which officer had been shot and whether he would recover. On hearing it was Crowe, Windvogel claimed Uithaalder fired the fatal shot. Before the mutineers opened fire, the latter was heard to boast 'that his ball would not touch the ground before it had drank blood'. Speelman reported this to O'Reilly, along with the mutineers' failed attempt to have him join them. The eighth and final witness was Ensign Jouzel who identified Lynx as one of four prisoners retaken on 22 February and escorted by him to Cypher Fontein where he handed them over to the Adjutants of the Cape Corps.

The case for the defence was brief. Lynx flatly denied the first two charges against him and tried to cast doubt on Human's evidence, the only evidence that directly incriminated him, simply by claiming the private was not telling the truth. He then asked the court martial to take into account his youth and record of good service, arguing that he had allowed himself to be unduly influenced by Antony Meyers and Stephanus Windvogel 'whose society I had not resolution to avoid'. Lynx then threw himself upon the mercy of the court with regard to the charge of desertion. He must have been reasonably convincing, as Lynx was recommended for clemency along with eight other mutineers. His death sentence was commuted to transportation to the Australian penal colonies for fourteen years.[4]

Three weeks after Lynx's court martial, Governor Sir George Napier personally oversaw the execution of Meyers and Windvogel, doing all he could to ensure the staged event was exemplary. As many Khoisan soldiers as could be spared from duty were assembled to witness it. Some among them, from the same Corps and holding the same rank as the condemned men, were ordered to carry out the grim task. The Khoisan soldiers were 'marched within view of the still quivering corpses', following which Napier spoke to them forcefully. He warned the assembled soldiers that any further insubordination would be met with severe punishment, telling them: 'if any similar case of mutiny should occur, I will order the execution of everyone concerned in it – should the number amount to one hundred'.[5]

Lynx was held at Robben Island with other convicted mutineers pending the arrival of convict transports to convey them to the Australian penal colonies. On 20 September 1840, the *Pekoe* called into Table Bay. Captained by Sampson Keen with Robert Bower as Surgeon Superintendent, the transport had left Dublin just over two months earlier. Four mutineers, Kevitt Stuurman, Hendrick Uithaalder, Vigiland Wessell (also recorded as Wessels Figiland) and Cobus Kivido who faced a court martial together on 30 August 1838, were taken on board. All had been sentenced to hang, but their sentences were commuted to transportation. Stuurman and Uithaalder were sentenced to fourteen years for mutiny, murder and desertion. Wessell and Kivido, guilty of the same offences, got seven years. Four other Khoisan soldiers joined them on the *Pekoe*. Stuurman Jantjes, Piet Faltyne and Keyser Stoffle were under life sentences for desertion. Hans Roman, also a deserter, was given fourteen years. Lynx, in the interim, was left at hard labour on Robben Island.[6]

The *Pekoe* arrived at Sydney on 6 November 1840. Surviving records indicate that Piet Faltyne received a ticket of leave sometime prior to June 1851. It was, however, rescinded in late June by the Yass Bench (a rural district inland from Sydney) after Faltyne absented himself from the district in which he was supposed to be residing. It is unclear what form of labour Faltyne was engaged in within the convict system. Nor is it evident what was required of Roman, Wessell, Stuurman and Stoffle, nor whether they were found guilty of further offences while in custody.[7]

More is known about Jantjes and Uithaalder. Stuurman Jantjes' first name was recorded as 'Haurman' on his convict indent. The 20-year-old Protestant left behind a wife and two children (a son and a daughter) at the Cape. He had a prior conviction that resulted in 21 days' imprisonment prior to receiving his life sentence for desertion at a court martial in Graham's Town on 13 March 1838. Jantjes was 5'1½" tall and bore a number of identifying marks. These included three blue dots between his eyebrows, three blue scars on his lower left arm, and scars across the left-hand side of his face that were evident on his left upper lip, eyebrow and temple. The top of his forefinger on his left hand was bent, and Jantjes' two front teeth were missing. With his 'copper' complexion and 'black and wooly' hair, Jantjes' description fits the category described by the colonial scribes as 'Hottentot' and matches the physical characteristics attributed to the seven other Khoisan ex-soldiers transported on the *Pekoe*.

Uithaalder, or Witnalder as he became known in the Australian penal colonies, was eight years older than Jantjes, but shorter at 4'7¾". He, too, was a Protestant and left behind a wife and daughter at the Cape. Witnalder's body bore a range of scars including a diagonal scar in the centre of his forehead, three small scars between his eyebrows, a blue spot on each side of his neck, two more blue spots on his left breast, and a scar on his upper arm. He also bore the scars from the one hundred lashes inflicted upon his body following an earlier conviction. Witnalder's court martial at Graham's Town on 30 August 1838 resulted in his fourteen-year sentence for playing a role in the Fraser's Camp mutiny.

Witnalder, possibly with some or all of the Khoisan convicts from the *Pekoe*, was housed at Hyde Park Barracks in Sydney for three years. Both Witnalder and Jantjes then became members of a small band of mounted police assembled by Commissioner of Crown Lands Stephen Simpson to patrol the northern boundaries of New South Wales during the 1840s. Simpson, a homeopath and public servant with a military background, arrived in Sydney with his wife Sophia in January 1840 carrying a letter from the Colonial Office recommending him to Governor George Gipps. Unfortunately, Sophia died soon after their arrival, having been married to Stephen for only two years following their twenty-year engagement. Simpson left Sydney, sailing north to Moreton Bay (Brisbane). He acted as Colonial Surgeon before being appointed Commissioner of Crown Lands for Moreton Bay where he was among the early settlers, initially living in one of the cottages at the former female penitentiary at Eagle Farm before moving to Redbank and, later, to Goodna. Simpson was said to have the best horse stud in the colony and was well respected. An Aboriginal man, in responding to the question 'Who is God?', replied 'Carbon white fellow, like it Doctor Simpson, sit down here'.[8]

Jantjes and Witnalder are both described in the convict records as having served in the Cape Mounted Rifles, so were presumably capable horsemen with the skills to become one of Simpson's mounted troopers. Witnalder's small stature cramped his style, though, as while he may have been skilled on horseback he needed help to climb up into the saddle. The two men were sent up from Sydney to join Simpson's force, which comprised other convicts as well as former convicts and ex-soldiers. Witnalder did not last long. He landed in hospital at Moreton Bay where he was treated for venereal disease and was dismissed from the police as 'a worthless little Hottentot'. On 3 December 1844, Witnalder was punished with fifty lashes after being found drunk.[9]

By the mid-1840s, Witnalder was working as a labourer for Mr Gaze in Brisbane. The men had an altercation over wages, but when the matter was taken up at the Police Office Witnalder's complaint was considered groundless. Witnalder exacted his revenge on Gaze. Despite being 'of very low stature and meagre appearance', Witnalder managed to rape his former master's wife, Eliza, on 6 February 1846 as the woman was returning home from town. It was suggested at his trial at the Central Criminal Court, held before Justice Therry on 15 April, Witnalder may have killed her if Captain Wickham and another magistrate had not arrived at the scene. Mr Dowling, who represented Witnalder at his trial, told the court that the defendant was 'one of the Hottentot bullock-drivers attached to the Garrison at the Cape of Good Hope' before being transported for mutiny. Witnalder was taken to be illegally at large in the colony when he committed the offence. However, he was a ticket-of-leave man whose ticket was rescinded when he was charged with rape. Dowling sought mitigation of the sentence given that Witnalder was of foreign origin, uneducated and 'probably ignorant of British laws and British customs'.[10]

When Witnalder came up for sentencing the following day, he told the court in broken English that Eliza Gaze's evidence at trial differed from her story at the Police Office. This was significant because the victim was the prosecution's sole witness. Witnalder assured the court that the Commissioner of Crown Lands, Simpson, his 'only friend', could attest to his good character as could Mr Lane, the Superintendent at Hyde Park Barracks. Nevertheless, Therry sentenced Witnalder to death. Within days, the Executive reprieved the condemned man, commuting his sentence to transportation for life.[11]

Witnalder arrived in Van Diemen's Land on the *Louisa* on 17 November 1846 where, when questioned, he told the convict authorities that he came from Graham's Town. He admitted to knocking down and raping his mistress after being the family's servant for six months. He was assigned to a work gang at Norfolk Island for four years' hard labour, and served just under a month at Port Arthur before being shipped there on 21 December 1846. On 14 May 1850, Witnalder arrived back at the Prisoners' Barracks in Hobart as a third-class prisoner. He was subsequently hired out to serve various masters in southern, eastern and northern Van Diemen's Land, including well-known horseracing identity James Lord at Quorn Hall in Campbell Town. He laboured briefly at Waterloo, Spring Bay, Richmond and Launceston, accruing a number of offences in the process. Witnalder was found drunk at divine service in October 1850, for which he spent six days in solitary confinement. Disturbing the peace in March 1853 earned him three hours in the stocks. He was also reprimanded after being found out after hours. Witnalder was punished for drunkenness twice more and spent a further ten days in solitary for disobeying orders in October 1853. On 6 January the following year, he was given six days' hard labour for repeating this offence.

Witnalder received his second ticket of leave on 19 December 1854. However, he accrued more offences as a ticket-of-leave man than he had as a third-class prisoner. Between 30 January 1855 and 7 September 1860, he was charged with twenty-three offences, the majority of which related to being found drunk, engaging in disorderly behaviour, using offensive language and disturbing the peace. He was also found guilty of assaulting a constable who apprehended him for being out after hours. For the most part, these offences were punished with fines although Witnalder was required to serve several short periods of hard labour and a few more stints in solitary confinement. By May 1858, Witnalder was such a regular at the Police

Office in Hobart that he was banned from living south of the midlands town of Oatlands after being found guilty, yet again, of disturbing the peace.[12]

This prohibition did not prevent Witnalder's return to Hobart where he was something of a local character. Known as the 'diminutive Caffre who goes about arrayed in military clothes', he attracted a mob of 200 people outside a Mr Ward's shop in Liverpool Street on Saturday 10 August 1861. The 'great noise' that resulted saw him back at the Police Office for disturbing the peace. Witnalder claimed none of the mob spoke to him and that although he wanted to go home, they would not let him out of their clutches. The unsympathetic authorities fined him 40 shillings or two months' labour in default, with the Mayor telling him that he was a public nuisance 'for although a little man he created a great disturbance'.[13]

Like other Khoisan ex-convicts in Van Diemen's Land, Witnalder had no means by which he could return home. He was destitute after being discharged from the convict system and became an object of ridicule to certain elements within the local populace. On 10 September 1862, he was before the bench on yet another charge of disturbing the peace. The Police Superintendent told the bench that Witnalder was 'constantly insulted by idle boys'. Another witness, Mr Jones, said that he had seen Witnalder 'insulted by mischievous boys'. Despite such evidence of bullying, the Stipendary Magistrate found the prisoner guilty and fined him 1 shilling. Superintendent Propsting took pity on the man and immediately paid the fine, kindly preventing Witnalder being returned to prison (from which he had only recently been released) for defaulting.[14]

Following a similar incident in early December 1862, Witnalder appeared before the bench to answer another charge of disturbing the peace. The 'eccentric little Kaffir, well-known for his military peculiarities' told the court that some boys had annoyed him thus causing the fracas. Provocation was not considered sufficient mitigation of his alleged crime. Witnalder was fined 10 shillings and costs, and was required to serve fourteen days in prison if he failed to come up with the money. Several weeks later, on 23 December 1862, Witnalder appeared before the Stipendary Magistrate AB Jones Esq, and Captain Bateman at the Police Court along with a 14-year-old boy, William (or Henry as his name was also reported) Collard. Both were charged with committing an 'unnatural offence' and were committed to face trial. The prisoners spent Christmas 1862 in gaol waiting to learn their respective fates.[15]

Witnalder and Collard (now referred to as Cornwall Collins) stood trial on Wednesday 28 January in the Supreme Court before the Chief Justice, Sir Valentine Fleming. In keeping with the sensibilities of the time, the newspapers reporting the case found the details to be 'quite unfit for publication'. Nevertheless, the boy had legal representation and much was made in evidence over whether the boy's mouth had been covered by Witnalder as the 'unnatural offence' (sodomy) was being committed. It was found that the boy had allegedly been silenced by the other prisoner, Witnalder, and was therefore a victim rather than a co-conspirator. The police constable was reprimanded for withholding this crucial evidence from the court. Collard was found not guilty, but retained in custody to bear witness against the older man. He was then sworn in, and tearfully gave evidence that he had been assaulted by Witnalder and had not consented to the man's attentions. The boy's ordeal in the stand lasted an hour, following which other witnesses were called. The jury retired for only ten minutes before returning a 'guilty' verdict. Witnalder once again faced the extreme penalty of the law.[16]

On Thursday 5 February 1863, the Executive Council met and considered Witnalder's case. It resolved that the death penalty would be carried into effect. Some members of the public expressed outrage (albeit muted because of the nature of the prisoner's alleged offence). The local Hobart newspaper implored 'the Councillors of the

Governor with whom rests the prerogative of mercy, to weigh well all the circumstances'. A submission from an unnamed advocate was reprinted in the *Mercury*'s columns, comparing Witnalder's predicament with Summers who after being convicted of sodomy in July 1862 had his death sentence commuted to transportation for life. Summers, the writer contended, had been in 'full possession of his senses'. The injustice in upholding the death sentence upon Witnalder, a man 'little better than a savage' was made apparent: 'Summers is surely more responsible than this half tamed brute. And as Summers was not hung, will not the sacrifice of Whitnalder's [sic] life be a Judicial or rather an Executive Murder?' The appeal failed, and several days later the *Mercury* reported that Summer's case had 'special circumstances' which did not apply to Witnalder's. The reading public was assured that despite the public deploring the application of the death penalty, the Executive had considered all facets of Witnalder's case in minute detail before deciding to uphold his sentence.[17]

The under-sheriff visited Witnalder at the Hobart Town Gaol to read the warrant for his execution. While there, he found the Protestant prisoner mistakenly had been attended by the Roman Catholic clergy since being condemned. On Friday 20 February 1863, Witnalder was roused from his cell at three thirty to prepare for death. He was joined by the Reverend Mr Hunter, who guided him in prayer. By eight that morning, a small crowd comprising the under-sheriff, keeper and under-keeper of the gaol, eight police constables and their sub-inspector, and reporters from the daily newspapers had assembled at the gaol. The only other witness was a Mr Lowe from Victoria. Witnalder emerged from his cell in Hunter's company, the prisoner's arms pinioned at his sides. The prayerful men were followed by the executioner. Because of Witnalder's diminutive size, heavy weights were attached to his feet so he would not suffer more than was necessary. Witnalder 'saluted' the onlookers with 'an abrupt bow', before the cap was drawn over his head, the noose adjusted, and the flooring removed from under his feet. He was said to have died easily, and had asked Hunter to tell those gathered that he was innocent of the crime for which he had suffered.[18]

In the meantime, Piet Lynx laboured at Robben Island following his court martial in April 1838 until late 1841 when *Prince Regent II* arrived at Table Bay from Dublin with a cargo of male convicts on board. Several died during the voyage, leaving room for prisoners from the Cape. Lynx was one, as was another Khoisan ex-soldier, Hendrick Keester. A former groom with the Cape Mounted Rifles, Keester was court martialled at Graham's Town on 4 September 1837 for deserting from his regimental headquarters at Cypher Fontein while on sentry duty on or about 21 November 1836. He also faced charges of taking his 'regimental necessaries' with him, including a double-barrelled carbine, regimental cloak, blanket, haversack, canteen and straps, and forty rounds of ball cartridge, re-entering the Corps under a false name and again deserting, and escaping from custody while under escort from Somerset to Cape Town on 8 April 1837, taking a regimental saddle with him. According to the Cape Mounted Rifles Adjutant Lieutenant Thomas Donovan, called as a witness, the 26-year-old private served in the military for one year and 111 days. Donovan described the man's character as 'exceedingly bad'. Despite Keester's plea to the contrary, he was found guilty of all charges. To signify his shameful status as a deserter from the military, he was sentenced 'to be marked with the letter D in the usual manner' and 'to be transported as a felon for life'.[19]

Lynx and Keester were among around 188 male convicts disembarked in Hobart from the *Prince Regent II* on 2 January 1842. Lynx, a Protestant aged 24, left behind his wife, Fakey, and their two children, Meikey and Sarkey, at the Cape. When questioned about his offence, he said the mutiny he helped lead was triggered by the pay sergeant refusing to pay the men. Keester, aged 23 and a Roman Catholic, also left a wife behind. Both men were illiterate, and both had worked as grooms within the military. Just as the convict authorities sometimes kept Aboriginal convicts together for their mutual support and wellbeing, it seems that a similar decision was taken in regard to Lynx and Keester. Initially, both were sent down Tasman's Peninsula for a two-year probationary period, Lynx to labour at the Coal Mines and Keester, whose health was suffering, to nearby Impression Bay. Before their probation expired, the men were shipped together to Sydney on the brig *Sir John Byng* and, from there, to Norfolk Island where they arrived on 18 March 1842.[20]

The men were returned to Van Diemen's Land on 6 June 1844 on the *Lady Franklin*. They were described as exhibiting 'good' behaviour at Norfolk Island where neither had accrued any offences and both had attained the third class in the probation system, just one step away from obtaining tickets of leave. On the indent recording their return, Lynx's marital status is 'single'. Perhaps the long-term separation from his family forced him to try and forget those he had left behind. Several weeks later, a colonial scribe jotted 'now dead' on Keester's conduct record. The note 'vide letter from Superintendent Prisoners' Barracks dated 28th July 1843' implies that he lived for less than two months after returning to Hobart. In the meantime, Lynx was sent to Perth in the island's northern midlands to labour. Over the eight years that followed, he was assigned to various settlers in the east of Van Diemen's Land, including N Young at Lake River on the Norfolk Plains (Longford), J Thompson at Charlie's Hope (now Black Charlie's Opening) and William Webb at Black Marsh, among others. Lynx also spent time labouring at convict stations at Picton in the Midlands and Sandy Bay in Hobart.[21]

During his time as an assigned convict servant, Lynx racked up twelve offences ranging from being drunk to neglecting his duties and being out after hours. For these various misdemeanours, he was punished with hard labour and also spent four hours in the stocks and four stints totalling thirty days in solitary confinement. On 7 September 1852, Lynx was awarded his Certificate of Freedom, written proof that he had become free as his sentence had expired.[22]

The last of the Khoisan transported from the Cape was Booy Piet, a 26-year-old illiterate Lutheran tried at Graham's Town on 5 July 1842 for desertion and stealing his regimental necessaries. The former private was sentenced to seven years' transportation. In August 1842, the convict transport *Waterloo* was wrecked in Table Bay, with only about 72 survivors among the 220 male convicts taken aboard at Sheerness. The shipwreck survivors, along with several convicts from the Cape including Piet, left the Cape on the *Cape Packet* on 10 October 1842 and arrived in Hobart on 24 November. When Piet was questioned on his arrival in Van Diemen's Land, he said he had spent seven years in the Cape Corps. His place of origin is recorded as 'Gaffrey Net' (that is, Graaf-Reinet). He is described as 5'5" tall with curly black hair, short and high cheekbones, a broad nose, and large, thick lips. Both thumbs bore scars.

Piet spent a little under three years in the convict system, during which time two offences were recorded against him. On 29 December 1843 he was ordered to do two months' hard labour in chains for being absent from Norfolk Bay convict station, a railway station that functioned as a supply route to and from Port Arthur. The following month, on 10 January 1844, he was found guilty of misconduct because he had a box in his possession that belonged to the storekeeper. This earned Piet fourteen days' solitary confinement. On 16 June he was transferred to Brown's River Probation Station, south of Hobart, where the men were housed in separate cells in a stone prison modelled on the Pentonville system. The building, comprising two tiers of single cells radiating out from the Superintendent's Quarters, stood atop a forested hilltop overlooking the Derwent River. The convicts laboured for twelve-hour days sawing trees and shouldering heavy timber through the dense undergrowth. When Piet completed the first stage of his probation in January 1845 he was returned to the Prisoners' Barracks in Hobart. This was as far as Piet progressed through the system because on 5 July he was admitted to the General Hospital in Hobart where he died on 28 August 1845.[23]

15

'Black Peter' the bushranger

Peter Haley (or Caley) arrived free in Sydney in 1839, only to end up in penal servitude in Van Diemen's Land a little over a decade later. In 1850, the Khoisan groom was a notorious horse thief in South Australia where he was known as 'Wolf' or 'Heddy'. After stealing George Conran's grey mare with her bridle at Port Adelaide, valued at £30, Alexander Buchanan's £25 mare, and a £2 saddle from Frederick Hansborough Dutton at Albany during September 1850, Haley was gaoled. He was tried in the Supreme Court in Adelaide on 25 November 1850. With twelve months' hard labour already on his record, Haley was punished with a sentence to ten years' transportation. He arrived in Hobart on 2 January 1851 on the *Antares*.[1]

When Haley was questioned about his offence, he told the Vandemonian authorities he was transported for 'stealing a horse at Mr Bagot's mines at Adelaide'. Charles Bagot ran a copper mine at Kapunda in the Flinders Ranges, inland from the South Australian capital. Haley made no mention of Conran's mare or Dutton's saddle. The 5'6" tall 24-year-old Presbyterian was illiterate and is recorded in the convict records as being single. His place of origin, or 'native place', is recorded as Symonds Bay (Simonds Bay, near Cape Town). A 'copper' coloured man with black, woolly hair, Haley had a distinguishing feature: 'P' on his right arm.[2]

He was sent to Cascades on the outskirts of town to serve his fifteen months' probation, returning to the Hobart Prisoners' Barracks on 20 January 1852. Haley was assigned as a convict servant to

W F Manton at New Norfolk, a district where his proclivity for horse stealing again became evident. In February 1852, a £2 reward was posted for his capture. He was retaken, and on 12 April 1852 Haley was tried at New Norfolk for stealing a horse valued at £15 from Mr P Bond. On being found guilty, Haley's sentence was extended to transportation for life with an initial period of four years' probation to be served at the Cascades where he arrived on 5 May. On 31 October, he was transferred down Tasman's Peninsula to Salt Water River, returning to Cascades on 29 December 1853.

Haley became a pass holder on 27 March 1855. However, the following month he served fourteen days in solitary confinement at the Prisoners' Barracks in Hobart for being out after hours. In June, Haley was found guilty of being 'drunk and being on W Middleton's premises for some improper purpose', although he was acquitted of another charge of horse stealing. A sentence to six months' hard labour was imposed, and Haley continued living at the Prisoners' Barracks and working for Captain Hawkins at the Survey Department. After being transferred to work in the Penitentiary garden, Haley found another opportunity to abscond on 15 April 1856, and took it.

Like Scipio Africanus and Arnoldus Jantje, Haley sought refuge in the bush. But rather than simply living rough and surviving off the land, Haley joined a notorious gang of bushrangers. By the 1850s, bushranging 'in its more systematic character' was unknown in Van Diemen's Land, although isolated incidents of highway robbery still occurred. At least this was the situation until 'Wingy' and his gang became active. Wingy's gang comprised 'four desperadoes'. The leader, Daniel Stewart, hailed from Edinburgh. Aged about 38, he had a ruddy complexion, black hair and grey eyes. He was dubbed 'Wingy' because he had but one arm. His mate William Thornton had a convict past in New South Wales and was called 'Sydney Jim'. Their comrade in arms, William Ferns, was 'Flowers' (presumably in oblique reference to his surname). Sydney Jim and Flowers both got around wearing black billycock hats and cord trousers. One sported a velveteen coat while the other preferred pilot cloth. Haley became 'Black Peter'. His nickname referred to Haley's complexion but could also have implied associated characteristics because black people were stereotyped in unflattering ways in colonial Australia.[3]

All four men had done time in the Vandemonian convict system, with Sydney Jim and Flowers being twice convicted. Sydney Jim arrived in Sydney on the *Prince Regent* in 1837 after receiving a sentence to seven years' transportation for stealing poultry. After being found 'at large with firearms' at Stone Quarry he was sentenced to life transportation and shipped to Van Diemen's Land. Wingy was transported from Edinburgh in 1841 for theft and housebreaking, becoming free on 27 November 1848 after his seven-year sentence expired. Flowers was eventually transported for stealing lead, after racking up about eighteen stays in Her Majesty's prisons in England. He arrived in Van Diemen's Land on 28 November 1850, and was sent to Cascades in April 1851. He received a conditional pardon on 14 February 1854, but was tried again in Launceston on 27 May 1856 for robbery and given three years' gaol. A further year was added to his sentence for unlawfully and maliciously cutting and wounding another man. Flowers, at some point, escaped from Launceston Gaol. Both Flowers and Haley were at Cascades at the same time in 1851. It was probably this connection that got Black Peter into Wingy's gang half a decade later, after Haley absconded from the Penitentiary garden in Hobart.[4]

The gang ranged over the Midlands and up into the hilly country around Hamilton and Bothwell, keeping the locals 'in a state of constant dread and alarm'. Their robberies were very well planned and executed 'with a degree of daring effrontery, which betokened, at all events, a very perfect confidence in their own turpitude and resources'. Although parties of police were sent out after them, the bushrangers evaded them for months on end. The situation came to a head when, on 16 March 1858, Chief District Constable Richard Propsting saw Black Peter and Flowers as he was travelling with his family in a dog cart on the Midlands Highway between Ross and Tunbridge. The bushrangers told him to 'stop' or 'stand' (he was later unsure as to which word was used). Sydney Jim levelled his gun at the policeman, firing a shot as Propsting drove onwards. He hit the dog cart, which, on later inspection, had gained a dent on the right-hand wheel. Black Peter also shot at Propsting's party, wounding a horse in the neck. The constable, who was also conveying another woman and a 7-week-old infant, managed to flog his horse into outrunning the bushrangers although he lost his hat to Flowers in the process. Following this fracas, the Inspector of Police offered a £200 reward for information that would lead to the apprehension and conviction of Black Peter, Wingy and their two companions. This was later increased to £100 for each of the wanted men.[5]

'Black Peter' Haley was the first taken. He went to the Phillips' hut at the Bed Chambers, Macquarie Plains, in the Hamilton district around midday on 29 April 1858, asking for flour. Mrs Phillips, with 'great presence of mind' sent a girl to get her husband who was nearby ploughing a field. The enterprising couple managed to wrestle their unwelcome visitor to the floor, pinion his arms and disarm him. The bushranger was carrying two six-barrelled revolvers, a double-barrelled pistol and a double-barrelled gun, all loaded. He was kept overnight at the gaol in New Norfolk then transferred by coach the following day to Hobart. After being held in the Prisoners' Barracks in Hobart for just under three months, Haley was sent to Port Arthur. Mrs Phillips received £100 reward for his capture, twice the annual salary a married couple could expect to earn in Tasmania in 1858 (over and above their rations) for labouring on a farm.[6]

Just two days following the capture of Black Peter, John Brown from Cluny was 'seated comfortably by the fire' after travelling the

5 miles home from Bothwell on Saturday 1 May when Wingy, Flowers and Sydney Jim broke into his home. The bushrangers threatened Brown with a loaded gun, telling him he would be shot if he did not allow them to tie him up. Once the man was restrained, two of them went through the house taking whatever they might find a use for while the third stood guard. Brown lost his Deane and Adams No. 54 gun to the intruders along with a gold watch, a gutta-percha (india rubber coated cloth) coat, other clothing, food, and a gallon of rum. Wingy's gang sat around drinking Brown's port and took it in turns to venture into the kitchen where they had Brown's manservant Samuel Hall prepare food for them. In all, the ordeal lasted almost four hours with the bushrangers taking their leave at twenty to eleven that night. At the start of the following week, Brown wrote to the editor of the local newspaper describing the unwelcome intrusion.[7]

The gang then moved north and, going beyond their usual range, on 13 May they robbed the tollgate keeper at the Silwood tollgate on the main road to Westbury. A few months later, rumours began to circulate that had Wingy and Flowers heading north towards the Mersey district. Chief District Constable Jackson wrote to the editor of Hobart's daily newspaper in an effort to quash these rumours as he was concerned that such wild rumours were being put about to confound ongoing police searches for the wanted men. Aside from the incident at the Silwood toll gate, Wingy's gang was not known to be active in his district. Similarly misleading rumours circulated implying that the Government 'evidenced a disinclination' to pay the large reward promised for each of the remaining three bushrangers. However, these rumours were thought to have been made up to induce 'doubt in the minds of those in whose tracks these armed men are likely to be found', thereby eliminating any incentive to turn in the wanted men.[8]

By the end of the month following the tollgate affair, the gang was active back down the midlands. Near the end of June 1858,

Wingy, Flowers and Sydney Jim held up Mr Fletcher, the *Eagles Return* publican at Snake Banks (now called Powranna) on the Midlands Highway, robbing him of his gold watch and chain. His canny wife, who heard the commotion from upstairs, hid most of her money and jewellery under the bed. When the bushrangers demanded money, she gave them but three £1 notes and a few coins. On being questioned about the paucity of the sum, Mrs Fletcher said she had been to Launceston to pay the spirit merchant and brewer. Only that morning, she told the bushrangers, she had sent the rest of their cash off by coach. Wingy's gang seemed content with this explanation. They helped themselves to the tea standing ready for the guard and passengers from the evening stage coach before leaving the premises. The bushrangers then tried to hold up a gentleman on the road nearby, but after being ordered to stop the enterprising man simply drove his horses faster and made his escape, though not without the animals being wounded in the process. The guard from the southbound coach carried word of these nefarious events to Hobart where he arrived on 30 June.[9]

Wingy's numbers were further depleted in September 1858 when Flowers was captured. The bushranger was making his way to the coast when he was identified and captured by Chief District Constable Kidd of George Town at the top end of the island. The vigilant policeman also recovered some of the property stolen by the bushrangers, including Fletcher's gold watch. By 21 September 1858, Flowers was lodged in the Prisoners' Barracks in Hobart. From there, he was sent down Tasman's Peninsula to join Black Peter at Port Arthur while the authorities continued to pursue Wingy and Sydney Jim. His arrest must have been a relief to the Government and its police force. Their apparent inability to apprehend the bushrangers was discussed thoroughly within the columns of a local newspaper with both the 'inefficient government' and its 'extravagant police force' found wanting.[10]

Near the end of the month, Constables Shaw and Waller of the Inspector's Reserve Force under the command of Sergeant McIvor, 'an old officer of the Hobart Town Police', set up an operation to catch Wingy and Sydney Jim. They hid in shepherd Luke Bradley's secluded hut on Mr A Bisdee's property at Pine Tier in the Hamilton district to await an anticipated visit from the men. Bradley had 'been long suspected' of providing assistance to the bushrangers. Sure enough, Wingy and Sydney Jim turned up at about ten thirty on the night of 29 September armed with double-barrelled guns, revolvers and bowie knives. As the story later went, they had Mrs Bradley serve them with alcohol and tea then settled down for the night with their weapons close to hand. Working only by the light of the embers from the dying fire in the hearth, McIvor leapt from his hiding place and demanded that the bushrangers surrender. It was later claimed that Sydney Jim's response was a shot from his revolver. McIvor then fired at him and rushed him with his bayonet following which Sydney Jim 'instantly fell, and neither spoke nor moved afterwards'. Constable Waller and Wingy also exchanged gunfire, with Wingy becoming completely disabled when a shot entered his remaining arm. With Bradley's help, Waller bound the prisoner. The next day, Wingy and his dead mate were taken 60 miles to Hamilton where an inquest was held to determine Thornton's cause of death. A verdict of justifiable homicide was returned. Wingy was then conveyed to Hobart Town Gaol where Black Peter and Flowers joined him, having been brought back from Port Arthur to be examined by the police as a preliminary step towards facing trial.[11]

Not everyone was satisfied with the official version of Wingy's capture and Sydney Jim's death. The Launceston newspaper *Cornwall Chronicle* denounced it as 'a very lame account ... without doubt, false from beginning to end'. It was instead proposed that the three police officers with the aid of Bradley and his wife were more than a sufficient force to capture the sleeping men, 'one of whom had one arm only', without the need for such a violent confrontation. The newspaper claimed to have it on good authority that the police had deliberately fired upon the sleeping men. Indeed, the *Cornwall Chronicle* declared 'we do not hesitate to designate the death of Thornton [Sydney Jim] as cold blooded murder'. The newspaper refuted the coroner's finding, and cautioned against any praise or reward being given to the police who shot Sydney Jim while there was any doubt about their actions.[12]

The police had to wait almost two months before the wounded Wingy was sufficiently recovered to be examined. On Tuesday 24 November, Daniel Stewart *alias* Wingy, William Ferns *alias* Flowers and Peter Haley *alias* Black Peter appeared before the Police Magistrate A Kennerley and the Inspector of Police charged with 'feloniously shooting at Richard Propsting with intent to kill and murder him'. Propsting gave evidence against them, as did a labourer, Thomas Smith from Cleveland, who swore the three were part of a gang of four men who took him prisoner on the day Propsting's party was attacked. Smith told the Police Court that he and his wife had been held captive for three or four hours, only being released when Wingy's gang heard a gig coming along the highway and went to investigate. Smith reportedly heard shots being fired, then overheard the bushrangers discussing the bungled hold up when they returned. The armed men set Smith and his wife free, then headed off. Before the hearing concluded, a further charge of 'robbery under arms' was brought against Wingy and Flowers in relation to their involvement in robbing John Brown at Cluny, near Bothwell. All three prisoners were committed for trial.[13]

The trial, however, had to be postponed. The Tasmanian Parliament was recalled urgently to rectify a 'blunder cleverly made by our learned Attorney General' which created a situation whereby some of the provisions under the new Criminal Procedure Acts were at odds with 9th Geo. IV, or 'the Charter of Justice'. Until this situation was fixed, the prisoners could not be sentenced to death if found guilty of the alleged offences. One of Hobart's daily newspapers observed sarcastically that the 'Honorable Members must feel highly gratified at being thus summoned from their homes at so much inconvenience to themselves in order to assist the learned Attorney General in his laudable desire to hang Mr Wingy and his roving associates'. Shortly after this article was published, 'Enquirer' wrote to the editor of the *Hobart Town Daily Mercury* to inquire what answer the Attorney General would give if a writ of habeas corpus was brought as there was, at the time they entered their plea, no grounds on which Wingy and his companions could legally be retained in custody.[14]

Despite the legal hiccup, Stewart, Ferns and Haley eventually appeared before the Chief Justice, Sir Valentine Fleming, at the Supreme Court in Hobart on Wednesday 26 January 1859. Wingy's arm was still in a sling. Four charges were put to the prisoners: firstly that they had shot at Richard Propsting intending to kill him; secondly that they had shot a gun with intention to kill and murder; and thirdly and fourthly that they had shot with intent to cause grievous bodily harm. The prisoners pleaded not guilty. Propsting was the key witness for the prosecution and provided lengthy sworn testimony as to the events that transpired when the bushrangers tried to intercept his party on the Midlands Highway. The jury retired at three thirty in the afternoon, returning one and a quarter hours later to state that they found the prisoners guilty on the fourth count but not guilty in relation to the other three charges. The men were remanded in custody.[15]

At the start of the following week, on Monday 31 January, the three bushrangers appeared before the Chief Justice for sentencing. Such was the level of public interest in their fate, the doors of the courthouse had to be closed to keep the crowd at bay. The prisoners were asked if they had 'anything to say why the Court should not give you judgment to die according to law?' Stewart nominated the defence counsel, Mr Lees, to speak for him. Lees argued that Stewart was not present when shots were fired at Propsting and also put it to the court that all three prisoners had been involved only in minor offences and had 'borne excellent characters' up until the time at which the alleged offences were committed. Ferns spoke for himself, telling the court he was innocent of the crime of which he had been convicted in Launceston, so had absconded and taken up employment near Bothwell, working hard for two years before being recognised by a man and therefore having to flee into the bush. He denied that any of the bushrangers had fired at Propsting. Haley declined the opportunity to address the court.

Chief Justice Fleming addressed the prisoners at length, summarising their convict careers and informing them of the wrong choices they had made along the way. Stewart, on being returned from Norfolk Island, had become a pass holder and could have progressed to become a ticket-of-leave man had he not continued his 'career of rebellion and resistance to lawful authority'. At the time of sentencing, Ferns was just one year away from being 'as free as the air', yet instead of trying to make an honest living he had taken to the bush. Haley was told that when he was made a pass holder in March 1855 he could have 'made amends for the past', but instead chose to abscond and take up life in the bush. Fleming then summarised the impacts of the crimes the men had committed on those who were their victims, before announcing that all three were to be 'severally taken from hence to the place from which you severally came, and from thence to a place of execution, there to be severally hanged by the neck until your bodies be dead'. The three prisoners were then returned to the town gaol where they were visited daily by several city missionaries, and regularly by two clergymen.[16]

A petition signed by Propsting, members of the jury and members of the public unsuccessfully sought the commutation of the death sentences passed in relation to the surviving members of Wingy's gang. On the morning of Wednesday 16 February 1859, the under-sheriff went to the cells of the condemned men (the three bushrang-ers and two others) and oversaw the executioner as he pinioned the men's arms. A small crowd of gaol officials and newspaper reporters gathered in the gaol yard to watch the execution. A sombre mood prevailed as the bell from the nearby Trinity Church tolled, echoing around the prison walls. As the prisoners were led out to the scaffold, Stewart was defiant. Ferns and the other two condemned men were 'firm', but Haley 'appeared more dead than alive – his countenance was ghastly, and he seemed almost unconscious of what was passing around him'. Haley's old friend, Ferns, reached out towards him, tell-ing Haley: 'Give us your hand, Peter'.

The Reverend Mr Davenport, in a 'voice choking with emotion', read from the penitential psalms, following which the bolt was drawn back by the executioner causing the drop to fall. A heavy thud was the only audible sound to mark the moment that the men became suspended from the ends of their respective ropes. As the clergyman sank to his knees to pray for the men's departing souls, the bodies of Haley and one of the other men quivered while Stewart, Ferns and the fifth man seemed to have died instantly. The bodies of the two men hanged alongside the bushrangers were sent to the General Hospital and St Mary's hospital respectively for dissection, a further punishment considered befitting to the crime of murder of which both had been convicted. Stewart's, Ferns' and Haley's bodies were taken to the Campbell Street burying ground to be interred.[17]

- III -
NEW ZEALAND

16

In open rebellion

In the early 1840s, newly arriving Pākehā coveted the lush river valley extending east from the natural harbour at the bottom of New Zealand's North Island. Legend has it that the extensive valley was created when one of two local taniwha (large mythological serpents) unfurled its tail as it thrust south to escape the confines of the lake that contained it. Its manoeuvre created a passage to the ocean (and freedom) and also formed the valley that Māori called 'Awakairangi', which translates as 'river of food from the sky'.

The heavily forested valley was home to a variety of plant and bird life that formed an integral part of the Māori diet along with the watercress, eels and crayfish taken from local waterways. Since the early decades of the nineteenth century, the valley had come under the jurisdiction of Ngāti Toa rangatira (chief) Te Rauparaha. Te Rauparaha led his people on an arduous journey south from Kawhia after the invasion of their former lands in 1820 during the bitterly contested musket wars. Forced from their lands by an invading army of 5000 Māori warriors, by the end of their long journey Ngāti Toa dominated the west coast of the lower North Island. From here, they were strategically placed to take advantage of early European trade and to launch taua (war parties) against South Island tribes.

As the early decades of trade gave way to systematic colonisation under the New Zealand Company, early European settlers at Port Nicholson renamed the desirable river valley to the east of the nascent township of Wellington after its principal river, the Hutt.

The waterway had been named after Oxbridge scholar and English politician Sir William Hutt, a founding member, director and chairman of the New Zealand Company. The Hutt Valley met all of the requirements specified in the instructions given to the Company's principal agent, William Wakefield, to buy from local Māori 110 000 acres of flat, fertile land in the vicinity of the new harbour settlement.

In September 1839, Wakefield signed a deed for the purchase of Port Nicholson with Te Ati Awa rangatiras Te Puni and Te Wharepouri. Wakefield was, during this early phase of colonisation, 'living in one corner of a large store-house built by Te Puni in the pā [fortified village] at Petone'. The deed provided for one tenth of the land in the agreement to be set aside exclusively for Te Ati Awa. However, this provision was never honoured. On concluding the deal, the New Zealand Company believed that it had rights to all the land extending from the waterfront across to the Tararua Ranges, including the Hutt Valley. However, Wakefield was later informed by Ngāti Toa that Te Ati Awa did not have the authority to enter into any agreements over the land in question. Rather, this was the prerogative of Te Rauparaha and his nephew Te Rangihaeata.[1]

Ostensibly, Te Rauparaha was a British ally. He signed the Treaty of Waitangi on 14 May 1840 along with other chiefs in the Wellington region. However, while the paramount chief may have accepted British sovereignty or at least some kind of formal relationship with the colonists, he did not see the Treaty as providing the settlers with unlimited access to Māori land. Not long after signing the Treaty, he built a large pā at Plimmerton to the north of Wellington and swore that he would prevent the settlers taking over the Hutt Valley.

In the meantime, another New Zealand Company settlement was being established at Nelson at the top of the South Island. Like their lower North Island counterparts, the early South Island settlers located a fertile valley they desired for themselves. Surveyors began to intrude on the Wairau Valley. However, Te Rangihaeata obstructed the surveyors because settlement was vehemently opposed by the uncle and nephew, who had interests in the land there. An armed encounter initially known as the Wairau Massacre but now referred to as the Wairau Affray took place in the South Island valley on 17 June 1843. In what was the first armed conflict between Māori and Pākehā after the conclusion of the Treaty of Waitangi, and the only battle of the New Zealand wars to be fought on South Island soil, twenty-two of the British surveying party were killed. The four Māori who died during the conflict included Te Rangihaeata's beloved wife Te Rongo, Te Rauparaha's daughter.

Tensions between Māori and Pākehā escalated. Te Rauparaha unsuccessfully urged his Ngāti Awa neighbours further up the coast at Waikanae to attack the British settlement at Wellington. Early the following year, on 12 February 1844, the recently arrived Governor Robert FitzRoy – who famously captained Charles Darwin's ship the *Beagle* – met with Te Rauparaha and admitted the colonists were to blame for the conflict at Wairau. Te Rauparaha and Te Rangihaeata both accepted payments of £200 from FitzRoy in return for waiving their rights to the Hutt Valley. Lacking insight into the complexities of Māori land ownership, the colonists assumed that overcoming Ngāti Toa chiefly objections cleared the major obstacle standing in the way of their taking over the valley, in keeping with the deal made with Te Ati Awa. As per the original agreement, local Māori were to retain some rights to their pā sites and established cultivations.

As part of the negotiations following Te Rauparaha's migration south, he reached agreements with Ngāti Rangitahi (a group with connections further up the North Island's west coast at Whanganui) and Ngāti Tama that they could cultivate land in the Hutt Valley. They had since established villages in the valley where they also tended their vegetable plantations. Gradually, white settlers began to encroach on their lands. The first New Zealand Company colonists arrived on the *Aurora* in January 1840. They initially camped at a place known to Māori as Pito-one, or the belly button of the earth, and called the new settlement 'Petone'. The initial settlement flooded and was soon abandoned. Some colonists headed west to establish Wellington, others migrated east up the Hutt Valley, and just a few stayed behind to farm land at Petone.

When Edward Jerningham Wakefield, son of Edward Gibbon Wakefield – the principal advocate behind the New Zealand Company – toured New Zealand between 1839 and 1844, he visited the fledgling settlement at the Hutt. He described how 'at high water, the ship's long-boats and private cargo-boats brought quantities of goods up to the owners' locations; the labourers and masters worked altogether at the casks, bales, and other heavy things; the natives lent their willing aid, being very handy in the water, then returned, either to a job at hut-building, or to hawk about their pigs and potatoes, which they brought in canoes to this quick market'. Each settler had a small retinue of labourers from his own part of Britain, as well as 'a native or two', attached to them.[2]

As the colonial intrusion into the Hutt Valley progressed, a military presence was established to protect the early pioneers. A contingent of soldiers guarded the bridge the colonists had erected across the Hutt River, while the most advanced party of troops was stationed 2 miles distant at Boulcott's Farm. Fifty men from the 58th Regiment served there under Lieutenant GH Page who, along with his servant, was lodged in a cottage on the property. Boulcott's barn was the centre of their defences, and housed about half of the troops. A wooden stockade erected around the barn provided an outer defence system and was loopholed to allow the soldiers to fire their muskets at approaching enemies. The remainder were quartered in small slab huts and tents.

The pioneer Joseph Boulcott cleared the land on his block down as far as the river. His back-breaking labour had seen the dense native bush give way to grass. Burned-out tree stumps stood in testament to his physical exertions. The farmer marked out his boundary roughly with partially burned logs and stumps. His land was bordered on one side by the Hutt River and on the remaining three sides by dense forest, mostly the giant rimu and rata that dominated the landscape. A rough track through the bush connected Boulcott with other colonists whose clearings peppered the landscape along the route to Wellington. Over time, initial dwellings built of raupo or nikau palm, often with assistance from Māori and influenced by indigenous architecture, gave way to houses constructed of timber hewn from the bush and topped with shingled roofs.

As 1840 progressed, the New Zealand Company shipped increasing numbers of colonists out to the new settlement. At the end of the year, in December, the New Zealand Company ship *Olympus* left Gravesend in England bound for New Zealand. Travelling on board as cabin passengers were Thomas Mason, the 22-year-old Yorkshire-born son of a tea dealer, and his newly wedded wife Jane. With a background in farming and business, Mason would have been considered well equipped to become a pioneer. Raised a Quaker, he resigned from the Society of Friends before setting sail because his marriage was to a non-Quaker (for which he would otherwise have been disowned by the Friends).

Following a four-month sea voyage, the Masons arrived in New Zealand where Thomas purchased a block of land at Taita, further up the valley from Boulcott's Farm and protected by a small contingent of the Hutt Militia. Reminiscing about the early Hutt Valley years later, Wellington settler Ebenezer Maxwell described how 'at the time of the first settlement much of the valley was a swamp'. Trees grew thickly alongside the Hutt River, ensuring that its banks did not erode. This confined the river to a narrower course than its current pathway to the sea. In the first decade and a half of settlement, the Hutt River ran deep and could be readily navigated by large Māori waka (war canoes) and European boats alike. However, a geological fault-line runs through the Hutt Valley and the landscape changed irrevocably following a significant earthquake in 1855 that 'raised the level of the valley by several feet'. The elevation of the soil and the clearing of the land combined to convert much of what had been swampy ground into arable land. A much shallower, broader river with eroding banks also resulted that was no longer navigable by large watercraft.[3]

Late in 1841, as the Masons were becoming established on the land, around thirty Ngāti Rangatahi arrived in the district and settled on some of the land Mason had already put to the spade. The resulting contestation over who had rights of occupancy was settled by the Commissioner of Native Reserves who reached an agreement with Ngāti Rangatahi that saw them move elsewhere. With peace temporarily restored, Mason returned to tilling the soil, planting his potato crop, and scattering the seeds of various trees and shrubs familiar from 'home'.[4]

Despite the apparent success of the Commissioner in settling Mason's case, Ngāti Rangitahi and Ngāti Tama remained far from satisfied with the colonial intrusion onto the lands to which they had a prior claim, and were bolstered in their objections with tangible support from a section of Ngāti Toa led by Te Rangihaeata. Ngāti Rangitahi also enjoyed strong support from their relatives from Whanganui, led by the renowned chief Topine Te Mamaku. Both men commanded a great deal of respect from their followers and were feared by the colonists. While their combined forces totalled 200 warriors, the local press exaggerated the number, speculating that 900 men might go to war against Hutt Valley settlers.[5]

In the mid-1840s, rumours of impending Māori raids were spreading throughout the region. Many colonial women fled the Hutt Valley, taking their children to the comparative safety of nearby Wellington. As tensions rose, military reinforcements were shipped over from the Australian colonies. The 'genial, convivial and generous' Major Edward Last headed up the company of the 99th Regiment that crossed the Tasman Sea to join forces with the two flank companies already stationed in Auckland. The three companies set sail for Wellington on 2 February 1847, with the combined force of 600 men under orders to quell the Māori 'rebellion' in the southern region of the North Island.[6]

As well as being concerned about the likelihood of imminent war, Mason disapproved of the way in which the colonial authorities were conducting their relationship with local Māori. He had in fact become quite friendly with some of the indigenes and did not like the way they were being treated. His Quaker sensibilities no doubt swayed his opinion. Mason was also worried about his wife Jane's declining health. Rather than simply moving his family into town, he decided to relocate temporarily across the Tasman Sea to Van Diemen's Land.

In 1845 the Masons packed up and sailed to Hobart, the capital of Van Diemen's Land, where Thomas was initially employed as a bookkeeper. Happily for the Masons, the Society of Friends was well established in Hobart. In 1847, Thomas rejoined the Quakers, and his wife Jane was also accepted into the Society. Four years after their arrival, Mason opened a small school for Quaker children, a testament to the level of acceptance that the family found in their new circumstances.[7]

Within months, Mason's decision to absent himself and his family from their Taita property was vindicated. The rumours of impending warfare, no doubt fuelled by accounts of the Wairau Affray and the war in the far north of the North Island, proved to be accurate. As the Masons settled into their new life across the Tasman Sea, armed conflict broke out between local Māori and the Hutt Valley colonists. It was triggered, in part, by Grey's orders to destroy Makahinuku Pā and other Māori settlements in the Hutt Valley that the Governor 'thought were complicit in the continuing obstruction and harassment of Hutt Valley settlers'. Tensions also escalated over competing claims to land following the eviction of some Ngāti Rangatahi. The land at issue was taken over by the Gillespies. On 2 April 1846 a cohort of Ngāti Rangatahi attacked and killed Andrew Gillespie and his young son, an act of retaliation that was seen as open warfare by the increasingly alarmed colonists.[8]

The concerned settlers thought Te Rangihaeata was somehow responsible for the incident. Although not personally involved, they suspected him of ordering the attack on the Gillespies. Te Rangihaeata was, after all, a highly influential rangatira and was at enmity with the colonists following the Wairau Affray regardless of diplomatic negotiations that had since taken place between he and his uncle and Governor FitzRoy. FitzRoy had since been replaced by the former Governor of South Australia, George Grey. Grey, like his predecessor, initially used diplomacy to restore peaceful relations. He tried to mollify the displaced Ngāti Rangatahi and Ngāti Tama with a land grant of 300 acres at Kaiwharawhara (near Wellington) and agreed to pay for the loss of their crops.

Grey's diplomacy failed. Within about five weeks, some of Te Rangihaeata's followers at Pauatahanui, up the coast from Wellington, fired on a naval party reconnoitring in the area. The elderly chief Te Rauparaha warned military leaders Majors Richmond and Last in early May of an imminent attack at Heretaunga (the Hutt Valley). However, the elder statesman's warnings to concentrate the settlers into one area as a defensive tactic were not heeded. To the contrary, as a cost-saving measure Richmond decided to disband the Wellington Militia and to halve the number of men stationed at the Hutt.

In the second week of May 1846, Te Rangihaeata and his ally Te Mamuku began to put their plans of attack into action. To divert attention and resources from the Hutt Valley, a scout was sent up into the Tinakori Range above Wellington. The man lit a large fire then circled around it numerous times, creating the impression that a large band of warriors was gathering with an attack on Wellington being imminent. This had the desired effect, drawing colonial troops away from the Hutt to shore up Wellington's defences.

A rough and narrow bush track connected the Hutt Valley to Porirua, the area to the north and over densely forested hills where Te Rauparaha, Te Rangihaeata and their allies were based. It was over this war trail that a force of around 200 Māori under the command of Te Mamuku and following orders from Te Rangihaeata descended stealthily down the ridge to Boulcott's Farm under the cover of fog early on the morning of Saturday 16 May 1846. They were probably dressed similarly to the warriors who raided another Hutt Valley property in the same period: 'each man was stripped, save for the usual katika, or kilt, worn around the loins. Their oiled bodies glistened … while their faces, daubed over with red paint, were fearful to behold. Their black hair was tied up in a knot on top of their heads and ornamented with feathers. Several carried muskets and had their cartridge-boxes fastened around their waists; the others were armed with war-clubs and spears, some of which were wonderfully carved'.[9]

Some of the warriors in the taua that approached Boulcott's Farm were men who colonists such as Thomas Mason knew personally. Some of the many Whanganui warriors included the 6-foot tall Hohepa Te Umuroa, a Ngāti Hau man of high standing who already sported a partial facial moko (tattoo), as well as Te Kumete, Te Waretiti, Matiu Tikiahi and Te Rahui. At least one of these men, if not all, formed part of the large force that advanced stealthily upon Boulcott's Farm.

As the taua neared their target, the advance party concealed themselves behind foliage to camouflage their approach. Their strategy worked remarkably well. The sentry realised too late that the greenery seemed to be moving nearer as he watched. He barely had time to fire off his Brown Bess and give a warning cry 'Māoris!' before being fatally tomahawked as he frantically tried to reload. As he fell to the ground, fifty Māori-wielded guns opened fire on the tent to which he had been retreating. His companions all became casualties of the conflict.

In an iconic moment in the fight at Boulcott's Farm, one of the young soldiers in the tent who happened to be the company's bugler raised his bugle to his lips and sounded a warning note after hearing the sentry discharge his Brown Bess. In doing so, Bugler William Allen made a target of himself, and had his right arm almost severed by a Māori tomahawk. Felled to the ground, young Bugler Allen staggered to his feet and raised the bugle with his left hand only to be killed by a tomahawk blow to the head before he could sound another note. Allen was considered a hero, and his concerted efforts to warn his companions of the surprise attack were later memorialised in a coloured lithograph.

The warriors advanced rapidly on Lieutenant Page's cottage, surrounding it. Page, armed with a pistol and his sword, joined several other soldiers and they fought their way through the Māori contingent to join the main force in Boulcott's barn. Within the confines of the building, the regimental soldiers shot at the enemy through the stockade, retreating to the barn to reload their weapons. With the sounds of Allen's bugle and the sentry's Brown Bess being fired, the attackers had lost the element of surprise. Page and the bulk of the redcoats under his command took up their bayonets and emerged from behind the stockade to engage the enemy in hand-to-hand fighting.

Fortunately for the soldiers, seven men who had belonged to the recently disbanded Hutt Militia came to their aid. After an hour and a half of close combat, the warriors retreated and, at a distance, performed a haka (ceremonial posture dance) witnessed by the soldiers. In all, six soldiers died in the affray and four other men were seriously wounded. Two of the wounded, one a soldier and the other an employee of Boulcott's, later died of their wounds. The retreating

Māori warriors carried their dead and injured with them and accurate numbers of the deceased are not known. However, two Māori were reported to have been shot dead and at least ten others were wounded in the affray.

The attack, one of a series in the Hutt Valley between April and August 1846, demoralised the settlers. Boulcott wrote a letter home to his father in England on 27 May 1846 describing how 'here everything is in a state of alarm, everyone armed and all most [sic] all the outsettlers returning to town, so hard for this season the whole of our agricultural operations are suspended and how the poor people are ever supported I am quite at a loss to guess, unless the Government will come forward and ration them.' He was worried that if the rumours circulating in the colonies of impending war between Britain and either France or America were true, England would abandon the New Zealand settlers to their fate which, Boulcott predicted, would be 'massacre'.[10]

The official response within New Zealand to the attack at Boulcott's Farm was threefold. Grey stepped up the military presence in the region, arming civilians with muskets and swearing in many volunteers. The volunteers supplemented the regular military force and the militia. The Governor also cleverly exploited intertribal rivalries, arming his Te Ati Awa allies so that they could pursue the 'hostile' Ngāti Rangitahi and their Whanganui allies. About 250 Te Ati Awa warriors, albeit armed with inferior colonial weapons, set out on the offensive under the command of leaders such as Te Puni. Grey's final measure was to extend martial law (initially declared throughout the Wellington district, excluding the town itself, on 20 April 1846) over a larger area, including Whanganui.

A month after the attack on Boulcott's Farm, the naval frigate *Calliope* sailed up the west coast of the North Island as far as Plimmerton where some of its crew routed Te Rauparaha from his hut and took him into custody. The ageing rangatira was suspected by some of the colonial officials of double-dealing, although the missionary Richard Taylor thought the chief 'was initially neutral, but was suspected because he remained in contact with his relatives'. Grey tried to come up with charges to prefer against him. However, no legal proceedings were instituted against Te Rauparaha. As martial law was in place, he could be held in custody indefinitely without being tried. A farcical situation developed. The *Calliope* sailed aimlessly up and down the coast of the North Island for ten months with Te Rauparaha imprisoned on board. Eventually, he was taken ashore in Auckland and detained a further eight months. After repeated demands for his release from Ngāpuhi supporters from the far north, Te Rauparaha was eventually released and returned home in ill health.[11]

Winter approached. With Te Rauparaha out of the way, the colonists commenced a rear guard action against Te Rangihaeata and his supporters. A combined force of Hutt Militia and their Māori allies used the same path that the invading Whanganui taua had taken on its approach to Boulcott's Farm to cross the bush-clad hills to the west coast to intercept a large contingent of Whanganui Māori warriors rumoured to be heading down the coast. The opposing forces met at Pauatahanui, where one of the Whanganui rangatira, Te Wareaitu (also known as Matini Ruta or Martin Luther) was captured then handed over to the regular soldiers. His brother Te Rangiatea, who was too ill to escape his pursuers, was also taken captive. Both were related to Te Rangihaeata and also, more distantly, to Te Mamuku. Their capture, along with the arrest of Te Rauparaha, was therefore of strategic importance to the British and colonial forces because they aimed to reassert dominance. It bolstered their position, despite Te Rangihaeata remaining elusive.

In August 1846, the colonists heard that some of the Māori 'rebels' were leaving their position in the Horokiwi valley. Last ensured this intelligence was passed onto the police chief at Waikanae who asked

British ally Wiremu Kingi to intercept the wanted men. Inclement
weather made for little sustenance and uncomfortable living conditions. This drove some of the 'rebellious' Māori down to the coast
near Pari Pari in search of food. Pari Pari was, according to Jerningham Wakefield, the residence of Te Puke whose village was 'situated
on a terrace of the hill, about fifty feet above the beach'. When Wakefield visited there in 1840 he noted 'two or three canoes … hauled up
under some karaka trees' near the beach, while 'the old men of the pa
were sitting beneath their shade, enjoying their pipes'.[12]

On or about 16 August 1847, some of Kingi's men led by Apera-
hama Ngatou and Nepetarima Ngauru captured eight of the hungry
Whanganui warriors near Pari Pari. They found Hohepa Te Umuroa,
Te Kumete, Te Waretiti, Matiu Tikiahi, Te Rahui, Topi, Mataiumu
and Te Korohunga after smoke from their fire gave away the men's
location. According to Last, 'a good deal of firing was heard in the
direction of the Pari Pari', so Te Rangihaeata's forces put up some
resistance. The eight men who subsequently became known as the
Pari Pari prisoners were handed over to the Armed Police before
being transferred into British military custody. They were then incarcerated on the *Calliope* along with Te Rauparaha and seven other
captive 'chiefs'. In September 1846, the *Auckland Press* announced to
its readers that 'in consequence of the successes of our regular troops,
seamen, militia, and native allies, everything appears to a most sat-
isfactory aspect to the southward'. The Lower Hutt War was over.[13]

Grey had Last convene a court martial of officers from his British Regiment at Porirua, north of Wellington, to try Te Rangiatea
and his brother Te Wareaitu. Neither man was provided with any
legal representation. One of the Militia men acted as an interpreter
throughout the proceedings. Te Rangiatea pleaded guilty to 'being
found in possession of a spear', but denied a second charge of 'having
taken part in an attack and massacre of Her Majesty's troops at the
Hutt'. The ailing prisoner was found guilty of both charges and, in

a most unusual judgement, was sentenced to imprisonment for life on the grounds of insanity. Te Rangiatea was admitted to hospital in Wellington where he died just two months later.

Te Wareaitu was next to appear. He faced similar charges to his brother: 'that he had resisted and wounded a friendly Māori of the Ngāti awa [Te Ati Awa] tribe' and 'of aiding in rebellion by taking part in a skirmish in the Hutt Valley three months before'. The military officers found Te Wareaitu guilty of open rebellion. They also found that he had assisted in the Hutt Valley skirmish, although he had not personally taken part. The unfortunate prisoner was sentenced to death. The sentence attracted opprobrium from the press and some of the settlers, and the military had difficulty in finding somebody willing to take on the role of hangman. However, 'a purse of gold' was offered to a soldier who agreed to play the part of executioner. When the soldier-hangman drowned little more than a year later in shallow water, his comrades attributed his premature death to his role as executioner, claiming that his share 'in the killing ... had clung to him like a curse'.[14]

As they were captured in the context of war, the Pari Pari prisoners and the other captives ought all to have been treated as prisoners of war. According them this status would have seen the men incarcerated until hostilities ceased, following which they could have returned home. However, like his Australian counterparts, Governor George Grey was determined to have exemplary punishments inflicted upon them to deter other Māori from taking up arms against colonists. Rather than acknowledging their actions as being acts of war, he criminalised their activities and had them put on trial. Because Grey had imposed martial law over the region in which they were taken into captivity, the men were not brought before the civil courts but were instead subjected to a court martial.[15]

In declaring martial law, Grey was following precedents set in the Australian colonies where martial law was declared against Aboriginal people near Bathurst, New South Wales, by Governor Thomas Brisbane over a four-month period from August 1824, and across parts of Van Diemen's Land by Lieutenant Governor George Arthur in 1828 during the height of the Black War between Tasmanian Aborigines and settlers. Grey's declaration of martial law was publicly questioned by a commentator who wrote to the *Wellington Independent* using the nom de plume 'An Englishman'. The writer was careful to state that he was not censuring the Governor, but reminded readers that 'it is under the best rulers that the liberties of the people are most liable to be infringed'. He inquired whether circumstances in the Wellington region warranted martial law.

Imposing martial law was usually reverted to in extreme circumstances, such as on the eve of the threatened invasion of Elizabethan England by Spain. Its imposition resulted in the suspension of people's rights to be tried before the civil courts. The letter writer's concerns were twofold. Living under martial law 'tacitly allowed that Englishmen forgo their privileges on moving to a British colony'. With regard to the Māori prisoners taken following the Lower Hutt War, he noted 'they have now been in custody for over two months. They are not notorious criminals. They were taken in a foraging expedition. To try them now by court martial, and then hang them, now that there is no necessity for such a proceeding, would be a gross act of wanton barbarity'. He asked whether there was 'the slightest reason to suppose, either that witnesses would be intimidated, or that a jury would be unwilling to convict them if they were tried legally?'[16]

Grey was not swayed by public opinion. However, Last tried to abrogate any further responsibility by sending the eight Pari Pari prisoners to Wellington to be tried before the civil courts. Richmond refused to try the men on the grounds that the declaration of martial law had stripped him of the authority to do so. Grey had the prisoners sent back up the coast to be tried by a newly convened court martial presided over by Last and comprising four of his officers. It was held in Porirua on 12 October 1846.

Last's commanding officer, Lieutenant Colonel Hulme, decided to allow the youngest of the prisoners, Te Korohunga, his freedom. He was, after all, 'a mere lad'. The remaining seven faced three charges, including having 'been taken in arms, and in open Rebellion against the Queen's Sovereign Authority and Government of New Zealand', as well as 'aiding ... and assisting the Rebel Chief Te Rangihaeata' and being 'unlawfully ... in possession of a firelock, the property of Her Majesty the Queen, marked 58th Regiment H. No. 62 ... The said firelock having been so unlawfully detained since 16th May 1846 at which time it was in the possession of Private Thomas Bolt 58th Regt. Who was shot in the attack by the rebels on 16th May 1846'.[17]

As before, the prisoners were not provided with any legal representation. An interpreter was provided to ensure that the prisoners could be said to have understood the proceedings. During the course of the proceedings, four Māori witnesses were produced to attest to the guilt of the prisoners who had, in any case, pleaded guilty to all the charges that had been put to them. Three of the witnesses gave evidence under oath through the interpreter Ensign Servantes. The fourth witness, Te Witu, had not converted to Christianity but was nevertheless still allowed to give evidence after being 'cautioned to speak the truth'. Te Witu's evidence was also interpreted by Servantes who claimed that it was he who had taken the musket being the mark of the 58th Regiment from the prisoner Te Kumete.

Unlike the trials of Aboriginal prisoners in New South Wales, the Māori prisoners appear to have been given the right to cross-examine the witnesses produced against them. Te Kumete questioned Te Witu as to whether he was 'positive that you took the musket marked 58th Regt. 62 from me?' Te Witu answered in the affirmative, following which evidence was heard from several military men, one of whom had been at Boulcott's Farm and confirmed that the weapon in question had belonged to the deceased soldier Bolt and had not been seen again until found in the possession of the Pari Pari prisoners.

In their defence, the Pari Pari prisoners argued that they acknowledged being rebels and following Te Rangihaeata but denied that they had killed anybody. They were nevertheless found guilty of all charges and were sentenced 'to be transported as felons for the term of their natural lives'. The prisoners were shipped to Auckland on board the naval steamer *Driver* to await passage to Van Diemen's Land, the site at which their sentence was to be carried out. Grey then gave orders for Matiu Tikiahi and Topi to be detained in Auckland as potential witnesses against Te Rauparaha should charges be brought against the rangatira. For some reason, though, when *HMS Castor* set sail for Van Diemen's Land at the end of October 1846, Matiu Tikiahi was one of the five Māori prisoners on board while Matiaumu remained behind.

17

A merciful alternative

A little more than two weeks after departing the Port of Auckland, HMS *Castor* docked at Hobart on 16 November 1846. The arrival of the Māori prisoners created a minor sensation. Sympathetic citizens rushed to the docks to see Hohepa Te Umuroa, Te Kumete, Te Waretiti, Matiu Tikiahi and Te Rahui dressed in their traditional attire. The prisoners were taken to the Paddock to be interviewed. Each was allocated a prisoner number, ranging from 765 to 769. Te Umuroa and Te Kumete were recorded as able to read and write in Māori. The others were illiterate. The men's physical descriptions and details were entered meticulously into the convict register. Most were described as 'laborer', and all were 'single'. After processing, they were taken to 'Mr Gunn's depository for men of all castes' (the Hobart Penitentiary). The Vandemonian convict records state the men were intended for a work gang at the notorious penal station, Port Arthur.[1]

In a letter accompanying the prisoners, Grey reasoned that had the men been subjected to their own law for their 'several murders and many robberies', they would have been sentenced to death. Transportation was, in his view, a merciful alternative. Grey saw value in inflicting an exemplary punishment on the men. He thought 'a great advantage would result to this Country [New Zealand], if these men were from time to time really kept to hard labour, and if they could be allowed to correspond with their friends … In this manner many of the turbulent chiefs would ascertain that the Government really intended to punish severely all those who connected themselves with murderers and robbers, and would find from the letters of their friends in Van Diemen's Land, what the nature of that punishment of transportation really is'.[2]

Exemplary punishment was a common enough notion in colonial Australia, yet Grey found little sympathy among Hobartians. When news of the judicial execution of Te Whareaitu broke in Van Diemen's Land, the *Colonial Times* castigated Grey, printing that 'it is impossible to characterise in terms sufficiently expressive of abhorrence the detestable crime of Governor Grey (Captain, as he is, to the disgrace of the army, called), in the murder of the gallant New Zealand chief Wareaitu [sic]'.[3]

When Te Umuroa, Te Kumete, Te Waretiti, Tikiahi and Te Rahui arrived in Van Diemen's Land, *The Britannia and Trades' Advocate* condemned the British colonisation of New Zealand as 'unjust ... [and] an act by which the British name and character were tarnished'. This was a remarkable observation, given that the Tasmanian Aboriginal population was dangerously close to extinction following one of the most brutal frontier experiences in the Australian colonies. However, the Māori were understood locally to 'regard their British co-occupants, though settled with the sanction of compacts and treaties, as strangers and intruders' and were viewed as superior 'natives' fighting to defend their country. The *Colonial Times* declared Grey ought to have gone 'at the head of the troops' to 'fight the New Zealand patriots like a man'. His convening of courts martial was abhorred 'throughout the island' and considered 'the very quintessence of tyrannical cowardice'. The more conservative *Hobart Town Courier* claimed that it would not 'censure ... the decree which subjected a native chief [Te Whareaitu] to the heaviest penalty of the law', yet stated emphatically 'if we have nothing to say of the dead, we have much to plead for the living'.[4]

The newly arrived Māori convicts were admired as warriors but seen as naive 'children of nature'. They may have taken a few tentative steps towards civilisation, but their status was considered precarious. One of the principal concerns around town was that these intelligent yet 'simple-minded' men would be corrupted at Port Arthur. *Hobart Town Courier* staff visited the prisoners at the Penitentiary, conversing with them through an interpreter. The newspaper railed against the men being sent to 'mingle with masses of moral guilt and doubly-convicted crime', as would be the case if they were sent down Tasman's Peninsula. The Māori convicts ought not to be exposed 'to contaminating familiarization with the most horrible forms of vice', reasoned the newspaper, particularly given that 'their greatest offence seems to have been the defence of their country against what, with erring views, they conceived to be foreign aggression, or doubtful implication in a murder committed under the excitement of hostilities and in the reckless violence of warfare'. It was suggested that compared with the fate awaiting them at Port Arthur, 'the doom of their Chief was mercy'.[5]

The five were asked by the *Hobart Town Courier* whether they thought it wrong a New Zealand chief (Te Whareaitu) had been hanged. They did not express any opinion beyond one stating that he 'didn't know'. Te Umuroa, Te Kumete, Te Waretiti, Tikiahi and Te Rahui were 'unwilling to express freely any opinion on the hostilities in which they were engaged, or on the justice of their sentence'. They did, however, point out 'that they were only "fighting those who came against their country"' and said they had not committed murder.

When questioned about their living conditions, the men said that they had plenty of food and clothing. They were also not expected to labour and were getting enough sleep. But they were not particularly happy with their water. According to the *Hobart Town Courier*, the men described it as 'wimouri kakena', which the interpreter translated as 'very bad water'. The men were, after all, used to being able to 'quench their thirst from the crystal springs and rivulets' of New

Zealand. The reading public was reassured that the water provided was the best available in Hobart at the time. It was drawn up by pump from the town water supply and delivered immediately to the prisoners to ensure its freshness.[6]

William Duke, an artist who had previously lived in New Zealand, visited the men and painted Te Umuroa's portrait. He portrayed the man holding his tokotoko, a staff of office denoting his achievements and symbolising his power and authority to speak. Duke took some artistic licence with the image, completing in oils Te Umuroa's unfinished moko. Artist John Skinner Prout also visited the prisoners. Born at Plymouth, England, on 19 December 1805, Prout came out to Sydney with his wife Maria and seven children in 1840. While in New South Wales, he bought a lithographic plant and taught at the School of Art. Following a visit to Van Diemen's Land in January 1844, Prout relocated his family to Hobart Town. They arrived in April. Once settled, Prout made a living through delivering lectures on 'the cultivation of the fine arts, with practical illustrations', and publishing several volumes of sketches.

As well as country scenes, Prout painted watercolour portraits of Australian Aboriginal people. He also created poetic likenesses of the five Māori convicts, mostly relying on simple tones of black, sepia and white that create a light, ephemeral impression. The individual portraits show each man cloaked in his traditional attire. A pounamu (greenstone) ear-ring hangs from Te Kumete's right ear. He also has a moko, as do two of his companions, Te Waretiti and Te Umuroa. All of the men wore serious expressions, ranging from Tikiahi's rather pensive, downcast look to the forthright gaze of Te Kumete. When they were completed, each signed their respective portrait. These engaging, luminous watercolour paintings form part of a larger collection of thirty-six of Prout's works at the British Museum in London. (The portraits are reproduced in the colour section of this book.)

Prout and his wife, with several of their children, returned to

227

London in 1848. They left behind a son, Frederick, who died in 1845 at the tender age of ten after being struck by a stone. Their daughter, Matilda, also stayed behind. In March 1847 she consented to marry John Dandridge. In October 1847, those few Tasmanian Aborigines who survived incarceration on Flinders Island were transferred to an abandoned convict station at Oyster Cove, south of Hobart. Dandridge was later supervisor of the Oyster Cove Aboriginal Station. After most of its Aboriginal inhabitants had died, the station was shut down. Truganini, a woman widely but incorrectly touted as being 'the last of the Tasmanians', moved with the Dandridges, her guardians, in 1874 to a house in Macquarie Street, Hobart. Truganini became a local identity, instantly recognisable around the streets of Hobart with her dark features and red turban. She died on 8 May 1876, aged 64, at the Dandridges' house.[7]

Thomas Mason, the Hutt Valley settler who relocated temporarily to Hobart in the 1840s, became part of the inner circle of well-known Quaker missionary and humanitarian George Washington Walker. Walker, with Quaker minister James Backhouse, left England in 1831 to undertake a nine-year mission to the Cape Colony and the Australian colonies. He settled in Hobart in 1840 where, with Backhouse, he founded the Society of Friends in Van Diemen's Land.[8]

Shortly after Te Umuroa, Te Kumete, Te Waretiti, Tikiahi and Te Rahui arrived in Van Diemen's Land, Mason visited the men at the Penitentiary where he 'was immediately recognised as an old friend and received with great joy'. He noticed that since he had known the men in New Zealand, 'at least 3 have since been tattooed'. When the Comptroller General of Convicts, Dr John Hampton, asked Mason's advice about how to treat the men, Mason told him their taking the moko was 'a sign that they have thrown off the restraint of Christianity'. He claimed tattooing was 'strictly forbidden by the missionaries'. Despite this, all five men carried copies of the Bible printed in Māori, which they read. They possibly came into contact with the Catholic Church through Father Comte who established a mission at Otaki in 1844 and worked extensively with around 200 Māori associated with Te Rauparaha.[9]

Mason advised Hampton to keep the Māori convicts entirely separate from the rest of the convict population and to provide them with Christian instruction. He advocated taking the lightest possible approach in physically restraining the men. He also advised refraining from commenting on the fairness or otherwise of their court martial. If a pardon came from London, it could then be perceived as a boon rather than a right.[10]

The prevailing thinking that indigenous groups ought to be kept apart from the lower classes of colonial society for fear of contamination informed decisions made about the Māori convicts. While they were at the Hobart Penitentiary, the Administrator of Van Diemen's Land Charles La Trobe ensured the Māori were kept 'secure ... from association with the common herd of Prisoners'. La Trobe was concerned about the legality of the court martial under which the men were sentenced and decided to treat the five Māori convicts differently from other convicts arriving in Van Diemen's Land.[11]

Prisoners sentenced to life transportation were usually sent to Port Arthur or Norfolk Island. Public pressure mounted, resulting in La Trobe ruling out sending the Māori convicts to either location. He wrote to the Home Office on 30 November 1846 to draw Earl Grey's attention to the case. He told Grey that while procedure demanded it, 'I cannot resolve to send them either to Norfolk Island or [Port Arthur at] Tasman's Peninsula to be classed and associated with the transported felons congregated in those settlements'. To provide him with the background context, La Trobe enclosed a copy of Governor George Grey's letter and Mason's advice about how to treat the prisoners. He then had to wait for advice from London. In the meantime, the *Hobart Town Courier and Government Gazette*

reported it was 'glad to learn ... that the most repulsive provision' of
the men's sentence (sending them to Port Arthur) was being reversed.
They were to be sent to the probation station at Darlington on Maria
Island.[12]

The convict probation system was introduced after the British
House of Commons convened a committee to inquire into transportation. The Molesworth Committee, named after its Chair, Sir William Molesworth, devised a new system for dealing with convicts.
Convicts were to progress along a pathway of five stages towards
rehabilitation into society. Newly arrived convicts experienced strict
prison discipline for the first several years of their sentence, working
in gangs under an overseer. Communication was restricted. Tobacco
and other luxurious items were banned. At the other end of the spec-
trum, convicts at the fourth of the five stages of probation received
a 'ticket of leave'. This functioned as a pardon valid only within the
colony in which it was granted. Ticket-of-leave men or women could
live almost as though they were free. If they committed any misdemeanours their ticket could be revoked. To earn their ticket, convicts
usually had to have served at least half of their sentence. In the case
of life sentences, this meant serving twelve years.[13]

Its relative isolation made Maria Island a suitable location for
felons. Some infrastructure was already available at Darlington,
adding to its attractiveness as a potential probation station. The
island had housed convicts between 1825 and 1830. During this
earlier convict period, men were treated more brutally. Some were
flogged so severely that they did not survive. It was brutality such
as this that led to the British Government trying to improve the
convict system. The probation station at Maria Island was quite new
when La Trobe decided to send Te Umuroa, Te Kumete, Te Waretiti,
Tikiahi and Te Rahui there. It had been opened only five years.

The special treatment meted out to the Māori convicts extended
beyond sending them to a probation station. They were fast-tracked

through the probation system and, as instructed by the Colonial Office, the men were 'allowed all the freedom enjoyed by the holders of Tickets of Leave'. This was very advantageous. Significantly, it meant that the men would immediately be eligible to be considered for the free pardon La Trobe was seeking on their behalf from London if it were approved. In the meantime, their status as ticket-of-leave holders entitled them to greater privileges than other convicts.[14]

The intention was to have the Māori convicts remain segregated from other convicts in the interests of their wellbeing while at Darlington. As a precursor to relocating them, the authorities sought a suitable person to become their overseer. Thomas Mason was the obvious choice, but as he had commitments that necessitated remaining in Hobart, the authorities were forced to look elsewhere for an appropriate candidate. The man chosen for the role was also a colonist with prior experience in New Zealand. Indeed, one of the local Tasmanian newspapers described John Jennings Imrie as having been 'many years a resident amongst the tribe and well acquainted with their language, and [able] to afford them every facility and advantage of religious and moral instruction'.[15]

In fact, Imrie had lived at Nelson, the New Zealand Company settlement at the top of the South Island, rather than at Whanganui from where the Māori convicts originated. This was just one of a number of inconsistencies evident in Imrie's life story when key details published in his obituary are compared with his documented life events. When he died in Brisbane, Queensland, in March 1901, an article celebrating the life of 'an old colonist' told how 'Dr Imrie' 'took his degrees at Edinburgh University' and served in the army as a Medical Officer during both the first Indian Mutiny and the Spanish Peninsula Wars. It was claimed that the Imries were the first white settlers at Nelson where John Jennings had 'built the first house ... having taken the materials out with him'.

The biggest tragedy revealed in Imrie's obituary was the loss of £40 000 worth of merchandise that the unfortunate man apparently lost when the ship conveying his goods struck rocks off the coast from Nelson and 'went to pieces before the eyes of the owner'. Being 'one of the few settlers who escaped being murdered' during the Wairau Massacre, so the account went, Imrie and the rest of the Nelson settlers barely escaped with their lives and abandoned Nelson (and all their property) to flee to Hobart when 'a schooner put into Nelson on her way to Tasmania'.[16] In reality, Imrie lived in New Zealand between 1841 and 1843 where he owned a shop, 'JJ Imrie & Co', in Bridge Street, Nelson. When the Imrie family sailed for Van Diemen's Land on the brigantine *Sisters* on 30 September 1843, their relocation was well planned and fully funded.[17]

By the time Imrie was employed as overseer to the Māori convicts, the Scotsman's English wife Etty was several months into her fourth pregnancy. When the family sailed for Maria Island on the Government schooner *Mary* with Te Umuroa, Te Kumete, Te Waretiti, Tikiahi and Te Rahui, La Trobe and Hampton accompanied them, presumably to see their high profile prisoners settled in and to check that the Darlington Probation Station was running smoothly.[18]

The mountainous and heavily forested Maria Island, named by Abel Tasman in 1642 after Dutch East India Company official Anthony Van Diemen's wife Maria, lies north-east of Hobart. It is clearly visible from the Tasmanian coastline. Cleared land around Darlington at its northern extremity is dwarfed by 'Bishop and Clerk', the island's second highest peak. A slim isthmus connects the northern part of the mountainous island to its southern sister. Tasmanian Aboriginal reed canoes plied the waters between Maria Island and the Tasmanian mainland long before Europeans arrived. The Oyster Bay Tribe regularly visited the island they called Toarra-marra-monah where they obtained ochre from a mine near the isthmus. The red pigment was valued by indigenous people for use in decorating their bodies. It was used in conjunction with grease by the women in creating elaborate hairstyles for the men. The women kept their hair very short to keep it out of the way as they dived for shellfish, an exclusively female occupation. The highly significant red pigment was also used in some of the indigenous people's bark paintings.

By the time the Māori convicts arrived at Maria Island on Sunday 20 December, it had long since been abandoned by the Oyster Bay people whose numbers declined dramatically following colonisation. In 1846, Maria Island was home to 291 convicts. These men were worked in gangs cultivating wheat, hops, potatoes, flax and vegetables or producing goods such as baskets and rope mats. During the summer months, Maria Island convicts rose at five thirty each morning and laboured until six in the evening.[19]

The Māori convicts, who were initially housed about half a mile from the probation station at Darlington, were not required to adhere to such a strict regimen. In the middle of the week following their arrival, their overseer Imrie's diary entry for Wednesday 23 December reads: 'At 6 am visited the Māoris hut all fast asleep'. Later in the morning, they spent time reading and writing, received several visitors, and hunted unsuccessfully for crayfish in the afternoon.

The Friday following their arrival was Christmas Day, 1846. When Imrie went to visit his charges at seven in the morning, he 'found them all reading'. Young Henry Imrie had already spent two hours visiting Te Umuroa, Te Kumete, Te Waretiti, Tikiahi and Te Rahui. In the afternoon, they all 'took a walk in the bush'. The day ended, as usual, with evening prayers in the men's hut. On Boxing Day, a general muster was scheduled for all convicts. The men cleaned their hut before being inspected and included in the count.

Within days of their arrival, Imrie had the men building new huts. This kept them usefully occupied until the end of January 1847. The final week of December and the early weeks of January were spent selecting and cutting timber for these huts. Construction began on Tuesday 12 January. After four days, framework for at least one of the rooves was already up. The following week, they spent several days gathering wattle for the huts. Gathering wattle on the damp and cloudy Tuesday 19 January resulted in all the men becoming 'very fatigued'. The next day found Te Waretiti 'indisposed from the fatigues of the preceding day'. He remained unwell throughout February and March.

During the last fortnight in January, the walls for the new huts were built using the wattle and daub construction method typical of colonial housing. Latticed frameworks for the walls were constructed from strips of wood. The men then spent several days thatching the rooves. They also made a mixture from clay and other locally available materials that was later used by plasterers to finish the walls. The men moved into their new hut on Sunday 7 February then helped the Imries move into their new home. Later in the week, the men were busily employed building an outhouse. The construction work took its toll on Matiu Tikiahi, who cut his thumb quite severely.

The weather throughout February was very warm and brought a steady stream of visitors to Imrie's hut. At one point, a bushfire erupted in the foliage beyond Imrie's hut and became a minor spectacle. After this, the men cleared the land around their huts. When not employed sawing timber or in other construction tasks, the Māori convicts were busy cleaning, doing laundry or carrying water. The occasional half day was devoted to lessons in reading and writing with Imrie. Weekends were more relaxed, sometimes including fishing expeditions or opossum hunts. Sunday mornings were spent in prayer with Imrie.

The men created and fenced a vegetable garden in March and spent their days tilling the soil and planting seeds. With Te Waretiti still ailing, from Monday 15 March Imrie had the men labour only during the early part of the day. They knocked off at half-past twelve, following which they spent their afternoons in a leisurely manner. Sometimes they would go fishing, catching crayfish as well as fish. Other times, they would read or take a walk in the bush or along the beach with the Imries. The gentler routine did not help Te Waretiti, so at the end of March Imrie 'applied a blister' to the man's neck. On 2 April 1847, Dr Brownell visited. It is unclear from Imrie's diary whether this was solely a social visit (it was Good Friday and Brownell's family accompanied him) or whether the doctor was available to Te Waretiti for a consultation. Fortunately, by Easter Sunday Imrie was able to record 'Waretiti much better'.

One wet Monday in mid-April, Te Umuroa complained of pain in his side. Imrie was immediately solicitous and arranged a footbath, as well as a dose of salts. While his companions cut and carried wood and sowed peas in the newly dug garden, Te Umuroa was confined to bed. By Saturday 24 April, his health appeared to be improving and he joined the others on their afternoon stroll after prayers the next day. However, Monday saw Te Umuroa confined once again – this time with 'severe Rheumatic pains'. The following day, Tuesday 27 April, Etty Imrie gave birth to a son named John after his father. The happy occasion was celebrated by the Māori convicts taking a day's holiday.

On Saturday 1 May, Dr Brownell and his wife visited. This enabled the doctor to check on Mrs Imrie's and her baby's health, as well as to look in on Te Umuroa whose health was continuing to decline. Throughout May, as the men were employed in planting out cabbages, lettuces, gooseberry cuttings and potatoes, Te Umuroa's health seemed to improve. However, as May gave way to June he fell ill. After rallying briefly, Te Umuroa's health declined dramatically. Brownell visited on Friday 25 June and found the man's lungs 'in a very bad state'. The doctor ordered a blister, but the treatment failed to elicit any improvement. After several more visits, the patient remained gravely ill, afflicted with tuberculosis.

On Sunday 18 July, Te Umuroa asked to see Etty Imrie. They read prayers together. Imrie was sufficiently concerned to stay with Te Umuroa until midnight. When he returned to the men's hut at four o'clock the following morning, he found 'Hohepa very nearly gone'. An hour later, the patient 'breathed his last without a struggle'. A wet morning followed, but sunshine broke through in the afternoon as Te Kumete, Te Waretiti, Tikiahi and Te Rahui and the Imries mourned the loss of Hohepa Te Umuroa. The following morning, the funeral was held at the cemetery on Maria Island where Imrie 'read the service in his [Hohepa's] native language'. In an extremely unusual measure for a deceased convict, Imrie had a headstone erected over the grave inscribed in both Māori and English.

Following their companion's death, the remaining men continued working in the garden and cutting and carting firewood. Their lives as convict labourers were punctuated with prayer, fishing expeditions, and walks along the beach and in the bush. Yet some of their Sunday walks were now to the cemetery north-east of the probation station at Darlington. Several of the men suffered minor ailments in the months that followed. In September 1847, Te Waretiti experienced swelling in his neck that required lancing and a poultice. In November, Te Rahui and Te Kumete suffered from flu.[20]

In the meantime, official correspondence was exchanged between London, New Zealand and Van Diemen's Land. In May 1847, the Home Office wrote to Governor Grey about the Māori prisoners. London officials conjectured that 'it must have been some Proclamation by you of martial law under which they were tried' and thought it a 'question of grave doubt' that under such circumstances the men 'could lawfully be treated as Convicts in V.D. Land'. Courts convened during times of martial law were not 'legal tribunals'. The problems arising over the probable illegality of the original sentences could be addressed only by an Act of Parliament, a difficult and inappropriate course of action. Similar sentiments were conveyed to La Trobe in response to his initial inquiry to the Colonial Office.[21]

Early the next year, in February 1848, welcome news arrived from England that the Māori convicts had been pardoned. The surviving men were free to return to New Zealand once arrangements could be made for them to do so. In the meantime, Imrie took them to see Te Umuroa's gravestone. On Sunday 12 March, Thomas Mason arrived at Maria Island to visit the freed men. He spent several days with them, departing the following Tuesday. The next day, the *Lady Denison* collected the Imries and their former charges. Their journey home had begun.

'Under Dr Imrie's attentive care', reported Hobart's *Colonial Times*, 'the prisoners were as comfortable as they could be rendered consistently with their situation, the loss of liberty and their expatriation being their principal sources of sorrow and regret'. Indeed, their incarceration under Imrie was represented to Hobart's reading public as beneficial. In captivity the men had 'become perfectly European in their habits and general demeanour' through following Imrie's example. However, the wonderful outcome (in colonial terms) achieved by Imrie was undercut by the observation that the men were 'admirable mimics, and extremely quick in catching any new fashion or mannerism'. In the colonial period, when indigenous people were seen to have adopted colonial ways, they were not considered to have become 'civilised' (despite this being the avowed goal of the colonising population). Rather, through imitating colonial people, 'mimic men' were thought to be subverting the authentic and pure controlling force of colonialism.[22]

In a letter to the Colonial Office in London, the new Lieutenant Governor of Van Diemen's Land William Denison reported that in compliance with a request from Grey, he was repatriating the remaining four Māori to their homeland. 'I was better the pleased in being able to do so', wrote Denison, 'inasmuch as one of the five had been carried off by consumption, a few months since, and the others had for some time … evinced symptoms of despondency … which would have before long caused them to follow their companion'. Te Kumete, Te Waretiti, Matiu Tikiahi and Te Rahui sailed for New Zealand on the *Lady Denison* on 10 March 1848.[23]

Several years later, in 1851, the Masons returned to Taita. Thomas, who became known as 'Quaker Mason', had a substantial house and outbuildings erected. When it turned out that his buildings had been mistakenly built on Māori land, he paid rent to the rightful owner and later had his buildings moved. The Masons ran sheep and cattle in the Wairarapa and Hawke's Bay regions as well as the Hutt. Mason was renowned for his extensive gardens, which included 150 fruit trees from Tasmania.[24]

After returning to New Zealand, Mason may have heard about Te Ahuru, also known as Haimona Pita (Simon Peter), who was brought before the Supreme Court in Wellington in September 1851 charged with stealing. He was sentenced to seven years' transportation, following which Governor Grey and Colonial Secretary Alfred Domett signed documentation transferring the man's labour to the Lieutenant Governor of Van Diemen's Land for the period of the man's sentence. Later that month, Te Ahuru was shipped to Hobart on the *Munford* where he arrived on 10 October 1851. The prisoner's details were recorded, with Te Ahuru being described as a 5'5" illiterate pagan who was unmarried. He was admitted to the Colonial Hospital while the authorities determined his fate.

Denison felt bound by a despatch dated 28 September 1850 sent by Earl Grey to Governor Fitzgerald at the Swan River Colony in which the Secretary of State for War and the Colonies issued instructions to keep Aboriginal prisoners sentenced to hard labour separate from the general convict population. This requirement saw Rottnest Island off the Western Australian coast near Perth function as a prison solely for Aboriginal people. Upwards of 3670 men and boys were shipped there from 1838 into the early decades of the twentieth century. Denison was concerned about the costs and impracticalities of separately accommodating Te Ahuru and decided to repatriate him to New Zealand within a week of his arrival in Hobart. He was sent back to New Zealand on the *Perseverance*. The master of the vessel successfully negotiated with Grey to retain the man as part of his crew. Te Ahuru was eventually issued with a conditional pardon on 21 December 1855. Following this, Grey made arrangements for Māori prisoners that did not involve transportation to the Australian penal colonies.[25]

18

Repatriating Hohepa
Te Umuroa, 1988

Hohepa Te Umuroa's headstone has intrigued visitors to the small colonial cemetery near Darlington for more than a century and a half. Throughout the different eras of occupation on Maria Island, thousands of visitors have paused to read the words still visible on the ageing headstone: Dei Roarei Tokotoia Metau Tinana Ehoa [Here lie the remains of] Hohepa Te Umuroa, Native of Wanganui, N.Z., who died July 19, 1847.

A generation after the probation station shut down, Anthony Trollope Robinson and two companions, Brown and Jones, spent five days on Maria Island in February 1876 to test the accuracy of rumours about lead and tin to be found on the island. Earlier, Brown had accompanied explorer Hamilton Hume (the boyhood companion of the Aboriginal convict, interpreter and guide Duall) on an expedition in Queensland. So it naturally fell to Brown to lead the small expeditionary party on Maria Island. Jones was delegated cook. Robinson took on the roles of 'hewer of wood and fetcher of water' and historian.

Robinson took his role seriously, recording the men's prospecting surveys along the coastline around Long Point where they found 'a solitary grave' that they thought might have belonged to a whaler. They had in fact stumbled across the final resting place of Rene Mauge, a French zoologist who died in February 1802 during the

Baudin expedition to Australia. He was buried by fellow crewmen at a place that became known as Point Mauge on Maria Island. The three prospectors visited Ah Sing, a man Robinson described as 'a good natured Celestial who gains a livelihood by catching and curing mutton-fish for the China market'. They shared a cup of tea with him and his wife before returning to their camp. The presence of Chinese abalone divers such as Ah Sing at Maria Island in the 1870s is commemorated in the placename 'Chinaman's Bay'.

Failing to find tin in the south, the men tried their luck looking for lead at Darlington at the northern end of Maria Island. They inspected unfruitful gold diggings around the island's highest peak, Mt Maria, en route. At Darlington, they were disappointed by the lack of potential mineral wealth but intrigued by the extensive ruins of the convict probation station and associated buildings. On a visit to the former Parsonage, Robinson could not help but notice the expansive view across to Freycinet Peninsula and other Tasmanian landmarks from its hilly site. 'At its foot', wrote Robinson, 'is God's acre'. The men descended to the cemetery and 'with some difficulty read the inscriptions on the tombs'. After visiting a number of other headstones, the three companions came across a solitary headstone 'in the corner, hard by the "phantom moaning of a circle sea"'. In describing the headstone, Robinson reproduced the transcription that informs viewers about the origins and death of Te Umuroa. After reading it, he and his companions 'turned away sadly from the grave of this stranger who sleeps in a strange land'.

Robinson deplored the deteriorating condition of the graveyard. While 'over some [graves] the roses were blooming; others are hidden by luxuriant salt-bushes. The fences and walls have fallen down, and cattle trample over the remains of those who once, perchance, were loved'. He suggested that if the Government would not see to the upkeep of the Maria Island cemetery, then surely friends and relatives of the deceased could do something about it. 'Better, far better, to level it to the ground, to wipe it out of man's remembrances', wrote Robinson, 'than to leave it as it is at present – a disgrace to Government and to those whose relatives are buried there'.[1]

The following decade, Italian entrepreneur Diego Bernacchi obtained a long-term lease over Maria Island and established manufacturing and tourist enterprises, including grape growing, a cement works, hotel and coffee palace. A 'special correspondent' for Hobart's *Mercury* newspaper visited the island in August 1884, concluding that it 'is a proper place for capital to join hands with labour in, and resolve into a densely inhabited productive appendage, instead of, as heretofore, a mere fluky sheep run, which under the system followed since its desertion as a penal settlement has by rapid degrees gone far towards resuming its primeval state'. After discussing the island's suitability for depasturing stock, and for the various other businesses proposed by Bernacchi, the correspondent devoted a final paragraph to the Maria Island cemetery.

Many of those buried at Maria Island lie in unmarked graves, as was the custom for convict burials. The writer remarked: 'where the last resting place of many prisoners who died there, one old man, Tom McDonald, employed by Mr Bernacchi, knows but will not tell'. In the late nineteenth century, most Tasmanians were keen to forget the island's convict past. In 1884 the state of known graves was deplorable. Within the crumbling walls of the cemetery many tombs were in a poor state of repair and 'overrun with briars'. Te Umuroa's grave was one of those affected. 'In a corner by himself sleeps a Māori. His headstone, almost lost amid briars', wrote the correspondent. Much to his disgust, stock roamed freely among the dead. 'Pigs and cattle', he wrote, 'do not look well in any burial ground'. Although he wryly observed that on his last visit to Hobart sheep were being depastured at the cemetery in the middle of town. With an upfront cost estimated at £20 and ongoing costs of around £2 per annum to see to the cemetery's upkeep, the correspondent demanded 'Will some

Minister or member ask this sum for decency's sake?'[2]

The 1890s depression spelt an end to the Bernacchi era on Maria Island, although the cement works he founded continued to operate until 1930. In 1938, another visitor to the island asked if it was to be left to stagnate. Signs from various layers of its colonial past were abundant, particularly around Darlington where 'many of the old brick convict settlement buildings remain to tell their silent story of the time when the island was used as a penal settlement' and where the functioning guest house was the former home of 'picturesque figure … Signor Bernacchi'. The natural landscape was well suited to exploring, as was the colonial cemetery. 'The most interesting headstone still decipherable', wrote the author 'AFG', 'is a Māori chief who died in 1847 in exile'. Touting tourism as the answer to fulfilling Maria Island's latent potential, 'AFG' recounted a little of Te Umuroa's story, noting how the headstones in the small graveyard reveal the history of early settlement on the island. The writer urged that 'steps should be taken to preserve these relics of the past'.[3]

During and after World War Two, farming and fishing were mainstays for the few families who continued living on Maria Island. Eventually, as Tasmanian concerns for endangered species increased, people began to talk about the island being set aside as a nature reserve. This became a reality in 1971 when Maria Island became a National Park. With its mix of natural attractions including bush-clad mountains, intriguing cliff formations, long white beaches, abundant marine and bird life, and free-ranging marsupials as well as its built environment dating back to the convict era, Maria Island became popular with tourists and school groups. Under the management of the Parks and Wildlife Service, a fence was erected around the long-neglected cemetery and the graves were tended with care.

In the early 1970s, Tim Hume from Launceston in the north of Tasmania became intrigued with the life story of Te Umuroa after seeing his headstone. His interest had a practical outcome. Hume corresponded extensively with John (Jack) Tattersall at the Hawke's Bay Museum & Art Gallery in Napier, New Zealand. The men shared knowledge from their different cultural backgrounds and geographic contexts that enabled both to build a more complete picture of the circumstances surrounding the transportation and incarceration of the Māori convicts. Much of this material was later included in a pamphlet published by Tattersall's employer. Correspondence exchanged by the men, and between Tattersall and other notable researchers such as Ian Wards and Ian Brand, is currently held at Archives New Zealand in Wellington.[4]

In the decade that followed, Hohepa Te Umuroa's headstone continued to command attention from those who stood before it in the long, dry grass. Times were changing. With the Australian bicentenary approaching in 1988, Australians of settler descent were increasingly interested in their convict ancestry. No longer a matter of shame, some vied with others for the prestige of being descended from the highest number of convict ancestors. Finding a convict ancestor dating back to the First Fleet was celebrated in some quarters. Perhaps this phenomenon arose in part from an increasing national consciousness about the impacts of colonisation on Australia's indigenous peoples. As some Aboriginal people had observed in the early colonial period, 'prisoners [convicts] were obliged to come here against their will, but the immigrants came of their own accord, to rob the black man of his land'.[5]

New Zealand society was also changing. The country became bilingual, with Māori becoming recognised alongside English as an official language. The 1975 *Treaty of Waitangi Act* was amended in 1985. It became possible for Māori to make retrospective claims over contested resources and commenced a process of reconciliation that is ongoing in the present day. Increasing state recognition of Māori aspirations were welcomed by some Pākehā but decried by others. Nevertheless, Māori continued to assert claims for more equitable treatment and to seek redress for the iniquities of the shared colonial past.[6]

Significantly for both countries, indigenous cultural resurgences and assertiveness in the 1980s coupled with increased European awareness of some of the more problematic outcomes of colonisation saw the start of lengthy processes of negotiation that have resulted in the repatriation of indigenous remains from various overseas institutions. Conditions were finally ripe for Te Umuroa to return home after 140 years in exile.

The visit that triggered moves to have Te Umuroa repatriated was different from the other reported visits. This time it was schoolchildren moved by the experience of seeing the headstone while on a school trip to the island in 1985 who told their father, expatriate New Zealander Chris Heald, about it when they got home. At the time, Heald worked for Australian Federal Minister for Justice Senator Michael Tate. He was well positioned to inquire into the circumstances surrounding Te Umuroa's internment and repatriation, although when Heald began to ask questions he had little idea it would take three long years for matters to resolve. He worked closely with Chris Batt, a Tasmanian parliamentary candidate from New Norfolk (west of Hobart), to campaign for the remains to be repatriated. Heald later revealed both men were concerned the complex and drawn out negotiations between the Tasmanian Government, Australian Federal Government, New Zealand Government and Whanganui people might amount to nothing.[7]

An obstacle arose over who would fund the repatriation if it were to go ahead. Ultimately, the New Zealand Government agreed to bear the cost, providing Heald and Batt with their 'first optimistic sign' that the venture might prove successful. The Government's decision was not without controversy. Consistent with some Pākehā dissatisfaction with the changing socio-cultural landscape in New Zealand, at least one correspondent wrote to the Minister of Māori

Affairs, the Honourable Koro Wetere, to query the costs involved to taxpayers with regard to the proposed repatriation. Wetere responded, providing an overview of the circumstances that led to the men being exiled. He pointed out that the Government of the day had treated the exiles unjustly. 'Today's Government', he wrote, 'had an inherited responsibility which required it to take appropriate action in order that some redress be made for the wrong done all those years ago'. And that action was to ensure that Te Umuroa's remains were repatriated to New Zealand.[8]

Another challenge facing the authorities was to locate living relatives of the deceased. Once it was established that Te Umuroa was a member of Ngāti Hau of Te Ati Haunui-a-Paparangi from Hiruharama (Jerusalem) on the Whanganui River, local kaumatua (elders) became involved in seeking the return of their tipuna (ancestor). Arrangements were made for six kaumatua – Matiu and Lei Mareikura, Hoana Akapita, Te Otinga Te Peehi (George Waretini), Joseph Wanihi and Nohi Wanihi – to travel to Maria Island in July 1988. The New Zealand delegation also included John Tahuparae, a cameraman with Television New Zealand's Māori language news bulletin *Te Karere* with Whanganui connections, and David Cresswell from the Department of Māori Affairs. A send-off from family, friends and other well-wishers was followed by an overnight stop in the South Island city of Christchurch from where the contingent flew to Hobart, Tasmania.[9]

On Saturday 30 July 1988, after a three-hour flight delay, the New Zealand delegation arrived at the modest Hobart International Airport building. Despite their late arrival, a large group had gathered to greet them. Tasmanian Aboriginal elders Dawn and Athol Smith welcomed them onto country and presented the New Zealanders with an Aboriginal flag. The vivid red band that lies horizontally across the lower half of the flag is often referred to as representing Australia's red soil. On this occasion, it was also read as symbolising

'Aboriginal blood spilt', and, according to anthropologist Karen Sinclair who has worked closely with Whanganui Māori, this explanation 'resonated' with the kaumatua. Parliamentarian Chris Batt (now an elected Member of the House of Assembly) was also on hand to greet the esteemed visitors and to present them, on his own and Chris Heald's behalf, with a print of Prout's evocative watercolour portrait of their ancestor. Hobart-based Adam Ranui, representing the Māori community living in Tasmania, also welcomed the Whanganui Māori to Tasmania and wished them a successful outcome to their quest.[10]

Questions about whether Te Umuroa may already have been repatriated to New Zealand over the intervening decades since his burial on Maria Island plagued the planning process that preceded the New Zealand contingent's arrival in Tasmania. Confusion over the whereabouts of his remains arose in part because Roderick Bernacchi, son of the entrepreneurial Diego, was known to have said that the remains had been removed from the grave and returned to New Zealand.[11]

Australian Government officials also raised doubts about the integrity of the site. During the colonial period, grave-robbing was a common occurrence with the remains of indigenous people sought after for lucrative, illicit sales to overseas research institutions and private collectors. There was also a suggestion that the headstones at the Maria Island cemetery had been shifted around, so there was no guarantee that Te Umuroa's headstone marked the actual location of the grave. Despite such concerns, Heald's thorough research reaching back into the colonial period turned up no evidence to indicate the repatriation or removal of remains or any relocation of the headstone. He remained confident in the integrity of the site.

The New Zealanders were honoured guests at a hangi (traditional Māori feast) on their first evening in Tasmania. On Sunday morning the visitors, being practising Christians like their tipuna, attended

Mass. The next step on their journey was a visit to the remarkably intact Port Arthur down Tasman's Peninsula, the infamous penal station where Te Umuroa and his companions initially were going to be sent. After this visceral experience, the contingent travelled the winding road up Tasmania's east coast, following it through a narrow gorge until they arrived at Orford. Maria Island lay clearly visible across the water that sets it apart from the Tasmanian mainland.

At daybreak the following day, Monday 1 August, the visiting Māori walked the short distance from their accommodation at Orford to the nearby beach to pray. This began a pattern of morning and evening prayers that framed each of the following five days, emulating the prayerful lives their ancestors led as convicts on Maria Island. On the first day, prayers were said over *Crescent*, the fishing boat used to ferry them daily to and from Maria Island, and over the waters across which they were to travel. Sinclair interpreted their 'attention to protocol' as something that helped to sustain the kaumatua. Through domesticating the event, 'the search for a long-dead ancestor in a foreign land became encompassed in the familiarly Māori'. Heald, who joined the kaumatua along with journalists and government officials, remembered how 'the little fishing boat ... was sung across the sea as Hohepa's relatives called to him', greeting him and letting him know they were coming to take him home. Tears flowed freely as the *Crescent* plied her way across the calm sea towards Maria Island.[12]

As the kaumatua approached the cemetery where their tipuna had been awaiting them for so long, the other members of the contingent hung back out of respect. The sounds of prayers and chanting filled the air as the Whanganui Māori greeted Te Umuroa. This opening ritual was later described rather poetically on the front page of one of Melbourne's major daily newspapers: 'while wild Cape Barren geese honked nearby, two Māori women sat by the [head]stone, bowed their garlanded heads and wept'. Prayers were also said for others who rested in the cemetery with thanks being given for their care of Te Umuroa during his time among them. Photographs of the kaumatua by Te Umuroa's headstone graced the front page of *The Age*.[13]

After the ceremony, 'the first sod was turned by a Māori hand', then archaeologists Richard Morrison and Brian Prince assisted by Darryl West (a Tasmanian Aborigine with expertise in recovering ancestral remains) began the official dig. Two days passed. On the third day, West indicated wordlessly that he had located the head of the coffin. While the designated diggers took a long lunch, the 'Wanganui River archaeologists took over' and when the official team returned the earth had been removed down to the level of the coffin. Around the middle of the following day, Thursday 4 August, a long, narrow coffin with faint lettering beginning with 'H' was exposed. The kaumatua had found their tipuna.[14]

On Friday 5 August 1988, Te Umuroa returned to Hobart for the first time in more than 140 years. He rested temporarily within the sacred confines of St Joseph's Church, an elegant convict-built sandstone structure with pews hewed from New Zealand Kauri. St Joseph's opened in 1841, making it Hobart's oldest Catholic Church, and was only five years old when Te Umuroa and his companions first arrived in Hobart. The following day, Te Umuroa's relatives accompanied him back to New Zealand where he initially rested at St Mary's Cathedral in Christchurch, a magnificent domed structure that has since suffered extensive earthquake damage in September 2010 and February 2011.

When Matiu and Lei Mareikura, Hoana Akapita, Te Otinga Te Peehi, Joseph Wanihi, and Nohi Wanihi arrived home the following day with their tipuna, a crowd of around one hundred people gathered to meet them. After appropriate protocol was followed, the mourning party followed the hearse along the road to the Patiarero marae (meeting place). More protocol followed, with a full tangi (funeral) for Te Umuroa, involving haka, taiaha, whaikōrero and waiata, being held throughout the night of 7 August.

Monday 8 August dawned grey and damp. The weather suited the sombre mood of people gathered to bury one who had been so wronged during the colonial period and who had spent so long waiting for his people to find him and bring him home. The Reverend Father Wiremu Te Awhitu, who when he was ordained in 1944 became the first Māori Catholic priest, officiated at Te Umuroa's burial. Te Awhitu had a long association with Jerusalem and led the priests in celebrating James K Baxter's requiem Mass in 1972.

As Te Awhitu led the congregation in prayer for Te Umuroa, three different sets of male pallbearers took it in turns to carry the coffin to the prepared grave at the Roma cemetery at Jerusalem. Women wreathed in leaves signifying mourning called out Te Umuroa's genealogy, binding him 'once and for all to the people of Whanganui'. The younger generation participated in the ceremony under the guidance of their elders. With solemnity and grace their ancestor was finally laid to rest in his homeland at a site overlooking his beloved Whanganui River. Images of the event were reproduced in the local newspaper, the *Wanganui Chronicle*. As Matiu Mareikura revealed to the journalist who attended the ceremony, 'we felt he was calling us to come and take him home ... And it's finished. His long 141-year wait has finally come to an end'.[15]

Conclusion

One of the most striking features of transportation within and to the Australian penal colonies for Aboriginal, Khoisan and Māori convicts, aside from their presence in the convict system, was the vastly different outcomes exhibited by each cohort. Many Aboriginal convicts from New South Wales died after spending a relatively short time in captivity, sometimes within weeks of being sentenced. The deaths of men such as Jackey in 1834 and Yanem Goona in 1848 were no doubt expedited by wounds received when being taken into custody. Leg irons bit sufficiently deeply into Jackey's leg to expose his bone while the man lay naked on the deck of a river steamer en route to Sydney Gaol. Goona nursed wounds too severe to allow his transfer from the Grampians to Melbourne Gaol until his injuries improved. Even when an Aboriginal overseer and a missionary were provided at Goat Island, the death rate exhibited by those tried in relation to the Brisbane Water district frontier war remained high. Following a review sparked in 1851 by a cluster of Aboriginal deaths in custody, some of the circumstances of their confinement were ameliorated. Until then, only very, very few lived long enough to be returned home.

Most Khoisan convicts survived within the Australian penal colonies for long enough to commit numerous further offences within the convict system. They were punished with the lash, had their diets restricted to bread and water while doing hard labour, or spent time in solitary confinement. Some were considered sufficiently incorrigible to be transferred to Port Arthur or Norfolk Island. Most of their offences amounted to escapism. Some regularly imbibed alcohol to numb the impacts of being so far from home in such degrading conditions. Others physically removed themselves from their labour and lodgings through absconding. Most lived long enough to attain conditional freedom, yet unlike their Australian and New Zealand counterparts, Khoisan received no assistance to return home after their sentences expired. They were left with few options. Willem Pokbaas begged a living on the streets of Launceston. Willem Hartzenberg was committed to institutions reserved for paupers. Hendrick Witnalder (Uithaalder) got around Hobart in a cast-off military uniform, and was regularly bullied by local lads, until his life ended at the end of the hangman's rope.

While treated favourably compared with other aboriginal convicts, the health of those few Māori transported to Van Diemen's Land nevertheless suffered in captivity. Despite the care provided by John Jennings Imrie, an overseer conversant with Māori language and who prayed and socialised with them regularly, the men continued to experience bouts of poor health. Their labour, mostly gardening and building their own dwelling, was the lightest required of any aboriginal convicts. They were also taken on regular walks to the beach and went fishing. The men had access to a relatively healthy diet through being encouraged to grow their own vegetables and supplementing their protein intake with locally caught fish. These were no doubt contributing factors in ensuring the majority survived long enough to be returned home. They did, however, leave Hohepa Te Umuroa behind in the small cemetery on the outskirts of Darlington. One hundred and forty years passed before his people arrived to take him home.

The life narratives of aboriginal convicts are stories of tenacity. Men from similar cultural contexts formed alliances within and beyond the convict system to aid each other's survival. Billy Roberts and Warrigal Jemmy, men from different parts of New South Wales, joined forces in Van Diemen's Land to abscond from captivity. Likewise, when Scipio Africanus turned to the bush to eke out a living beyond the convict system, he met up with Arnoldus Jantje, also from the Cape. The two Khoisan aided each other's survival over several years, before being taken back into custody for theft. The men from the Brisbane Water district held on Goat Island befriended Purimal, initially using sign language to facilitate communication and gradually learning to speak the man's language. With their help, some limited communication between the missionary Langhorne and Purimal became possible.

Care and concern for each other extended beyond the immediate networks formed by aboriginal men within the convict system to wider colonial and imperial networks. Duall was recalled early from Van Diemen's Land at Charles Throsby's behest. Throsby, through earlier having stuck his neck out for Aboriginal people at the Cowpastures, was secretly reported to London by Governor Lachlan Macquarie as one of the official's enemies. Other Cowpastures settlers such as the Superintendent of Wild Cattle John Warby and explorer Hamilton Hume's uncle John Kennedy also did what they could to protect local Aboriginal people from military recriminations for retaliatory actions Aborigines had taken against colonists. When the initial group of Māori prisoners arrived in Hobart, their old friend Thomas Mason was on hand to visit and intercede for them. Such was the movement of people (as well as goods and ideas) between the various colonies, that John Jennings Imrie – initially from Scotland – had lived for several years in New Zealand but was, by the time the men arrived, on hand in Hobart and available to oversee the Māori prisoners at Maria Island. Colonial philanthropist Saxe Bannister, while at the Cape, was likewise able to intercede on behalf of the Stuurman children albeit too late for their father, David, who meanwhile had died in custody in Sydney.

Working relationships were established between numerous Aboriginal people and colonists across New South Wales, particularly with small landholders. Tommy, helping the Cosgroves with their wool dray, received what little help they could offer him when he came under attack from warriors from another Aboriginal tribe. Numerous Aboriginal people laboured as child carers and fetchers of wood and water in return for basics such as food, shelter and clothes. Ironically, it was when these relationships soured that those who had been closest to the colonists were later dealt with through the courts. Only those well known to the colonists could be recognised, with colonial witnesses coming forward to attest positively to their identities in court. And interpreters could be procured only for those sufficiently close to the colonists to have had someone become conversant with their language, thus allowing their trials to go ahead. Unknown numbers of Aboriginal people with more distant relationships with the encroaching colonists were dealt 'summary justice' well beyond the eyes and ears, and reach, of the law.

Across all three settler colonies, aboriginal people were incorporated into forces designed to uphold and enforce colonial law and/or to defend the colony. 'Friendly' Māori warriors were utilised in New Zealand to augment imperial and colonial regiments in waging war against the 'hostile' tribes. It was Māori with colonial allegiances who captured the Pari Pari prisoners later transported to Maria Island. At the Cape, the British identified men among the Khoi with whom they found it most expedient to deal, investing them with staffs of office. Numerous Khoisan were incorporated into dedicated military regiments to shore up British defences at the Cape against attack from Xhosa and other military foes. When Khoisan were treated badly by the Cape Corps and mutinied, it earned them a one-way trip, some to the scaffold and others to the Australian penal colonies.

In the Australian colonies, Aboriginal men were invested as native police or troopers, being given guns and horses and training under white officers on how to use them. These men were involved in tracking and capturing Aboriginal men, some of whom were later incorporated into the convict system, particularly across the Port Phillip District. Despite their successes, these men were not considered the equal of white police. Sergeants Stapleton and Bennett caused an uproar in Melbourne when, on Monday 10 April 1843, they engaged in a brawl to settle 'a ticklish point' as to the 'merits of their respective commands'. Stapleton of the white police took exception when Bennett, who was in charge of a 'squadron of mounted black beetle', suggested his native police were the equal of their white counterparts. Public outrage generated by this event did not relate to whether Aboriginal people were the equal of whites. In fact, the *Melbourne Times* described Stapleton as 'very naturally horrified' at such a suggestion. Rather, it was the police decision to hold the inquiry into the matter behind closed doors that attracted the opprobrium of the press.[1]

Efforts to incorporate aborigines into colonial society saw them, for the most part, located within its lower echelons. Even within the convict system in its early years, Musquito, Bull Dog and possibly Jackson were situated on the lowest rungs of the ladder, working as assistants to the convict charcoal burners at Norfolk Island. The British Empire's aboriginal subjects were far from being seen, and treated, as equals. To cite just one among numerous examples, in his reminiscences, retired Chief Justice Roger Therry (counsel to the Attorney General during the trials following the Myall Creek Massacre) raised the spectre of men recently discharged from the colony's gaols being allowed the vote. He then delineated what, for him, amounted to an even worse possible scenario:

a wild black fresh from the Bush, with whose intelligence a
gorilla might well vie, if he but reside six months in a district, has
an equal right to vote with the wealthiest and most intelligent
commoner in the land. ... Several of the half-caste inhabitants of
New South Wales ... have been placed on the electoral roll under

the universal manhood suffrage system. These persons are known to be imbued with the wandering habits, and follow the forest life, of the aboriginal parent. When required on the day of the election at the polling booth, they may probably be found up a gum tree, chasing an opossum, or cooking a kangaroo in the bush of Australia. As no property is required to qualify a man either to vote or to be a *Représentant de people*, "The Honourable Billy, the black fellow," from Illawarra, or the Honourable "Moon-eyed Jemmy," from the Clarence, may enter the House of Assembly, and rise to be a minister of state.

Because of their allegedly low intelligence and lack of religious precepts, he considered Aboriginal defendants as 'objects of great commiseration', particularly in instances where they were condemned to death. Like his fellow judges, Therry advocated equality before the law but admitted Aboriginal men 'suffer[ed] loss of life for offences for which the white man only suffers transportation or hard labour on the roads'.[2]

Colonial Governors at New Zealand, the Cape and New South Wales oversaw judicial systems that, despite orders to the contrary from London, dealt with aboriginal offenders more harshly than with other prisoners. The legality of the court martial that saw the Pari Pari prisoners transported to Van Diemen's Land was called into question in Van Diemen's Land and in London. Imposing transportation, effectively for life, on Khoisan who were involved in relatively minor thefts was harsh punishment indeed. Many left wives and children behind at the Cape, knowing they would never see their families or their homeland again. Following the Myall Creek Massacre and the resultant hangings, the New South Wales law courts dealt more harshly with Aboriginal offenders than previously. Justice Alfred Stephen, influenced by his early childhood in a slave colony and formative experiences in Van Diemen's Land in the early stages of his legal career, seemed bent on sentencing to death any Aborigines who entered his courtroom, even trying unsuccessfully to extend his influence to procure the death of Koort Kirrup in the Port Phillip District.

Court-imposed sentences are always intended as exemplary. But in the case of aboriginal convicts, sentences to transportation went beyond making a general example of the alleged offenders. Rather, these sentences were imposed in part to mollify disgruntled colonists who might otherwise be tempted to take the law into their own hands. Sentencing aborigines to transportation was also a tactic designed to manage aboriginal cohorts within each of the settler colonies. Removing aboriginal men from their communities effectively reduced the resources available to those resisting colonisation. Their removal, through transportation, was also designed to cause alarm. At the Cape and in New South Wales, authorities thought the impacts of having people effectively vanish would act as a greater deterrent to aboriginal resistance than offenders being held prisoner virtually within view of their communities or being hanged. Not knowing what had become of their kin would surely aid the authorities in subjugating dissident aborigines. In New Zealand, the Governor hoped the Pari Pari prisoners, who were literate, could be encouraged to write letters home. He reasoned that learning the details of their fate could subdue Māori resistance.

Despite the use of transportation against aboriginal people in New South Wales, the Cape Colony and New Zealand, conflict between colonists and aborigines continued well into the nineteenth century. Grievances from the early colonial period through to the twentieth century are still in the process of being resolved today. Little attention, either scholarly or more general, has been given to aboriginal convicts before now. Some attention has been paid to Musquito within Australia, particularly in relation to the latter stages of his career as a leader of the tame mob in Tasmania. David Stuurman has excited some interest among researchers at the Cape Colony.

To date, Hohepa Te Umuroa has attracted more attention than any other aboriginal convict, in part because of the presence of his headstone at Maria Island and also because of his repatriation to New Zealand in 1988. In addition to a pamphlet and several articles, aspects of his story have been told in 'Maria Island Dreaming', a musical performance with visual images performed in Hobart by local artists. More recently, New Zealand author Witi Ihimaera's controversial book *The Trowenna Sea* provided a fictionalised account of the lives of the Pari Pari prisoners. Ihimaera's device of fictionalising a wife, Te Rai, for Hohepa Te Umoroa has since been incorporated into an opera, *Hohepa*, written by Jenny McLeod. *Hohepa* premiered in Wellington, New Zealand, in March 2012.[3]

The main aim of *Aboriginal Convicts* is to facilitate these life narratives becoming more widely known. At key sites where aboriginal convicts lived and laboured in captivity, including Port Arthur and Cockatoo Island, there is currently no interpretive information acknowledging or commemorating their presence. In a hut at Darlington on Maria Island, three of the five portraits of the Pari Pari prisoners are on display. Together with Hohepa Te Umuroa's headstone and Musquito's name on a monument erected in St David's Park, Hobart, to commemorate Norfolk Island convicts, these images are one of few tangible traces of the existence of aborigines within the convict system. Scholars are yet to embrace the term 'aboriginal convicts'. This, though, is surely the most apt name by which these people ought to be remembered.

Notes

Abbreviations
HRA Historical Records of Australia
HRNSW Historical Records of New South Wales
PROV Public Records Office Victoria
SRNSW State Records of New South Wales
TAHO Tasmanian Archive and Heritage Office

Introduction

1   Clark, Anna, 'History in Black and White: A Critical Analysis of the Black Armband Debate', *Journal of Australian Studies*, Vol. 26, No. 75, pp. 1–11.
2   *R v Dundomah and Others 1840, Decisions of the Superior Courts of New South Wales, 1788–1899*, Bruce Kercher (ed), Division of Law, Macquarie University, Sydney, accessed 18 December 2004 at www.law.mq.edu.au/research/colonial_case_law/nsw/cases/case_index/1840/r_v_dundomah_and_others/.
3   Kercher, Bruce, *An Unruly Child: A History of Law in Australia*, Allen & Unwin, Sydney, 1995, p. 16.
4   Connor, John, *The Australian Frontier Wars, 1788–1838*, UNSW Press, Sydney, 2002, p. 26.
5   *Hobart Town Gazette and Southern Reporter*, 14 November 1818, p. 1; Convict Death Register, 4/4549, Reel 690, pp. 113, 115, 171, SRNSW.

1   Banishing Musquito, Bull Dog and Duall

1   Governor John Hunter to the Duke of Portland, 2 January 1800, Enclosure No. 1, 'Trial for the Murder of Two Natives', *HRA*, Series I, Volume II, p. 413.
2   *Sydney Gazette*, 19 May 1805, p. 2. The terminology used to describe Musquito and the deeds attributed to him around Sydney have been the subject of historical debate, as has the existence of another man known as Musquito (with variant spellings) to whom some of the Aboriginal convict's deeds could be attributed. See in particular Parry, Naomi, 'Many Deeds of Terror', Contested History Forum, *Labour History*, Issue 85, 2003, accessed on 27 February 2006 at www.historycooperative.org/journals/lab/85/parry.html; Windschuttle, Keith, 'Guerilla Warrior and Resistance Fighter? The Career of Musquito', *Labour History*, Issue 87, 2004, pp. 221–35; and Parry, Naomi, '"Many Deeds of Terror": Response to Windschuttle's Defence of his View of Musquito', *Labour History*, Issue 87, 2004, pp. 236–38. Academic argument has also ensued over which Musquito was sketched during the Baudin expedition. Brian Plomley claimed the portrait 'under the name Y-erran-gou-la-ga' depicted the man

known to the settlers as Musquito who was later 'deported to Norfolk Island' and 'sent to Van Diemen's Land where he was assigned as servant to various masters'. See NJB (Brian) Plomley, *Weep in Silence: A History of the Flinders Island Aboriginal Settlement*, Blubber Head Press, Hobart, 1987, p. 10. See also footnote 4 below.

3   *Sydney Gazette*, 30 June 1805, p. 2.
4   Governor Philip Gidley King to Lord Camden, 20 July 1805, *HRA*, Series I, Volume V, pp. 497, 503. (Emphasis in the original.) See Smith, Keith, *Mari Nawi: Aboriginal Oydsseys*, Rosenberg, 2010, pp. 68–75 regarding Petit's sketches on which Barthelemy Roger's later engravings of Musquito and Bull Dog were based.
5   *Sydney Gazette*, 11 August 1805, p. 2.
6   King to John Piper, 8 August 1805, *New South Wales Colonial Secretary's Office Correspondence*, Reel 6040, p. 41, TAHO.
7   Nobbs, Raymond, *Norfolk Island and its First Settlement, 1788–1814*, Library of Australian History, North Sydney, 1988, pp. 192, 198; Maxwell-Stewart, Hamish, 2008, *Closing Hell's Gates: The Death of a Convict Station*, Allen & Unwin, Sydney, p. 30.
8   Nobbs, *Norfolk Island and its First Settlement*, pp. 192, 198; Musquito Correspondence File, TAHO; Walker, James, *Early Tasmania: Papers Read Before the Royal Society of Tasmania During the Years 1888 to 1899*, Government Printer, Hobart, 1989, p. 166; Donohue, James, *The Forgotten Australians: The Non-Anglo or Celtic Convicts and Exiles*, self-published, Sydney, 1991, p. 35. Donohue's suggestion that Henry, convicted at the Sydney District Assizes on 6 January 1840, was Aboriginal is incorrect. His conduct record states his native place was Calcutta. See CON35/1/1, TAHO.
9   King to Portland, 28 September 1800, Enclosure No. 5, 'General Orders', HRA, Series I, Volume II, p. 624; Plomley, NJB (Brian) (ed), *Jorgen Jorgenson and the Aborigines of Van Diemen's Land*, Blubber Head Press, Hobart, 1991, p. 74.
10   Thomas Campbell to Lieutenant Governor Thomas Davey, 17 August 1814, New South Wales Colonial Secretary's Office Correspondence, Reel 6004, p. 251, TAHO; Bonwick, James, *The Last of the Tasmanians, or the Black War of Van Diemen's Land*, (London, 1870), reprint, Libraries Board of South Australia, Adelaide, 1969, p. 93; *Hobart Town Gazette*, 24 February 1818, p. 2.
11   Lieutenant Edward Lord, a folder of notes compiled by WH Hudspeth (1874–1952), an amateur local historian, NS690/29, TAHO. See George Frankland's 1835 map of Van Diemen's Land and Leventhorpe Hall's 1884 map of Tasmania.
12   *Hobart Town Gazette*, 24 February 1818, p. 2; Parry, '"Many Deeds of Terror"', pp. 208, 211; 'Government Public Notice and Order: Civil Department', *Sydney Gazette*, 3 August 1816, p. 1; Brook, Jack, *The Parramatta Native Institution*, UNSW Press, Sydney, 1991, p. 27.
13   Kohen, James, *The Darug and their Neighbours*, Darug Link, Blacktown, 1993, p. 63; Reynolds, Henry, *The Other Side of the Frontier*, Penguin, Melbourne, 1981, p. 9.

14 'State of the Settlement in 1795' (reprinted from *Saunders' News-Letter*, 30 January 1797), *HRNSW*, Volume II, p. 820; Reynolds, *The Other Side of the Frontier*, p. 9; Liston, Carol, 'The Dharawal and Gandangara in Colonial Campbelltown, New South Wales, 1788–1830', *Aboriginal History*, Volume 12, 1988, p. 50. Unfortunately, vandals have destroyed the paintings in Bull Cave.

15 Atkinson, Alan, *Camden: Farm and Village Life in Early New South Wales*, Oxford University Press, Melbourne, 1988, p. 8; 'Letters from Sydney', 8 April 1797, *HRNSW*, Volume III, pp. 203–204; Kohen, James, *The Darug and their Neighbours*, p. 63; Root, Deborah, *Cannibal Culture: Art, Appropriation, and the Commodification of Difference*, Westview Press, Boulder, CO, 1996, p. 159. There are numerous examples of such depictions in colonial newspapers. See, for example, *Geelong Advertiser*, 5 December 1840, p. 3.

16 'State of the Settlement in 1795', *HRNSW*, Volume II, p. 820.

17 Liston, 'The Dharawal and Gandangara in Colonial Campbelltown', p. 60. According to James Jervis, this claim was made in a letter to the *Monitor* of 15 December 1826. See Jervis, James, *A History of the Berrima District 1798–1973*, Library of Australian History, Sydney, 1973, p. 9; *Sydney Morning Herald*, 3 April 1843, p. 3.

18 Macquarie to Earl Bathurst, 18 March 1816, *HRA*, Series I, Volume IX, pp. 52–53; Liston, 'The Dharawal and Gandangara in Colonial Campbelltown', p. 50.

19 *New South Wales Colonial Secretary's Office Correspondence*, Reel 6044, pp. 213–32, TAHO.

20 John Warby (c 1767–1851), *Journeys in Time 1809–1822: The Journals of Lachlan and Elizabeth Macquarie*, Macquarie University, accessed 9 March 2006 at www.lib.mq.edu.au/all/journeys/people/profiles/warby.html; *New South Wales Colonial Secretary's Office Correspondence*, Reel 6044, pp. 213–32, TAHO.

21 Liston, 'The Dharawal and Gandangara in Colonial Campbelltown', p. 51; Roxburgh, Rachel, *Throsby Park: An Account of the Throsby Family in Australia 1802–1940*, Macarthur Press, Sydney, 1989, p. 7.

22 Macquarie, Lachlan, 'Government and General Orders: Civil Department 18 June 1814', *New South Wales Colonial Secretary's Office Correspondence*, Reel 6038, pp. 501–505, TAHO; *Sydney Gazette*, 23 March 1816, p. 2; Macquarie, Lachlan, 'List of Hostile Natives', *New South Wales Colonial Secretary's Office Correspondence*, Reel 6005, p. 44, TAHO.

23 Macquarie, Lachlan, 'Instructions to Schaw, Wallis, and Dawe', *New South Wales Colonial Secretary's Office Correspondence,* Reel 6045, pp. 149–50, TAHO; Connor, John, *The Australian Frontier Wars, 1788–1838*, UNSW Press, Sydney, 2002, pp. 13, 49.

24 Macquarie, 'Instructions to Schaw, Wallis, and Dawe', Reel 6045, pp. 150, 152, 155, 164, 165, TAHO; Connor, *The Australian Frontier Wars*, p. 49.

25 Lachlan Macquarie. 'Instructions to Captain Wallis', *New South Wales Colonial Secretary's Office Correspondence*, Reel 6045, p. 8, TAHO; Liston, 'The Dharawal and Gandangara in Colonial Campbelltown', p. 52.

26 Parsons, Vivienne, 'Throsby, Charles (1777–1828)', *Australian Dictionary of Biography*, Volume 2, Melbourne University Press, Melbourne, 1967,

pp. 530–31.

27 Roxburgh, *Throsby Park*, pp. 5, 7; Macquarie to Bathurst, 1 December 1817, Enclosure, 'List of the Names, Designations, &c., of Persons residing at present in the Colony of New South Wales, who have always manifested an Opposition to the Measures and Administration of Governor Macquarie', *HRA*, Series I, Volume IX, p. 500.

28 Wallis to Macquarie, 9 May 1818, *New South Wales Colonial Secretary's Office Correspondence*, Reel 6045, pp. 51–56, TAHO. Variant spellings for Kinabygal include Conibigal, Carnambaygal and Cannaboygal.

29 Turnbull, Paul, '"Outlawed Subjects": The Procurement and Scientific Uses of Australian Aboriginal Heads, ca. 1803–1835', *Eighteenth Century Life*, 22.1, 1998, pp. 158, 166; Mackenzie, George, *Illustrations of Phrenology*, A. Constable & Co., Edinburgh, 1820, p. 235, cited in Turnbull, 'Outlawed Subjects', p. 237.

30 Throsby to Wentworth, 5 April 1816, *D'Arcy Wentworth Correspondence*, Mitchell Library, Sydney, MLA752 CY699, pp. 183–86; Lieutenant AE Parker to Macquarie, 'Report of a Detachment of the 46th Regt. from the 22nd April to the 5th May 1816', Reel 6045, pp. 60–61, TAHO. Quayat is a spelling variant for Quiet.

31 Macquarie, 30 April 1816, *New South Wales Colonial Secretary's Office Correspondence*, Reel 6045, pp. 20–21, TAHO; *Sydney Gazette* (Supplement), 11 May 1816, p. 2; Kohen, *The Darug and Their Neighbours*, p. 68.

32 Connor, *The Australian Frontier Wars*, p. 52; Brook, *The Parramatta Native Institution*, p. 31.

33 Connor, *The Australian Frontier Wars*, p. 52.

34 *Sydney Gazette*, 3 August 1816, p. 1; *Sydney Gazette* (Supplement), 3 August 1816, p. 2.

35 Macquarie to Brevet Major James Stewart, 31 July 1816, *HRA*, Series III, Volume II, p. 471.

2 Diverging destinies

1 Macquarie to Davey, 31 July 1816, *HRA*, Series III, Volume II, p. 156; Lieutenant Governor William Sorell to Macquarie, 8 December 1817, *HRA*, Series III, Volume II, p. 289; Sorell to Commandant Gilbert Cimitiere, 2 September 1819, *HRA*, Series III, Volume II, pp. 527–89; Sorell to Cimitiere, 3 December 1819, *HRA*, Series III, Volume II, p. 540.

2 Maxwell-Stewart, Hamish, *The Bushrangers and the Convict System of Van Diemen's Land, 1803–1846*, unpublished PhD thesis, University of Edinburgh, 1990, pp. 5–6, 9; Macquarie to Earl Bathurst, 7 May 1814, *HRA*, Series I, Volume III, p. 250.

3 Sorell to Macquarie, *HRA*, Series III, Volume II, pp. 340–41; Macquarie to Sorell, *HRA*, Series III, Volume II, p. 354. For further details about the unruly colonial garrison and their insubordinate commandant, see Sargent, Clem, *The Colonial Garrison 1817–1824*, TCS Publications, Canberra, 1996, p. 60; Branagan, Jack, *The Historic Tamar Valley: Its People, Places and Shipping, 1798–1990*, Regal Publications, Launceston, 1990, pp. 3–4; Bethell, Llewelyn Slingsby, *The Story of Port Dalrymple: Life and Work in Northern Tasmania*,

Government Printer, Hobart, 1957, p. 15. See also *HRA*, Series III, Volume II.

4 Reynolds, John, 'Sorell, William (1775–1848)', *Australian Dictionary of Biography*, Volume 2, Melbourne University Press, Melbourne, 1967, pp. 459–62; Wells, Thomas, *Michael Howe, The Last and Worst of the Bushrangers of Van Diemen's Land: Narrative of the Chief Atrocities Committed by This Great Murderer and his Associates, During a Period of Six Years in Van Diemen's Land*, (Hobart, 1819), reprint, Review Publications, Dubbo, 1979, pp. 9–10.

5 *Hobart Town Gazette*, 31 January 1818, p. 1.

6 Wise, Christine, 'Black Rebel Musquito', *Rebels & Radicals*, Eric Fry (ed), Allen & Unwin, Sydney, 1983, p. 3. Spelling variants for Worrrell include Worral and Worrill; Wells, *Michael Howe*, p. 13. For reference to Mary's surname, see *Hobart Town Gazette*, 12 April 1817, p. 2; 'Bushrangers Captured', *Hobart Town Gazette*, 16 August 1817, p. 2.

7 Maginn, William, *The Military Sketch-Book: Reminiscences of Seventeen Years in the Service Abroad and at Home by an Officer of the Line*, (second edition), Henry Colburn and Richard Bentley, London, 1831, p. 300; Davey to Macquarie, 30 April 1815, Enclosure No. 2, 'Informations, D. McCarty and Christopher Hacking, on Charles Carlisle's Death', *HRA*, Series III, Volume II, pp. 92–98.

8 Sorell to Macquarie, 13 October 1817, *HRA*, Series III, Volume II, pp. 283–84. Given the issues surrounding Aboriginal people providing evidence in court (they were not considered Christians and were precluded from taking the required oath), it is unclear how Cockerill's testimony was to be heard. No records pertaining to cases relying on her evidence appear to have survived.

9 See, for example, West, John, *The History of Tasmania with Copious Information Respecting the Colonies of New South Wales, Victoria, South Australia, &c.*, (Launceston, 1852), reprint, Angus & Robertson, Sydney, 1971, p. 267; Melville, Henry, *The History of the Island of Van Diemen's Land from the Year 1824 to 1835 Inclusive to Which is Added a Few Words on Prison Discipline*, (London, 1835), reprint, Libraries Board of South Australia, Adelaide, 1967, p. 25; Turnbull, Clive, *Black War: The Extermination of the Tasmanian Aborigines*, (London, 1948), reprint, Sun Books, Melbourne, 1974, p. 62; Sorell to Macquarie, 13 October 1817, *HRA*, Series III, Volume II, p. 283. The convict's name has been transcribed as 'Mr Gill' but was more likely to have been 'McGill' because a convict of that name took part in expeditions against bushrangers, including Howe, and later received a free pardon for his services. See 'List of Twelve Conditional Pardons Granted by His Excellency Governor Macquarie (on the recommendation of His Honor the Lieutenant Governor of Van Diemen's Land) for Persons in that Dependency bearing date 4th June 1819', CON13/1/2, pp. 1–2, TAHO.

10 Whitcoulls Limited, *A Bloodthirsty Banditti of Wretches: Informations on Oath Relating to Michael Howe and Others Between 1814 and 1818*, Sullivans Cove, Adelaide, 1985, pp. 100–101.

11 Canteri, Carl, *The Origins of Australian Social Banditry: Bushranging in Van Diemen's Land, 1805–1818*, BLit thesis, Oxford, University of Oxford, 1977, pp. 36, 102, 176 cited in Maxwell-Stewart, *The Bushrangers and the Convict System of Van Diemen's Land*, 1990, p. 161; Whitcoulls, *A Bloodthirsty Banditti*

of Wretches, 1985, pp. 100–101. It is claimed in this text that Cockerill was with McGill and Musquito. This seems unlikely as Cockerill was shipped to Sydney in October 1817 and was in hospital there in December 1818. It is possible, though, that she may have returned to Van Diemen's Land in the interim; *Hobart Town Gazette*, 24 October 1818, p. 2; Wells, *Michael Howe*, 1979, p. 38; Sorell to Macquarie, *Sorell Dispatches*, 20 October 1818, Mitchell Library, CY1096, pp. 91–95; 'List of Twelve Conditional Pardons Granted by His Excellency Governor Macquarie', CON13/1/2, pp. 1–2, TAHO; *Hobart Town Gazette* (Supplement), 9 January 1819, p. 1.

12 *New South Wales Colonial Secretary's Office Correspondence*, Reel 6006, pp. 188–89, TAHO. Cockerill was subsequently returned to Van Diemen's Land where she died in the Colonial Hospital in Hobart Town on 29 June 1819. See the *Hobart Town Gazette*, 3 July 1819, p. 1; 'Transfer of Dicall [Duall] from Port Dalrymple to Sydney', *New South Wales Colonial Secretary's Office Correspondence*, Reel 6006, p. 188, TAHO; 'Arrival in Sydney from Port Dalrymple per "Sindbad"', *New South Wales Colonial Secretary's Office Correspondence*, Reel 6006, p. 296, TAHO.

13 Throsby, 'Journal of a Tour to Bathurst Through The Cow Pastures', Reel 6038, pp. 88–89, TAHO. Breastplates were based on military gorgets. Often crescent shaped, they were inscribed metal plaques that hung from chains and were worn around the recipient's neck.

14 Macquarie, 'Government and General Orders', 31 May 1819, pp. 48–49; Webster, Robert, *Currency Lad: The Story of Hamilton Hume and the Explorers*, Leisure Magazines, Sydney, 1982, p. 19; 'The Corroborie at Parramatta', *The Australian*, 19 January 1826, p. 3; 'Return of the Cowpasture Aborigines for 1833', 4/6666.3 SRNSW, cited in Liston, Carol, 'The Dharawal and Gandangara in Colonial Campbelltown, New South Wales, 1788–1830', *Aboriginal History*, Volume 12, 1988, pp. 58–59.

15 Horton, Reverend William, Letter to the Secretaries of the Wesleyan Missionary Society, 3 June 1823, *Wesleyan Missionary Papers*, Mitchell Library, BT 52, Volume 4, pp. 1269–74.

16 *Hobart Town Gazette*, 16 July 1824, p. 2; *Hobart Town Gazette*, 6 August 1824, p. 2.

17 *Hobart Town Gazette*, 3 December 1824, p. 3; Melville, Henry, *Australasia and Prison Discipline*, J. Effingham Wilson and Chas. Cox, London, 1851, p. 352.

18 *Hobart Town Gazette*, 3 December 1824, p. 2; Cox, Robert, *Steps to the Scaffold: The Untold Story of Tasmania's Black Bushrangers*, Cornhill Publishing, Pawleena, 2004, p. 61; Melville, *Australasia and Prison Discipline*, p. 352. (Emphasis in the original.)

19 *Hobart Town Gazette*, 25 February 1825, p. 2; Melville, *Australasia and Prison Discipline*, pp. 351–53.

20 West, *The History of Tasmania*, p. 266. According to West, white people 'persuaded the natives that the lighter hue of their half-caste children resulted from the too free use of flour'; Bonwick, *The Last of the Tasmanians*, pp. 92–93; West, *The History of Tasmania*, p. 267; Giblin, Ronald, *The Early History of Tasmania, Volume II*, Melbourne University Press, Melbourne, 1939, p. 163.

3 Jackey's pitiful state

1 *The Australian*, 6 May 1834, p. 2; *Sydney Monitor*, 7 May 1834, p. 3.

2 'William IV Paddle Steamer', *Monument Australia*, accessed 12 January 2012 at http://monumentaustralia.org.au/monument_display.php?id=20788&image=0.

3 Martin, James, *Memorandums: Escape from Botany Bay, 1791: Being 'Memorandums' by James Martin: introduction and notes by Victor Crittenden*, Mulini Press, Canberra, 1991.

4 Huntington, Henry, 'History of Newcastle and the Northern District No. 4', *Newcastle Morning Herald*, 17 August 1897, accessed 30 May 2006 at www.newcastle.edu.au/Resources/Divisions/Academic/Library/Cultural%20 Collections/pdf/huntington1796.pdf.

5 McCarthy, FD, 'Bungaree (– 1830)', *Australian Dictionary of Biography*, Volume 1, Melbourne University Press, Melbourne, 1966, p. 177.

6 Duke of Portland to the Right Hon. Henry Dundas, 19 December 1798, *HRNSW*, Volume III, pp. 517–18; Newcastle Family History Society (NFHS), *Early Newcastle: The Fettered and the Free*, Newcastle Family History Society, Lambton, 2005, pp. 27, 38.

7 Bigge, John, *Report of the Commissioner of Inquiry into the State of the Colony of New South Wales*, Volume I, Ordered by the House of Commons to be printed, 1822, p. 117; Roberts, David, 'Aborigines, Commandants and Convicts: The Newcastle Penal Settlement', *Awaba*, University of Newcastle, accessed 3 June 2006 at www.newcastle.edu.au/centre/awaba/awaba/group/amrhd/awaba/history/convicts.html.

8 Roberts, 'Aborigines, Commandants and Convicts'; *R v Boatman or Jackass and Bulleye 1832*, *Decisions of the Superior Courts of New South Wales, 1788–1899*, Bruce Kercher (ed), Division of Law, Macquarie University, Sydney, accessed 1 June 2006 at www.law.mq.edu.au/research/colonial_case_law/nsw/cases/case_index/1832/r_v_boatman_or_jackass_and_bulleye/.

9 'Burrigan Stabbed by John Kirby; died', *New South Wales Colonial Secretary's Office Correspondence*, Reel 6067, pp. 135–37, 143, 150, TAHO; 'John Kirby Convicted by Court of Criminal Jurisdiction of Murder of Burrigan', *New South Wales Colonial Secretary's Office Correspondence*, Reel 6023, p. 31, TAHO; *R v Ridgway, Chip, Colthurst and Stanly 1826*, accessed 1 June 2006 at www.austlii.edu.au/au/special/NSWSupC/1826/62.html; Niel Gunson (ed), *Australian Reminiscences & Papers of L. E. Threlkeld: Missionary to the Aborigines 1824–1859*, Volume II, Appendix XI: Saxe Bannister's Observations on the Aborigines of New South Wales (1830), Australian Institute of Aboriginal Studies, Canberra, 1974, p. 358; Currey, CH, 'Bannister, Saxe (1790–1877)', *Australian Dictionary of Biography*, National Centre of Biography, Australian National University, accessed 28 March 2012 at http://adb.anu.edu.au/biography/bannister-saxe-1738/text1919.

10 Bairstow, Damaris, *A Million Pounds, A Million Acres: The Pioneer Settlement of the Australian Agricultural Company*, D. Bairstow, Sydney, 2003, pp. 1–4.

11 Hannah, Mark, 'Aboriginal Workers in the Australian Agricultural Company, 1824–1857', *Labour History*, Issue 82, 2002, pp. 17, 20, 24.

12 'Report from Mr Robert Dawson to The Governor and Deputy Governor of the Australian Agricultural Company, Sydney, 4 February 1826', accessed 1 June 2006 at http://libguides.newcastle.edu.au/content. php?pid=94330&sid=746705.
13 'Dr Alexander Nesbit's Report', *Australian Agricultural Company Despatches*, B905–B906.
14 Bairstow, *A Million Pounds, A Million Acres*, p. 369.
15 Reece, Bob (RHW), *Aborigines and Colonists: Aborigines and Colonial Society in New South Wales in the 1830s and 1840s*, Sydney University Press, Sydney, 1974, p. 19; Bairstow, *A Million Pounds, A Million Acres*, p. 88.
16 Bairstow, *A Million Pounds, A Million Acres*, p. 89.
17 John Gladstone to William Huskisson, 11 March 1828, *HRA*, Series I, Volume XIV, p. 30; Huskisson to Ralph Darling, 18 March 1828, *HRA*, Series I, Volume XIV, p. 30.
18 Gladstone to Huskisson, 11 March 1828, *HRA*, Series I, Volume XIV, p. 30; Ford, RL, *William's River: The Land and its People*, RL Ford, Clarencetown, 1995, p. 40.
19 Lord Stanley to Darling, 24 November 1827, *HRA*, Series I, Volume XIII, p. 625; Ford, *William's River*, pp. 38–40.
20 'Hunter's River', *Sydney Monitor*, 23 April 1834, p. 3; Reece, *Aborigines and Colonists*, p. 17; Ford, *William's River*, pp. 34, 127.
21 *R v Jackey 1834*, *Decisions of the Superior Courts of New South Wales, 1788–1899*, Bruce Kercher (ed), Division of Law, Macquarie University, Sydney, accessed 1 October 2005 at www.law.mq.edu.au/research/colonial_case_law/nsw/cases/case_index/1834/r_v_jackey/; 'Old Newcastle Gaol', accessed 15 May 2006 at www.jenwilletts.com/Newcastle%20Gaol.htm.
22 *The Australian*, 6 May 1834, p. 2; *Sydney Monitor*, 7 May 1834, p. 3; 'Imprisonment for Debt, Rules', *Decisions of the Superior Courts of New South Wales, 1788–1899*, Bruce Kercher (ed), Division of Law, Macquarie University, Sydney, accessed 17 June 2006 at www.law.mq.edu.au/research/colonial_case_law/nsw/cases/case_index/1834/imprisonment_for_debt_rules/.
23 'Sydney Gaol', *Sydney Monitor*, 14 March 1834, p. 2.
24 Reece, *Aborigines and Colonists*, pp. 8, 10.
25 'Society in Sydney New South Wales', *Sydney Monitor*, 11 April 1834, p. 4.
26 Reece, *Aborigines and Colonists*, p. 11.
27 *R v Jackey 1834*.
28 *R v Binge Mhulto 1828*, *Decisions of the Superior Courts of New South Wales, 1788–1899*, Bruce Kercher (ed), Division of Law, Macquarie University, Sydney, accessed 15 October 2007 at www.law.mq.edu.au/research/colonial_case_law/nsw/cases/case_index/1828/r_v_binge_mhulto/.
29 Baxter to Colonial Secretary, 19 December 1828, 28/10171 4/2005, SRNSW.
30 *R v Jackey 1834*; GP Walsh, 'Nichols, George Robert (1809–1857)', *Australian Dictionary of Biography*, Volume 5, Melbourne University Press, Melbourne, 1974, pp. 335–36.
31 *R v Jackey 1834*.
32 *Sydney Gazette*, 2 September 1834, p. 2; 'A Return of Five Male Convicts

Embarked on the Currency Lass for Van Diemen's Land', CON13/1/6, p. 303; 'Jackey', CON31/1/26, p. 16, TAHO.

33 Sen, Satadru, *Disciplining Punishment: Colonialism and Convict Society in the Andaman Islands*, Oxford University Press, Oxford, 2000, p. 94. As the Colonial Hospital in Hobart Town was not required to keep detailed records of dissections until later in the nineteenth century, it is not possible to confirm whether this was Jackey's fate.

4 Dancing in defiance

1 Connor, John, *The Australian Frontier Wars, 1788–1838*, UNSW Press, Sydney, 2002, p. 16; *R v Monkey and Others 1835*.

2 See Justice Burton's case notes for the trial of Hobby and Maitland Paddy held at Sydney in the Supreme Court of New South Wales on 5 August 1835. Hobby was found guilty of 'robbery in the dwelling house of Alfred Hill Jaques' and sentenced to 'death recorded', while Maitland Paddy was found not guilty. Justice Burton, *Notes of Criminal Cases*, 2/2420, Volume 19, pp. 4, 6, SRNSW.

3 *R v Long Dick, Jack Jones, Abraham, and Gibber Paddy 1835*, *Decisions of the Superior Courts of New South Wales, 1788–1899*, Bruce Kercher (ed), Division of Law, Macquarie University, Sydney, accessed 1 October 2005 at www.law. mq.edu.au/research/colonial_case_law/nsw/cases/case_index/1835/r_v_long_dick/; *The Australian*, 31 October 1834, p. 2; *R v Monkey and Others 1835*, *Decisions of the Superior Courts of New South Wales, 1788–1899*, Bruce Kercher (ed), Division of Law, Macquarie University, Sydney, accessed 1 October 2005 at www.law.mq.edu.au/research/colonial_case_law/nsw/cases/case_index/1835/r_v_monkey/.

4 Threlkeld, Lancelot, 'Fourth Annual Report of the Aboriginal Mission at Lake Macquarie, New South Wales', 7 November 1834, *Australian Reminiscences & Papers of L E Threlkeld: Missionary to the Aborigines 1824–1859*, Niel Gunson (ed), Australian Institute of Aboriginal Studies, Canberra, 1974, p. 120; Threlkeld to FA Heley, 26 November 1834, *Australian Reminiscences & Papers of L E Threlkeld*, p. 255; Threlkeld to MacLeay, 26 May 1834, *Australian Reminiscences & Papers of L E Threlkeld*, p. 255.

5 Berndt, Ronald & Berndt, Catherine, *The World of the First Australians*, Ure Smith, Sydney, (1964) 1977, pp. 180–81; *Australian*, 6 March 1835, p. 2; *Sydney Monitor*, 14 February 1835, p. 2; *R v Mickey and Muscle 1835*, *Decisions of the Superior Courts of New South Wales, 1788–1899*, Bruce Kercher (ed), Division of Law, Macquarie University, Sydney, accessed 1 October 2005 at www.law.mq.edu.au/research/colonial_case_law/nsw/cases/case_index/1835/r_v_mickey_and_muscle/.

6 Swancott, Charles, *The Brisbane Water Story, Parts 1 to 4*, Brisbane Water Historical Society, Booker Bay, 1953–61, Part 1, p. 13; *The Australian*, 31 October 1834, p. 2; Cape to McLeay, 28 October 1834, 34/7867, SRNSW; Connor, *The Australian Frontier Wars*, p. xxi.

7 'A Dreadful Sufferer', 'The Blacks', *Sydney Herald*, 27 November 1834, p. 2. See also a reference to a military force being in the Brisbane Water district in a letter to the Colonial Secretary dated 7 November 1833 from a correspondent

in Maitland. The presence of the military caused some of the Brisbane Water men to go to Wollombi near Maitland where they were engaged in 'outrages' against colonists in the area. A reward of £10 each was posted for the capture of 'The Brisbane Water Chief', Joe the Marine, Jemmy Jackass, Charcoal, Charcoal's Brother, Bilo, Mickey and Young Price. A convict absconder, John Newton, was thought to be with them and was also sought by the authorities. See 34/8237 4/2251.2, SRNSW; 'Arcadia at Our Gates', *Town and Country Journal*, 6 March 1875, pp. 379–80.

8   'A Dreadful Sufferer', 'The Blacks', *Sydney Herald*; J Smith, 'The Blacks of Brisbane Water', *Sydney Herald*, 25 December 1834, p. 2.

9   Cape to McLeay, 28 October 1834, 34/7867, SRNSW; 'Extracts', *Sydney Herald*, 27 November 1834, p. 2. The unnamed correspondent may have been Donnison, a local Justice of the Peace who provided assistance to Lieutenant Owen. On 30 August 1834, the *Sydney Monitor* had reported on an earlier spate of attacks involving Bloodsworth's and Hely's farms.

10 Threlkeld to Bannister, 16 August 1826, *Australian Reminiscences & Papers of L. E. Threlkeld*, p. 93.

11 Cape to Harrington, 31 October 1834, 34/7958, SRNSW; Stokes, John, *Discoveries in Australia with an Account of the Coasts and Rivers Explored and Surveyed During the Voyage of HMS Beagle in the Years 1837, 38, 39, 40, 41, 42, 43*, T and W Boone, London, 1846, p. 283.

12 *New South Wales Government Gazette*, 19 November 1834, p. 811; *New South Wales Government Gazette*, 26 November 1834, p. 825; *New South Wales Government Gazette*, 17 December 1834, p. 881. It is not clear whether the Colonial Secretary was reckoning these relationships in accordance with Aboriginal kinship systems or European notions; Cape to MacLeay, 29 October 1834, 34/7915, SRNSW; *New South Wales Government Gazette*, 17 December 1834, p. 881.

13 Swancott, *The Brisbane Water Story*, Part 1, p. 24. Aboriginal names identified in Blair and Fenton, 'Darkinjung: Our People NSW Supreme Court 1820s–1840s', p. 135.

14 *R v Long Dick, Jack Jones, Abraham, and Gibber Paddy, 1835*; Swancott, *The Brisbane Water Story*, Part 1, pp. 24–25.

15 *Sydney Monitor*, 4 April 1835, p. 2.

16 *R v Monkey and Others 1835*.

17 Justice Burton, *Notes of Criminal Cases*, 2/2418, Volume 17, p. 35, SRNSW; *R v Monkey and Others 1835*; *Sydney Monitor*, 14 February 1835, p. 2. Having been recaptured, Jack Jones was tried before Justice Dowling in the Supreme Court of New South Wales. He also faced a charge of committing robbery at the dwelling house of Alfred Jaques. He and his co-defendants Long Dick, Abraham and Gibber Paddy were found guilty and sentenced to 'death recorded'. See *R v Long Dick, Jack Jones, Abraham, and Gibber Paddy 1835*.

18 See *R v Monkey and Others 1835*, Note 1.

19 *Australian*, 13 February 1835, p. 2.

20 Backhouse, James, *A Narrative of a Visit to the Australian Colonies*, Hamilton, Adams, London, 1843, p. 387.

21 *R v Binge Mhulto 1828*; Baxter to Colonial Secretary, 19 December 1828, 28/10171 4/2005, SRNSW.

22 Backhouse, *A Narrative of a Visit to the Australian Colonies*, p. 387.

23 *R v Lego'me 1835*, *Decisions of the Superior Courts of New South Wales, 1788–1899*, Bruce Kercher (ed), Division of Law, Macquarie University, Sydney, accessed 1 October 2005 at www.law.mq.edu.au/research/colonial_case_law/ nsw/cases/case_index/1835/r_v_legome/; Lego'me's trial being conducted before a military jury is recorded in the *Australian*, 17 February 1835, p. 2; *Sydney Monitor*, 14 February 1835, p. 2; *Sydney Gazette*, 14 February 1835, p. 2. Variant spellings for Lego'me include Leggamy and Liggamy. It is possible that he may have yelled 'let go of me' when captured, resulting in his name being misunderstood as 'Lego'me'.

24 *Sydney Gazette*, 14 February 1835, p. 2; *Australian*, 17 February 1835, p. 3; *R v Little Freeman 1835. Informations and Other Papers*, 11 February 1835, T41, Bundle 45, SRNSW; *Sydney Monitor*, 14 February 1835, p. 2; *R v Toby 1835. Informations and Other Papers*, 11 February 1835, T41, Bundle 43, SRNSW.

25 *Launceston Advertiser*, 26 March 1835, p. 4; *Hobart Town Courier*, 20 March 1835, p. 2.

26 *Australian*, 17 February 1835, p. 2.

27 Foucault, Michel, *Discipline and Punish: The Birth of the Prison*, translated by Alan Sheridan, Penguin Books, London, (1977), 1991.

28 *Sydney Gazette*, 27 June 1835, p. 2.

29 Governor Richard Bourke to Lieutenant Governor George Arthur, 14 February 1835, *Arthur Papers*, Volume 8: Correspondence with Sir R. Bourke, 1831–6, Reel 3, A2168, Law Library, University of Tasmania.

30 Hannah, Mark, 'Aboriginal Workers in the Australian Agricultural Company, 1824–1857', *Labour History*, Issue 82, 2002, pp. 17–33; King, Hazel, *Richard Bourke*, Oxford University Press, Melbourne, 1971, pp. 74, 123; Mostert, Nëel, *Frontiers: The Epic of South Africa's Creation and the Tragedy of the Xhosa People*, Pimlico, London, 1992, pp. 33–35.

31 *R v Mickey and Muscle 1835*, *Decisions of the Superior Courts of New South Wales, 1788–1899*, Bruce Kercher (ed), Division of Law, Macquarie University, Sydney, accessed 1 October 2005 at www.law.mq.edu.au/research/colonial_ case_law/nsw/cases/case_index/1835/r_v_mickey_and_muscle/. Hanshall's name also appears as Hansall. Charley Muscle was also known as Charley Myrtle or Murphy. Toby 'of the Ilalaung tribe' was tried on 12 February 1835 before Burton and a civil jury in relation to the same incident. He was found guilty of assaulting Mr John Lynch and was remanded for sentence. See the *Sydney Monitor*, 14 February 1835, p. 2.

32 Threlkeld, 5th Report, *Australian Reminiscences & Papers of L. E. Threlkeld*, p. 122.

33 'At a Council Held at the Council Room Hobart Town on the 31st day of March 1835', *Minutes of the Proceedings of the Executive Council*, Reel EC4/3, pp. 408–409, TAHO.

5 Exiled to Goat Island

1 Bourke to Secretary of State, *HRA*, Series I, Volume XVII, p. 718. It is unclear as to why Bourke mentioned eight Aboriginal convicts when there had been nine intended for Van Diemen's Land. Possibly one of the men died in custody prior to the rest being sent to Goat Island.

2 Sen, Satadru, *Disciplining Punishment: Colonialism and Convict Society in the Andaman Islands*, Oxford University Press, Oxford, 2000, p. 89.

3 *Australian*, 6 March 1835, p. 2.

4 *Australian*, 17 February 1835, p. 2.

5 George Langhorne to the Colonial Secretary, 30 August 1835, Bundle 4/2322.2, Reel 2204, SRNSW; *Australian*, 1 May 1835, p. 3; Backhouse, James, *A Narrative of a Visit to the Australian Colonies*, Hamilton, Adams, London, 1843, p. 457.

6 Sheriff's Office to the Colonial Secretary, 6 July 1835, 35/5095 4/2298, SRNSW; Sheriff's Office to the Colonial Secretary, 9 July 1835, 35/5167 4/2298, SRNSW; Langhorne to the Reverend Richard Hill, 31 December 1835, Mitchell Library, State Library of New South Wales, Sydney, Add. 117. The two unnamed Aboriginal convicts who died in custody along with Charley Muscle or Myrtle were Lego'me and Currinbong Jemmy. See the register of convict deaths and burials compiled by the Principal Superintendent of Convicts Office, Fiche No. 749–751, 4/4549, SRNSW.

7 Parsons, Vivienne, 'Cunningham, Richard (1793–1835?)', *Australian Dictionary of Biography*, Volume 1, Melbourne University Press, Melbourne, 1966, pp. 268–69; *HRA*, Series I, Volume XVIII, pp. 235–37; Langhorne to Hill, 31 December 1835.

8 Threlkeld, 6th Report, *Australian Reminiscences & Papers of L. E. Threlkeld*, p. 133. Variant spellings are Boorimul and Boromil; Langhorne to Hill, 1 February 1836.

9 Threlkeld, 5th Report, *Australian Reminiscences & Papers of L. E. Threlkeld*, p. 122; Threlkeld to Parker, 15 November 1836, *Australian Reminiscences & Papers of L. E. Threlkeld*, p. 132.

10 Freeman, James, Convict Death Register, 4/4549, Reel 690, SRNSW; Threlkeld to Parker, 15 November 1836, *Australian Reminiscences & Papers of L. E. Threlkeld*, p. 132.

11 Threlkeld, 6th Report, *Australian Reminiscences & Papers of L. E. Threlkeld*, p. 133; Threlkeld to M'Leay, 17 November 1836, *Australian Reminiscences & Papers of L. E. Threlkeld*, pp. 258–59.

12 Governor Darling to Right Hon. W. Huskisson, Enclosure No. 2, Mr ES Hall to Sir George Murray, 26 November 1828, *HRA*, Series I, Volume XIV, p. 597; Threlkeld to M'Leay, 17 November 1836, *Australian Reminiscences & Papers of L. E. Threlkeld*, p. 259.

13 *Australian*, 12 December 1839, p. 2; *Australian*, 19 December 1839, p. 2; *Australian*, 21 December 1839, p. 3.

14 *Australian*, 19 December 1829, p. 2; HHS Browne to Colonial Secretary, 28 December 1850, 191/50 4/3379 with enclosure 'A Return Shewing The

Number Of Aboriginal Natives Who Have Been Received On Cockatoo Island From The 1st Of January 1839 To The 16th December 1850' prepared by Charles Ormsby, Superintendent, 50/12485 4/3379 SRNSW.

15 Threlkeld, 7th Annual Report, *Australian Reminiscences & Papers of L. E. Threlkeld*, p. 137.
16 Langhorne to Bourke, 26 November 1836, *Historical Records of Victoria*, Volume 2A, p. 157.
17 Langhorne to the Colonial Secretary, 15 December 1836, 36/10534 4/2367.2, SRNSW.
18 Samuel Perry to the Colonial Secretary, 20 December 1836, 36/10797 4/2367.2, SRNSW; William Watson to the Colonial Secretary, 16 January 1837, 37/1169 4/2367.2, SRNSW.
19 Plomley, NJB (Brian), *Weep in Silence: A History of the Flinders Island Aboriginal Settlement*, Blubber Head Press, Hobart, 1987, pp. 582–85; Swancott, Charles, *The Brisbane Water Story, Parts 1 to 4*, Brisbane Water Historical Society, Booker Bay, 1953–61, Part 4, p. 67; Threlkeld, 8th Report, *Australian Reminiscences & Papers of L. E. Threlkeld*, p. 144.

6 Driving out the white fellows

1 'An Emigrant Mechanic' [Alexander Harris], *Settlers and Convicts, or Recollections of Sixteen Years' Labour in the Australian Backwoods*, (London, 1847), Melbourne University Press, Melbourne, 1954, p. 212; Duffield, Ian, 'Martin Beck and Afro-Blacks in Colonial Australia', *Journal of Australian Studies*, Issue 16, 1985, p. 3; Flanagan, Roderick, *The Aborigines of Australia*, Edward F. Flanagan and George Robertson and Company, Sydney, 1888, p. 130.
2 *Hunter River Gazette*, 8 April 1843, p. 2.
3 'Namoi River', extract of a letter from Mr B Doyle, of the Namoi, to his father, CM Doyle, Esq., dated 19 January 1843.
4 *Maitland Mercury*, 28 January 1843, p. 2.
5 *Maitland Mercury*, 8 April 1843, p. 2.
6 Gray, Nancy, 'Scott, Helenus (1802–1879)', *Australian Dictionary of Biography*, Volume 2, Melbourne University Press, Melbourne, 1967, pp. 428–29; Gray, Nancy, 'Scott, Robert (1799?–1844)', *Australian Dictionary of Biography*, Volume 2, Melbourne University Press, Melbourne, 1967, pp. 428–29.
7 Wilson-Miller, James, *Koori, a Will to Win: The Heroic Resistance, Triumph and Survival of Black Australia*, Angus & Robertson, Sydney, 1985; *Depositions Related to Murders Committed by Blacks*, 43/2053 4/4562.5, SRNSW; 'Horrible Outrage Committed By The Blacks', *Maitland Mercury*, 11 February 1843, p. 2.
8 *Depositions Related to Murders Committed by Blacks*, 43/2053 4/4562.5, SRNSW.
9 Collins, William, 'Melville and Harry', article submitted to Alex Morrison, *The Budget*, Singleton, 1895, A6725(ix), The Percy Haslam Collection, University of Newcastle Library; *Maitland Mercury*, 11 February 1843, p. 2.
10 *Maitland Mercury*, 16 September 1843, p. 3.
11 *Sydney Morning Herald*, 19 September 1843, p. 2; *Depositions Related to Murders Committed by Blacks*, 43/2053 4/4562.5, SRNSW.

12 *Maitland Mercury*, 16 September 1843, p. 3; *Depositions Related to Murders Committed by Blacks*, 43/2053 4/4562.5, SRNSW.
13 *Hunter River Gazette*, 12 March 1842, p. 4.
14 Johnstone and Boydell to the Colonial Secretary, 2 October 1843, 43/7456 4/2624.2, SRNSW; *Maitland Mercury*, 18 March 1843, p. 3.
15 Johnstone and Boydell to the Colonial Secretary, 2 October 1843, 43/7456 4/2624.2, SRNSW.
16 *Maitland Mercury*, 16 September 1843, p. 2.
17 *Maitland Mercury*, 17 June 1843, p. 4.
18 *Maitland Mercury*, 16 September 1843, p. 2.
19 *Maitland Mercury*, 26 August 1843, p. 3.

7 The hanging judge

1 *Maitland Mercury*, 16 September 1843, p. 2.
2 King, Peter, *Crime, Justice, and Discretion in England, 1740–1820*, Oxford University Press, New York, 2000, pp. 334–35.
3 *Maitland Mercury*, 16 September 1843, p. 2.
4 Rutledge, Martha, 'Stephen, Sir Alfred (1802–1894)', *Australian Dictionary of Biography*, Volume 6, Melbourne, Melbourne University Press, 1976, pp. 180–87. See, for example, McFarlane, Ian, *Aboriginal Society in North West Tasmania: Dispossession and Genocide*, PhD thesis, University of Tasmania, Tasmania, 2002; Ryan, Lyndall, *The Aboriginal Tasmanians*, Queensland University Press, Brisbane, 1981; Reynolds, Henry, *Fate of a Free People*, Penguin, Melbourne, 1995; Windschuttle, Keith, *The Fabrication of Aboriginal History: Volume One, Van Diemen's Land, 1803–1847*, McLeay Press, Sydney, 2002.
5 *Colonial Times*, 24 September 1830, p. 3.
6 Levy, Michael, *Governor George Arthur: A Colonial Benevolent Despot*, Georgian House, Melbourne, 1953, p. 102.
7 Assistant Protector William Thomas to Resident Judge Roger Therry, 14 May 1845, 46/2561 4/2742, SRNSW; Robinson, George Augustus, Saturday 19 July 1845, *The Journals of George Augustus Robinson, Chief Protector, Port Phillip Aboriginal Protectorate, Volume Four: 1 January 1844 – 24 October 1845*, Ian D Clark (ed), Heritage Matters, Clarendon, 1998, pp. 321–22.
8 *Australian*, 17 April 1841, p. 2.
9 *Maitland Mercury*, 16 September 1843, p. 3.
10 *Maitland Mercury*, 16 September 1843, p. 3; *Maitland Mercury*, 11 February 1843, p. 2.
11 Collins, William, 'Melville and Harry', article submitted to Alex Morrison, *The Budget*, Singleton, 1895, A6725(ix), The Percy Haslam Collection, University of Newcastle Library, p. 2.
12 *Maitland Mercury*, 14 October 1843, p. 3; Sheriff to the Colonial Secretary, 14 October 1843, 43/7395 4/2631 SRNSW.
13 *Maitland Mercury*, 14 October 1843, p. 3; *Maitland Mercury*, 21 October 1843, p. 2.
14 *Maitland Mercury*, 11 November 1843, p. 3.
15 Police Office Port Macquarie to the Colonial Secretary, 28 October 1843,

43/7968 4/2624.6, SRNSW.

16 *Maitland Mercury*, 14 October 1843, p. 3; 'A Return Shewing the Number of Aboriginal Blacks Who Have Been Received on Cockatoo Island From the 1st of January 1839 to the 16th December 1850', 28 December 1850, 50/12485 4/3379, SRNSW. In July 1824, Earl Bathurst had instructed Sir Thomas Brisbane to reopen a penal station at Norfolk Island 'for the purpose of employing there the worst class of convicts'. See Bathurst to Brisbane, 22 July 1824, *HRA*, Series I, Volume XI, p. 321; Gipps to Stanley, 23 February 1844, *HRA*, Series I, Volume XXIII, pp. 417–18.

17 Colonial Secretary to the Principal Superintendent of Convicts, 17 April 1844, 4/3691, Reel 1053, p. 241, SRNSW; CON22/1/6, p. 497, TAHO; Price to CG, 9 Oct 1846, MM62/18/6390, TAHO. Dr Timothy Causer generously shared information with me regarding the outcome for Sorethighed Jemmy.

18 CON17/1/1, p. 176–77, TAHO; CON37/1/3, pp. 669–70, TAHO; CUS36/1/347, TAHO; Colonial Secretary to the Principal Superintendent of Convicts, 21 September 1846, 4/3692, Reel 1054, p. 175, SRNSW; Colonial Secretary to the Principal Superintendent of Convicts, 28 September 1846, 4/3692, Reel 1054, p. 178, SRNSW.

19 *Maitland Mercury*, 14 March 1846, p. 4; *Sydney Morning Herald*, 17 March 1846, p. 2.

20 CON37/3, p. 620; CON16/3, p. 240, TAHO.

21 Therry, Roger, *Reminiscences of Thirty Years' Residence in New South Wales and Victoria*, (London, 1863), reprint, Sydney University Press, Sydney, 1974, pp. 286–87, 459.

22 *Maitland Mercury*, 19 September 1843. p. 1; *Sydney Morning Herald*, 22 September 1843, p. 4.

8 Exemplary punishments at Port Phillip

1 Robinson, George Augustus, Saturday 10 October 1840, Ian D Clark (ed), *The Journals of George Augustus Robinson, Chief Protector, Port Phillip Aboriginal Protectorate, Volume Two: 1 October 1840 – 31 August 1841*, Heritage Matters, Clarendon, 1998, p. 6.

2 Robinson, Sunday 11 October 1840, *Journals, Volume Two*, p. 7.

3 Robinson, Wednesday 21 October 1840, *Journals, Volume Two*, p. 18; Robinson, Monday 26 October 1840, *Journals, Volume Two*, p. 21.

4 For the release of some of the Aboriginal prisoners from Melbourne Gaol, including 20 men on 16 November 1840, see Robinson, Monday 16 November 1840, *Journals, Volume Two*, p. 29. See also *Geelong Advertiser*, 21 November 1840, p. 3; Robinson, Monday 16 November 1840, *Journals, Volume Two*, p. 31.

5 Robinson, Wednesday 6 January 1841, *Journals, Volume Two*, pp. 51–52; *Geelong Advertiser*, 9 January 1841, p. 3.

6 Gipps to La Trobe, 24 October 1840, *Gipps–La Trobe Correspondence*, p. 48; *Geelong Advertiser*, 23 January 1841, p. 3.

7 Robinson, Wednesday 20 January 1841, *Journals, Volume Two*, p. 59; Robinson, Tuesday 28 September 1841, *The Journals of George Augustus Robinson, Chief Protector, Port Phillip Aboriginal Protectorate, Volume Three: 1 September 1841 –*

31 December 1843, Ian D Clark (ed), Heritage Matters, Clarendon, 1998, p. 8.

8   Gipps to La Trobe, 6 February 1841, *Gipps–La Trobe Correspondence*, p. 57;
    La Trobe to Gipps, 16 February 1841, *Gipps–La Trobe Correspondence*, p. 62;
    Geelong Advertiser, 23 January 1841, p. 3.

9   Clark, Ian D, 'Koenghegulluc', *Aboriginal Languages and Clans: An Historical
    Atlas of Western and Central Victoria, 1800–1900*, Department of Geography and
    Environmental Science, Monash University, Melbourne, 1990, pp. 179–80; *R v
    Jacky Jacky 1844*, VPRS, 30/P/O, Unit 3, File 1-4A-1, PROV; *Melbourne Weekly
    Courier*, 18 May 1844, p. 3.

10 Robinson, Thursday 4 April 1844, *The Journals of George Augustus Robinson,
    Chief Protector, Port Phillip Aboriginal Protectorate, Volume Four: 1 January 1844
    – 24 October 1845*, Heritage Matters, Clarendon, 1998, p. 34.

11 See in particular *R v Murrell and Bummaree 1836*, *Decisions of the Superior
    Courts of New South Wales, 1788–1899*, Bruce Kercher (ed), Division of Law,
    Macquarie University, Sydney, accessed 18 October 2006 at www.law.mq.edu.
    au/research/colonial_case_law/nsw/cases/case_index/1836/r_v_murrell_and_
    bummaree/.

12 *R v Jacky Jacky 1844*, VPRS, 30/P/O, Unit 3, File 1-4A-1, PROV.

13 *Geelong Advertiser*, 29 April 1844, p. 3.

14 *Melbourne Weekly Courier*, 18 May 1844, p. 3.

15 CON37/1/2, p. 437, TAHO; Tuckfield 31/1/1844 in VPRS 19, PROV, cited in
    Clark, *Aboriginal Languages and Clans*, pp. 179–80.

16 Brisbane to Bathurst, 7 September 1825, *HRA*, Series I, Volume XI, p. 811;
    Gipps to Stanley, 23 February 1844, *HRA*, Series I, Volume XXIII, pp. 417–18;
    CON37/1/2, p. 437, TAHO.

17 Clark, *Aboriginal Languages and Clans*, pp. 94, 239; Bride, T (ed), *Letters from
    Victorian Pioneers: Being a Series of Papers on the Early Occupation of the Colony,
    The Aborigines, etc.*, Robert S Brain, Government Printer, Melbourne, 1898; CB
    Hall to Lieutenant-Governor Charles La Trobe, 6 September 1853, *Letters from
    Victorian Pioneers*, p. 222.

18 Clark, *Aboriginal Languages and Clans*, p. 95.

19 According to Robinson, flock losses in the Wimmera in 1843 had been
    attributed to station owner Hamilton and his men deliberately making local
    Aboriginal people aware that orders had been received that they were not to
    be 'molested' for taking sheep. It was claimed that 'ever since the natives have
    been most troublesome'. See Robinson, Tuesday 11 April 1843, *Journals, Volume
    Three*, p. 149; La Trobe to the Colonial Secretary, 13 June 1845, 45/4355
    4/2741, SRNSW.

20 *Maitland Mercury*, 10 January 1846, p. 2; *Maitland Mercury*, 5 October 1844,
    p. 4.

21 Fels, Marie, *Good Men and True: The Aboriginal Police of the Port Phillip District
    1837–1853*, Melbourne University Press, Melbourne, 1988, pp. 3, 7.

22 Dana to La Trobe, July 1845, 45/1379 4/2741, SRNSW. For the English
    interpretation of Yanem Goona's name, see Philip Rose to Lieutenant-
    Governor Charles La Trobe, *Letters from Victorian Pioneers*, p. 148. The
    boasting by Dana's men took place at Parker's station on the Loddon, as

mentioned in Parker to Robinson, 4 September 1845, in correspondence file VPRS 46/89, SIC, PROV; *Maitland Mercury*, 14 June 1845, p. 4.

23 *Geelong Advertiser*, 7 August 1845, p. 3. Thomas Bride provided a translation for 'borack', stating that it means 'no, not so'. See Bride (ed), *Letters from Victorian Pioneers*, footnote 1, p. 225.

24 *Melbourne Courier*, 17 October 1845, p. 2.

25 *Melbourne Courier* (Extraordinary), 17 October 1845, p. 1; Clark, *Aboriginal Languages and Clans*, p. 244; Robinson, Saturday 18 October 1845, *Journals, Volume Four*, p. 336.

26 Rose to La Trobe, *Letters from Victorian Pioneers*, p. 148; Vicary, David & Westerman, Tracy, '"That's Just The Way He Is"': Some Implications of Aboriginal Mental Health Beliefs', *Australian e-Journal for the Advancement of Mental Health*, 3.3, 2004, p. 5; CON37/1/2, p. 588, TAHO; CON16/1/2, p. 250.

27 Lord, Richard, *Impression Bay: Convict Probation Station to Civilian Quarantine Station*, Richard Lord and Partners, Taroona, Tasmania, 1992, p. 23; CON37/1/2, p. 588, TAHO.

9 Sentences to 'instil terror'

1 *Melbourne Courier*, 23 January 1846, p. 2; *Melbourne Courier*, 2 February 1846, p. 3.

2 CON37/1/3, p. 625, TAHO; Fels, Marie, *Good Men and True: The Aboriginal Police of the Port Phillip District 1837–1853*, Melbourne University Press, Melbourne, 1988, p. 269.

3 *Melbourne Argus*, 20 October 1846, p. 3.

4 AM Campbell to Charles La Trobe, 29 September 1853, Bride, T (ed), *Letters from Victorian Pioneers: Being a Series of Papers on the Early Occupation of the Colony, The Aborigines, etc.*, Robert S Brain, Government Printer, Melbourne, 1898, pp. 143–44.

5 Cannon, Michael, *Black Land, White Land*, Minerva, Port Melbourne, 1993, pp. 221–22; Robinson, George Augustus, Saturday 4 April 1846, *The Journals of George Augustus Robinson, Chief Protector, Port Phillip Aboriginal Protectorate, Volume Five: 25 October 1845 – 9 June 1849*, Ian D Clark (ed), Heritage Matters, Clarendon, 2000, p. 16; Robinson, 'Brief Report of an Expedition to the Aboriginal Tribes of the Interior Over More Than Two Thousand Miles of Country During the Five Months Commencing March to August 1846', *Papers, Volume Four: Annual and Occasional Reports 1841–1849*, Heritage Matters, Clarendon, 2001, p. 55.

6 *Maitland Mercury*, 24 October 1846, p. 1.

7 *R v Warrigle Jemmy 1846*, VPRS 30/P/O, Unit 5, File 1-28-8, PROV; *Melbourne Argus*, 22 September 1846, p. 2.

8 Robinson, Friday 18 September 1846, *Journals, Volume Five*, p. 111; *Melbourne Argus*, 20 October 1846, p. 3.

9 'Warrigle Jemmy', Convict Indent, 47/453 4/2779.3, SRNSW.

10 Parker to Robinson, 12 December 1846, 46/1896 4/2779.3, SRNSW.

11 Robinson to Lonsdale, 28 December 1846, 46/1896 4/2779.3, SRNSW; à

Beckett to Lonsdale, 6 January 1847, 47/28 4/2779.3, SRNSW.
12 Lonsdale to Colonial Secretary, 8 January 1847, 47/20 4/2779.3 SRNSW.
13 CON37/1/3, p. 912, TAHO; *Maitland Mercury*, 27 January 1847, p. 4.
14 *Sydney Morning Herald*, 29 December 1846, p. 2; *Atlas*, 2 January 1847, pp. 8–9; CON37/1/3, p. 864, TAHO.
15 CON37/1/3, pp. 864, 912, TAHO; Brand, Ian, *The Convict Probation System: Van Diemen's Land 1839–1854*, Blubber Head Press, Hobart, 1990, p. 86; CON33/1/33, p. 8039, TAHO.
16 *Hobart Town Gazette*, 27 June 1848, p. 568; Brand, Ian, *Penal Peninsula: Port Arthur and its Outstations, 1827–1898*, Regal Publications, Launceston, 1978, p. 2; CON37/1/3, p. 912, TAHO.
17 *Hobart Town Gazette*, 20 February 1849, p. 130; CON37/1/3, p. 912, TAHO.
18 *Hobart Town* Gazette, 19 September 1848, p. 837; CON37/1/3 p. 864, TAHO.
19 Clark, Ian D (ed), *The Papers of George Augustus Robinson, Chief Protector, Port Phillip Aboriginal Protectorate, Volume Four: Annual and Occasional Reports 1841–1849*, Heritage Matters, Clarendon, 2001, 1848 Annual Report, p. 156.

10 Aboriginal deaths in custody

1 Mundy, Godfrey, *Our Antipodes; Or, Residence and Rambles in the Australian Colonies: With a Glimpse of the Gold Fields*, Richard Bentley, London, 1852, p. 111; Gipps to Lord Glenelg, 8 July 1839, *HRA*, Series I, Volume XX, pp. 217–18; Governor George Gipps to Lord John Russell, 8 July 1839, *HRA*, Series I, Volume XX, pp. 216–18.
2 Parker, Roger, *Cockatoo Island*, Thomas Nelson, Melbourne, 1977; Mundy, *Our Antipodes*, p. 112.
3 See Visiting Magistrate H. H. Browne to the Colonial Secretary, 28 December 1850, 191/50 4/3379 SRNSW with enclosure 'A Return Shewing the Number of Aboriginal Natives who have been Received on Cockatoo Island from the 1st Of January 1839 to the 16th December 1850' prepared by George Ormsby, Superintendent, 50/12485 4/3379, SRNSW [hereafter Ormsby Return]; *R v Sandy and Others 1839*, *Decisions of the Superior Courts of New South Wales, 1788–1899*, Bruce Kercher (ed), Division of Law, Macquarie University, Sydney, accessed 1 June 2007 at www.law.mq.edu.au/research/colonial_case_law/nsw/cases/case_index/1839/r_v_sandy/.
4 *R v Sandy and Others 1839*.
5 *Sydney Gazette*, 22 August 1839, p. 2; *R v Sandy and Others 1839*.
6 Ormsby Return, 50/12485 4/3379, SRNSW; Parker, *Cockatoo Island*, p. 2.
7 Ormsby Return, 50/12485 4/3379, SRNSW.
8 *Maitland Mercury*, 31 October 1846, p. 2; *Maitland Mercury*, 7 October 1843, p. 3.
9 *Maitland Mercury*, 31 October 1846, p. 2.
10 *Maitland Mercury*, 7 July 1852, p. 2; Visiting Justice David Forbes to the Colonial Secretary, 13 May 1853, 53/4389 4/3198, SRNSW.
11 *Hunter River Gazette*, 5 February 1842, p. 3; *Hunter River Gazette*, 19 March 1842, p. 3.
12 *Sydney Morning Herald*, 14 September 1842, p. 2; Ormsby Return, 50/12485

4/3379, SRNSW.

13 *Maitland Mercury* (Supplement), 22 March 1843, p. 1; Ormsby Return, 50/12485 4/3379, SRNSW.

14 *R v Tallboy 1840, Decisions of the Superior Courts of New South Wales, 1788–1899*, Bruce Kercher (ed), Division of Law, Macquarie University, Sydney, accessed 1 June 2007 at www.law.mq.edu.au/research/colonial_case_law/nsw/cases/ case_index/1840/r_v_tallboy/.

15 *R v Kilmeister (No. 1) 1838, Decisions of the Superior Courts of New South Wales, 1788–1899*, Bruce Kercher (ed), Division of Law, Macquarie University, Sydney, accessed 22 June 2012 at www.law.mq.edu.au/research/colonial_case_ law/nsw/cases/case_index/1838/r_v_kilmeister1/; *R v Kilmeister and Others (No. 2) 1838, Decisions of the Superior Courts of New South Wales, 1788–1899*, Bruce Kercher (ed), Division of Law, Macquarie University, Sydney, accessed 22 June 2012 at www.law.mq.edu.au/research/colonial_case_law/nsw/cases/ case_index/1838/r_v_kilmeister2/.

16 Duffield, Ian, 'Martin Beck and Afro-Blacks in Colonial Australia', *Journal of Australian Studies*, Issue 16, 1985, p. 3; 'An Emigrant Mechanic' [Alexander Harris], *Settlers and Convicts, or Recollections of Sixteen Years' Labour in the Australian Backwoods*, (London, 1847), Melbourne University Press, Melbourne, 1954, p. 221.

17 *R v Tallboy 1840*. (Emphasis in the original.)

18 Colonial Secretary to the Principal Superintendent of Convicts, 19 November 1841, 4/3689, Reel 1053, p. 276, SRNSW; Ormsby Return, 50/12485 4/3379, SRNSW.

19 *R v Billy 1840, Decisions of the Superior Courts of New South Wales, 1788–1899*, Bruce Kercher (ed), Division of Law, Macquarie University, Sydney, accessed 1 June 2007 at www.law.mq.edu.au/research/colonial_case_law/nsw/cases/ case_index/1840/r_v_billy/.

20 Colonial Secretary to the Principal Superintendent of Convicts, 19 November 1841, 4/3689, Reel 1053, p. 276, SRNSW; Ormsby Return, 50/12485 4/3379, SRNSW.

21 Philip Gidley King to the Colonial Secretary, 16 February 1848, 48/22884/2817, SRNSW; Colonial Secretary to the Commandant at Port Stephen, 19 February 1848, 48/2288 4/2817, SRNSW.

22 *Maitland Mercury*, 13 September 1848, p. 2.

23 Gaoler, Newcastle Gaol to High Sheriff, Sydney, 16 November 1848, 48/12910 4/2826.3, SRNSW; Ormsby Return, 50/12485 4/3379, SRNSW; Browne to Native Police Office, 12 May 1849, 49/4630 4/2839.3, SRNSW.

11 A less destructive alternative

1 Browne to Native Police Office, 5 December 1850, 181/50 4/3379, SRNSW (also see annotation dated 7 December 1850).

2 Browne to Colonial Secretary, 28 December 1850 (with enclosure), 191/50 4/3379, SRNSW; Ormsby Return 50/12485 4/3379, SRNSW.

3 The data pertaining to non-Aboriginal male convicts transported to Van Diemen's Land has been supplied by Associate Professor Hamish Maxwell-

Stewart, University of Tasmania.

4   Browne to Colonial Secretary, 28 December 1850, 191/50 4/3379, SRNSW.

5   Dr Patrick Hill to the Colonial Secretary, 22 February 1851 (with enclosures), 51/2048 4/3379, SRNSW.

6   See the Colonial Secretary's annotations on Hill to the Colonial Secretary, 22 February 1851, 51/2048 4/3379, SRNSW; Circular, 20 March 1851, 51/2048 4/3379, SRNSW.

7   Watson to FitzRoy, 4 March 1851, 51/2470 4/2929, SRNSW.

8   Justice Roger Therry to the Colonial Secretary, 10 March 1851, 51/2471 4/2929, SRNSW.

9   Proceedings of the Executive Council on the 10ᵗʰ March 1851 relative to the Capital conviction of 'Peter' an aboriginal native convicted of Rape at the Bathurst Circuit Court, Minute No. 51/10 4/2932, SRNSW; Colonial Architect Blacket to the Colonial Secretary, 11 March 1851, 51/2494 4/2932, SRNSW.

10 Proceedings of the Executive Council on the 25ᵗʰ March 1851 relative to a letter from Mr. James Green Attorney at Law with respect to the Capital conviction of 'Peter' an aboriginal at the Bathurst Circuit Court for rape, Minute No. 51/12 4/2932, SRNSW; Justice Roger Therry to the Colonial Secretary, 7 April 1851, 51/3450 4/2932, SRNSW; Proceedings of the Executive Council on the 7ᵗʰ April 1851 relative to the commutation of the sentence of death passed upon 'Peter' an aboriginal at the late Bathurst Circuit Court, for rape, Minute No. 51/14, 51/3608 4/2932, SRNSW; Note determining Peter to be sent to Cockatoo Island, 51/3608 4/2932, SRNSW; Police Office Sydney to the Colonial Secretary, 4 August 1851, 51/7598 4/2942, SRNSW.

11 Visiting Magistrate, Cockatoo Island to the Colonial Secretary, 6 May 1853, 53/1938 4/3379, SRNSW (also see annotations).

12 Superintendent, Cockatoo Island to the Colonial Secretary, 29 May 1853, 53/1938 4/3379 SRNSW; Visiting Surgeon George West to the Colonial Secretary, 30 May 1853, 53/4773 4/3379 SRNSW (also see annotation); West to the Colonial Secretary, 2 July 1853, 53/1507 4/3379, SRNSW.

13 Inspector General of Police and Chairman of the Convict Classification Board Mayne to the Colonial Secretary, 7 June 1856, 56/5325 4/3328, SRNSW; File notes relating to Stupid Tommy and Peter, 56/7541 4/3337; Stupid Tommy and Peter, Tickets of Leave, 4/4231, Reel 892, SRNSW.

14 West to the Colonial Secretary, 24 April 1858, 58/5878 4/3379, SRNSW; Superintendent, Cockatoo Island to the Colonial Secretary, 27 May 1858, 58/5878 4/3379, SRNSW; West to the Visiting Magistrate, Cockatoo Island, 22 May 1858, 4/3379, SRNSW; Visiting Magistrate Cockatoo Island to the Colonial Secretary, 27 May 1858, 58/1938 4/3379, SRNSW.

15 Basket, Ticket of Leave 57/132, 4/4231, Reel 892; Billy, Ticket of Leave 56/25, 4/4230, Reel 892; John Bull, Ticket of Leave, 56/24, 4/4230, Reel 892; Du Key, Ticket of Leave 60/26, 4/4233, Reel 893; Michie, Ticket of Leave, 56/128, 4/4231, Reel 892; Tommy, Ticket of Leave 55/89, 4/4230, Reel 892; Duk, Ticket of Leave 57/132, 4/4231, Reel 892A; John Keating, Certificate of

Freedom 60/10, 4/4421, Reel 603; Paddy, Ticket of Leave 57/75, 4/4231, Reel 892; Jackey, Certificate of Freedom 69/9, 4/4221, Reel 1258; John Peacock, Certificate of Freedom 69/37, 4/422, Reel 1258, SRNSW; 'Maitland Circuit Court', *Maitland Mercury*, 4 August 1855, p. 2; 'Telegraphic Messages from our Correspondents: Mudgee', *Sydney Morning Herald*, 17 March 1865, p. 5; 'Bathurst Circuit Court', *Bathurst Times*, 25 September 1858, p. 5; 'Central Criminal Court', *Sydney Morning Herald*, 7 December 1855, p. 2.

12 From the 'Cockatoo of Cape Town' to Sydney

1   Mostert, Noël, *Frontiers: The Epic of South Africa's Creation and the Tragedy of the Xhosa People*, Jonathan Cape, London, 1992, p. xxv; Freund, William, 'The Cape Under the Transitional Governments, 1795–1814', in Richard Elphick & Hermann Giliomee (eds), *The Shaping of South African Society, 1652–1820*, Longman Penguin, Cape Town, 1979, pp. 220, 311.

2   Malherbe, Vertrees, 'South African Bushmen to Australia? Some Soldier Convicts Investigated', *Journal of Australian Colonial History*, Vol. 3, No. 1, 2001, pp. 104–105.

3   Freund, 'The Cape Under the Transitional Governments, 1795–1814', pp. 221, 379; Malherbe, Vertrees, 'David Stuurman: "Last Chief of the Hottentots"', *African Studies*, Vol. 39, No. 1, 1980, p. 49.

4   Malherbe, Vertrees, 'How the Khoekhoen Were Drawn into the Dutch and British Defensive Systems, to *c.* 1809', *Military History Journal*, Vol. 12, No. 3, 2002, p. 96.

5   Malherbe, 'David Stuurman', p. 50; Mostert, *Frontiers*, p. 350.

6   Malherbe, 'David Stuurman', pp. 48–61; Clarke, Marcus, 'Stuurman – Brothers, Patriots, and Hottentots', *Sydney Morning Herald*, 6 May 1879, p. 7.

7   Malherbe, 'David Stuurman', pp. 48–60; Duly, Leslie, '"Hottentots to Hobart and Sydney": The Cape Supreme Court's Use of Transportation 1828–38', *Australian Journal of Politics and History*, Vol. 25, Issue 1, 1979, p. 44.

8   Malherbe, 'David Stuurman', p. 60.

9   Sir Rufane Shawe Donkin to Earl Bathurst, letter dated 26 July 1820, *Records of the Cape Colony from January 1820–June 1821*, copied for the Cape Government, from the manuscript documents in the Public Record Office, London, by George McCall Theal, Volume XII, printed for the Government of the Cape Colony, 1902, p. 220.

10 Mayberry, Peter, 'Irish Convicts to New South Wales 1788–1849', accessed 11 February 2012 at http://members.pcug.org.au/~ppmay/cgi-bin/irish/irish.cgi.

11 *Australian*, 30 January 1829, pp. 2–3.

12 Indent for the *Brampton*, 1823, NRS12188, Bound Manuscript Indents, 1788–1842, 4/4003A, Microfiche 627, SRNSW.

13 *The Sydney Gazette and New South Wales Advertiser*, 1 May 1823, p. 2; *Hobart Town Courier*, 25 July 1829, pp. 2–3.

14 Convict Muster Records, 1825, Home Office: Settlers and Convicts, New South Wales and Tasmania, The National Archives Microfilm Publication HO10, Pieces 5, 19–20, 32–51, TNA; Indent for the *Brampton*, 1823,

NRS12188, Bound Manuscript Indents, 1788–1842, 4/4003A, Microfiche 627, SRNSW.

15   Pringle, Thomas, *Narrative of A Residence in South Africa*, Doppler Press, Brentwood, UK, (1834) 1986, pp. 84–85.

16   David Stuurman, Ticket of Leave, NRS12202, 4/4069, Reel 911, SRNSW.

17   Bannister, Saxe, *Humane Policy, or, Justice to the Aborigines of New Settlements Essential to a Due Expenditure of British Money and to the Best Interest of the Settlers with Suggestions How to Civilise the Natives by an Improved Administration of Existing Means*, Thomas and George Underwood, London, 1830, p. 55; Currey, CH, 'Bannister, Saxe (1790–1877), *Australian Dictionary of Biography*, National Centre of Biography, Australian National University, accessed 28 March 2012 at http://adb.anu.edu.au/biography/bannister-saxe-1738/text1919.

18   Pringle, *Narrative of A Residence in South Africa*, p. 85; *Convict Death Register*, 4/4549, Reel 690, SRNSW.

19   Clarke, 'Stuurman – Brothers, Patriots, and Hottentots', p. 7.

20   'Erin-go-bragh', 'The Last Hottentot Chief', Lessons in Modern Geography, Children's Corner, *The Queenslander*, 18 August 1900, p. 390.

21   'The Hottentots', *West Gippsland Gazette*, 9 February 1904, p. 4.

13   Indicted for the crime of theft

1   Bennett, J, 'Bigge, John Thomas (1780–1843)', *Australian Dictionary of Biography*, Australian National University, accessed 20 February 2012 at http://adb.anu.edu.au/biography/bigge-john-thomas-1779/text1999.

2   Duly, Leslie, '"Hottentots to Hobart and Sydney": The Cape Supreme Court's Use of Transportation 1828–38', *Australian Journal of Politics and History*, Vol. 25, Issue 1, 1979, pp. 39–40.

3   Duly, '"Hottentots to Hobart and Sydney"', pp. 41–44.

4   Kahn, A & Heunis, T, 'The Historical Development of the Supreme Court in South Africa', *A Review of the Administrative Recess System in the High Court*, accessed 20 February 2012 at www.justice.gov.za/reportfiles/court%20recess_2003/crr_ch1.pdf.

5   Allars, K, 'Burton, Sir William Westbrooke (1794–1888)', *Australian Dictionary of Biography*, National Centre of Biography, Australian National University, accessed 20 February 2012 at http://adb.anu.edu.au/biography/burton-sir-william-westbrooke-1857/text2159; William Burton to William Menzies, letter dated 1 November 1829, Personal Letters of Burton, J. Cape Colony, *Decisions of the Superior Courts of New South Wales, 1788–1899*, Bruce Kercher (ed), Division of Law, Macquarie University, Sydney, accessed 20 February 2012 at www.law.mq.edu.au/research/colonial_case_law/nsw/other_features/music_letters_poetry/personal_letters_of_burton_j-cape_colony/.

6   Executive Council, Cape of Good Hope, to the Lieutenant Governor of Van Diemen's Land, letter dated 12 September 1831 and enclosure, 'List of Convicts to be Transported to Van Diemen's Land in the Convict Ship *William Glen Anderson*', CON13/1/5, pp. 252–54, TAHO; Indents of Male Convicts, *William Glen Anderson*, CON14/1/2, pp. 85–88, TAHO.

7   CO396: no. 112, Burton to Cole and enclosure, 20 May 1831; CO396: no.
    113, Burton to Cole and enclosure, 24 May 1831; CO5175: 186, Bell to
    Superintendent of Police, 12 September 1831, cited in Malherbe, Vertrees,
    'Khoikhoi and the Question of Convict Transportation from the Cape Colony,
    1820–1842', *South African Historical Journal*, Vol. 17, Issue 1, 1985, footnote 28,
    p. 27.
8   *Hobart Town Courier*, 22 October 1831, pp. 2–4; 'Hobart Town News', *Sydney
    Herald*, 28 November 1831, p. 2.
9   Indents of Male Convicts, *William Glen Anderson*, CON14/1/2, TAHO,
    Hobart, Tasmania, pp. 85–88; *Hobart Town Courier*, 17 December 1831, pp. 2,
    3; Description List of Male Convicts, *William Glen Anderson*, CON18/1/21,
    TAHO.
10 Assignment Lists and Associated Papers, *William Glen Anderson*, CON13/1/5,
    TAHO; New South Wales and Tasmania, Australia, Convict Muster 1832
    record for Wildschut, Home Office: Settlers and Convicts, New South Wales
    and Tasmania, National Archives Microfilm Publication HO10, Pieces 5,
    19–20, 32–51, TNA; CON13/1/46, p. 134, TAHO; CON13/1/35, p. 82,
    TAHO; Muster of Convicts at Port Arthur Penal Settlement 1830–1832,
    CSO1/532/11581, TAHO; 'Man Found Dead', *Examiner*, 21 June 1848, p. 402.
11 Bonwick, James, *The Bushrangers: Illustrating the Early Days of Van Diemen's
    Land*, George Robertson, Melbourne, 1856, pp. 69, 74; Robson, Lloyd, 'Brady,
    Matthew (1799–1826)', *Australian Dictionary of Biography*, National Centre of
    Biography, Australian National University, accessed 23 February 2012 at http://
    adb.anu.edu.au/biography/brady-matthew-1822/text2089.
12 Adrian Van Wyk, Conduct Record, CON31/1/46, TAHO.
13 Morgan, Sharon, *Land Settlement in Early Tasmania: Creating an Antipodean
    England*, Cambridge University Press, Cambridge, 2003, p. 39; New South
    Wales and Tasmania, Australia; Convict Muster 1832 record for Klaas Loman,
    Home Office: Settlers and Convicts, New South Wales and Tasmania, National
    Archives Microfilm Publication HO10, Pieces 5, 19–20, 32–51, TNA; Klaas
    Zloman [Loman], Conduct Record, CON31/1/47, TAHO.
14 Petrow, Stefan, 'Policing in a Penal Colony: Governor Arthur's System of
    Policing in Van Diemen's Land, 1826–1836, *Law and History Review*, Vol. 18,
    No. 2, 2000, par. 66. Accessed 23 February 2012 at www.historycooperative.
    org/journals/lhr/18.2/petrow.html; Willem Hartzenberg, Conduct Record,
    CON31/1/20, TAHO.
15 CON94/1/1, p. 311, TAHO; CON32/1/1, p. 162, TAHO; Willem
    Hartzenberg, Conduct Record, CON31/1/20, TAHO; *Mercury*, 28 July 1876,
    p. 2.
16 Arnoldus Jantje, Appropriation List, CON27/1/5, TAHO; CON31/1/24, p. 48,
    TAHO; Home Office: Settlers and Convicts, New South Wales and Tasmania,
    National Archives Microfilm Publication HO10, Pieces 31, 52–64, TNA.
17 *The Sydney Herald*, 29 June 1837, p. 2; Gaol Record for Scipio Africanus,
    Description books [Sydney Gaol and Darlinghurst Gaol], Series 2523, Reels 857–
    889, SRNSW; *The Sydney Gazette and New South Wales Advertiser*, 9 September
    1837, p. 3; CON35/1/1, p. 8, TAHO.

18 CON37/1/1, p. 2256; CON37/1/7, p. 2135, TAHO.
19 CON31/1/24, p. 48, TAHO; *Mercury*, 28 July 1876, p. 2.
20 CON37/1/7, p. 2256, TAHO.
21 Mina Magerman, Warrant, NRS1155, 2/8255, Reel 2420, p. 155, SRNSW; Mina Magerman, Certificate of Freedom 38/0358, 4/4342, Reel 1000, SRNSW.
22 'Abstract of the Number of Inhabitants in the Colony of New South Wales, according to a Census taken the 2nd September, 1836, under an Act of the Governor and Council of 7th Wm. IV., No. 1, passed 5 July, 1836', accessed 29 February 2012 at http://hccda.anu.edu.au/pages/NSW-1836-census-01_83; *The Sydney Gazette and New South Wales Advertiser*, 14 October 1824, p. 4; Mina Magerman, Certificate of Freedom 38/0358, 4/4342, Reel 1000, SRNSW.
23 'The Durand's Alley Tragedy', *Empire*, 24 November 1859, p. 5; 'Coroner's Court', *Sydney Morning Herald*, 24 November 1859, p. 4.
24 Malherbe, 'Khoikhoi and the Question of Convict Transportation from the Cape Colony, 1820–1842', p. 27.
25 'Eden', NRS1155, 2420, 2/8256, pp. 163–224; Jan Aaron, Ticket of Leave, 4/4202, Reel 957; Kleinboy Adam, Ticket of Leave, 4/4207, Reel 959; Jan Bastaard, Ticket of Leave, 4/4202, Reel 957A, SRNSW.
26 Cobus Zeeland, Convict Indent, *Lady Nugent*, NRS12189, X638, microfiche 719, Ticket of Leave, 4/4153; Reel 941B; Jan Windvogel, Convict Indent, *Earl Grey*, NRS12189, X638, microfiche 719, SRNSW.
27 Duly, '"Hottentots to Hobart and Sydney"', p. 44.

14 Mutiny and desertion

1 See in particular Malherbe, Vertrees, 'How the Khoekhoen Were Drawn into the Dutch and British Defensive Systems, to *c.* 1809', *Military History Journal*, Vol. 12, No. 3, 2002.
2 Malherbe, 'How the Khoekhoen Were Drawn into the Dutch and British Defensive Systems', p. 95; Freund, William, 'The Cape Under the Transitional Governments, 1795–1814', in Richard Elphick & Hermann Giliomee (eds), *The Shaping of South African Society 1652–1820*, Penguin, Cape Town, 1979, p. 222.
3 Lewin Robinson, AM, 'Hottentots in New South Wales', *Africana Notes and News*, Vol. 19, No. 2, 1970, pp. 72–73; Theal, George, *History of South Africa Since September 1795*, Cambridge University Press, Cambridge, (1908), 2010, p. 175.
4 Private Piet Lynx, Court Martial Transcript, WO71/302, 281603, TNA; CON33/1/55, TAHO.
5 'Cape of Good Hope: Miscellaneous', *The Asiatic Journal and Monthly Register for British and Foreign India, China, and Australasia*, Vol. XXVI, May–August 1838, Part 2: Asiatic Intelligence, Wm. H Allen & Co, London, 1838, p. 232.
6 'List of Military Convicts to be Transported from the Cape of Good Hope to New South Wales in the Convict Ship *Pekoe*, Sampson Keen, Master', *New South Wales Convict Ship Muster Rolls & Related Records*, Series CGS 1155,

Reels 2417–2428, SRNSW; Lewin Robinson, 'Hottentots in New South Wales', p. 72.

7   'Tickets of Leave Cancelled', *Sydney Morning Herald*, 23 June 1851, p. 3.

8   'Law Intelligence, Central Criminal Court, Thursday, Before their Honors the Three Judges, Sentences', *Sydney Morning Herald*, 17 April 1846, p. 2; Iltis, Judith, 'Stephen Simpson (1793–1869), *Australian Dictionary of Biography*, National Centre of Biography, Australian National University, accessed 7 March 2012 at http://adb.anu.edu.au/biography/simpson-stephen-2666/text3715.

9   Personal communication between Alan Queale, Department of Justice, Brisbane and Vertrees Malherbe cited in Malherbe, Vertrees, 'South African Bushmen to Australia? Some Soldier Convicts Investigated', *Journal of Australian Colonial History*, Vol. 3, No. 1, 2001, pp. 121–23; Lewin Robinson, 'Hottentots in New South Wales', p. 72; CON37/1/3, p. 801, TAHO.

10 'Law Intelligence, Central Criminal Court, Wednesday, before His Honor Mr Justice Therry', *Sydney Morning Herald*, 16 April 1846, p. 2.

11 'Law Intelligence, Central Criminal Court, Thursday, Before their Honors the Three Judges, Sentences', *Sydney Morning Herald*, 17 April 1846, p. 2; *Sydney Morning Herald*, 5 May 1846, p. 3.

12 CON37/1/3, p. 801, TAHO.

13 *Mercury*, 13 August 1861, p. 3.

14 *Mercury*, 11 September 1862, p. 7.

15 *Mercury*, 3 December 1862, p. 2; *Mercury*, 20 December 1862, p. 4; *Mercury*, 24 December 1862, p. 5.

16 *Cornwall Chronicle*, 4 February 1863, p. 3.

17 *Examiner*, 7 February 1863, p. 5; *Mercury*, 17 February 1863, p. 2; *Mercury*, 19 February 1863, p. 2.

18 *Examiner*, 10 February 1863, p. 5; 'Execution at the Hobart Town Gaol', *Examiner*, 24 February 1863, p. 5; 'Execution of Hendrick Whitnalder', *Cornwall Chronicle*, 25 February 1863, p. 5.

19 Private Hendrick Keester, Court Martial Transcript, W071/299, TNA.

20 Piet Lynx, Indent, CON14/1/11; Conduct Record, CON33/1/15; Hendrick Keester, Indent, CON14/1/11; Conduct Record, 33/1/15; Appropriation List, CON27/1/9, TAHO.

21 Piet Lynx, Appropriation List, CON27/1/10; Conduct Record, CON33/1/55; Hendrick Keester, Appropriation List, CON27/1/10, Conduct Record, CON33/1/15, TAHO.

22 Piet Lynx, Appropriation List, CON27/1/10; Conduct Record, CON33/1/55, TAHO; *Examiner*, 18 September 1852, p. 8.

23 Booy Piet, Conduct Record, CON37/1/1, TAHO; Miller, Linus, *Notes of an Exile to Van Dieman's Land*, S.R. Publishers, Wakefield, Yorkshire (1846), 1968, pp. 286–87; Brand, Ian, *The Convict Probation System: Van Diemen's Land, 1839–1854*, Blubber Head Press, Hobart, 1990, pp. 197–98.

15 'Black Peter' the bushranger

1   'Criminal Sittings', *South Australian*, 25 November 1850, p. 2; Peter Haly

[Haley], Conduct Record, CON37/1/6; Indent, CON16/1/4, TAHO.

2 *South Australian Register*, 23 January 1852, p. 3.

3 Peter Haly [Haley], Conduct Record, CON37/1/6; *Cornwall Chronicle*, 24 March 1858, p. 4; *Courier*, 1 October 1858, p. 3; *Courier*, 6 October 1858, p. 3; *South Australian Register*, 28 October 1858, p. 3.

4 William Thornton, Conduct Record, CON35/1/2; Daniel Stewart, Conduct Record, CON33/1/19; William Ferns, Conduct Records, CON33/1/99 and CON37/1/8; Peter Haly [Haley], Conduct Record, CON37/1/6; TAHO.

5 'Hobart Town', *Examiner*, 29 January 1859, p. 2; 'Tasmania. Bushranging', *South Australian Register*, 28 October 1858, p. 3; *Cornwall Chronicle*, 24 March 1858, p. 4.

6 'Capture of "Black Peter" the Bushranger', *Hobart Town Daily Mercury*, 1 May 1858, p. 3; 'The Bushranger', *South Australian Advertiser*, 28 July 1858, p. 3; 'Imbecility of the Government: The Police Force: The Bushrangers', *Cornwall Chronicle*, 14 July 1858, p. 4; 'The Labor Market', *Hobart Town Daily Mercury*, 9 April 1858, p. 3; Peter Haly [Haley], Conduct Record, CON37/1/6; Indent, CON16/1/4, TAHO.

7 'The Bushrangers', Letter to the Editor of the *Hobart Town Daily Mercury* from John Brown, *Hobart Town Daily Mercury*, 5 May 1858, p. 3; 'The Bushrangers', *Argus*, 10 May 1858, p. 6.

8 'Bushrangers', *Hobart Town Daily Mercury*, 10 July 1858, p. 5; 'To the Editor of the Mercury', letter from J Jackson CDC, *Hobart Town Daily Mercury*, 20 September 1858, p. 3.

9 'The Bushrangers', *Portland Guardian and Normanby General Advertiser*, 9 July 1858, p. 3.

10 William Ferns, Conduct Record, CON37/1/8; 'Bushranging', *South Australian Register*, 28 October 1858, p. 3; 'Capture of Another Bushranger', *Courier*, 8 October 1858, p. 3; 'Imbecility of the Government: The Police Force: The Bushrangers', *Cornwall Chronicle*, 14 July 1858, p. 4.

11 *Courier*, 1 October 1858, p. 3; 'Inquest Upon Thornton [Sydney Jim]', *Courier*, 5 October 1858, p. 3; 'Bushranging', *South Australian Register*, 28 October 1858, p. 3.

12 'The Bushrangers – Wingy and Thornton', *Cornwall Chronicle*, 9 October 1858, p. 4.

13 'Examination of Wingy and His Confederates', *Courier*, 24 November 1858, p. 2.

14 'Meeting of Parliament', *Hobart Town Daily Mercury*, 4 December 1858, p. 2; 'Enquirer', letter to the editor, *Hobart Town Daily Mercury*, 9 December 1858, p. 3.

15 'Hobart Town', *Examiner*, 29 January 1859, p. 2.

16 'The Bushrangers: Sentence of Death', *Courier*, 31 January 1859, p. 2.

17 'The Condemned Bushrangers', *Courier*, 14 February 1859, p. 2; 'The Execution', *Courier*, 16 February 1859, p. 3.

16 In open rebellion

1 Stevens, Joan (ed), E. Jerningham Wakefield, *Adventure in New Zealand*,

Golden Press, Auckland, 1975, p. 80.

2 Wakefield, *Adventure in New Zealand*, pp. 85–86.

3 Brodie, James, 'Mason, Thomas – Biography', from *Dictionary of New Zealand Biography. Te Ara – The Encyclopedia of New Zealand*, updated 1 September 2010 www.TeAra.govt.nz/biographies/2m38/1; Maxwell, Ebenezer, *Recollections and Reflections of an Old New Zealander*, AH & AW Reed, Dunedin, NZ, 1937, p. 22.

4 Brodie, 'Mason, Thomas – Biography'.

5 *The Britannia, and Trades' Advocate*, 18 June 1846, cited in Hopkins, Jeffrey, '"Fighting Those Who Came Against Their Country": Maori Political Transportees to Van Diemen's Land 1846–48', Tasmanian Historical Research Association: *Papers and Proceedings*, Vol. 44, No. 1, March 1997, p. 57.

6 Woodhouse, A (ed), *Tales of Pioneer Women*, Whitcomb & Tombs, Christchurch, 1940, p. 106; Boggis, E, Typed extract from a letter dated 14 May 1973, NS776/1/18, Archives New Zealand; Gibson, Tom, *The Wiltshire Regiment (the 62nd and 99th Regiments of Foot)*, Leo Cooper, London, 1969, pp. 68–69.

7 Brodie, 'Mason, Thomas – Biography'.

8 Keenan, Danny, *Wars Without End: The Land Wars in Nineteenth-Century New Zealand*, Penguin, Auckland, 2009, p. 154.

9 Woodhouse (ed), *Tales of Pioneer Women*, p. 110.

10 Keenan, *Wars Without End*, pp. 152–56; Cowan, James, *The New Zealand Wars: A History of the Maori Campaigns and the Pioneering Period*, AMS Press, University of California, 1969, pp. 102–11; 'War in Wellington', Ministry for Culture and Heritage, accessed 14 January 2012 at www.nzhistory.net.nz/war/wellington-war; Joseph Boulcott to his father, letter dated 27 May 1846, in Louise Lawrence (ed), *The Penguin Book of New Zealand Letters*, Penguin Books, Auckland, 2003, pp. 98–99.

11 Collins, Hēni, *Ka Mate Ka Ora! The Spirit of Te Rauparaha*, Steele Roberts, Wellington, 2010, pp. 202–29.

12 Major Edward Last to Governor George Grey, letter dated 16 August 1846, *Wellington Independent*, 7 October 1846, p. 3; Wakefield, *Adventure in New Zealand*, p. 97.

13 Wilkie, Ruth, 'Te Umuroa, Hohepa – Biography', from *Dictionary of New Zealand Biography. Te Ara – the Encyclopedia of New Zealand*, updated 1 September 2010 www.TeAra.govt.nz/en/biographies/1t80/1; Last to Grey, letter dated 16 August 1846, *Wellington Independent*, 7 October 1846, p. 3; *Auckland Press*, 2 September 1846.

14 Tattersall, John, *Maoris on Maria Island*, Hawke's Bay Museum & Art Gallery, Napier, 1973, p. 7; Rusden, George, *History of New Zealand: Volume One*, Melville, Mullen & Slade, Melbourne, 1895, p. 411.

15 Tattersall, *Maoris on Maria Island*, p. 5.

16 *Wellington Independent*, 7 October 1846, p. 2. The correspondent's identity is unknown. However, it has been suggested that the argumentation in the letter emulates an earlier example of Bishop Selwyn's work. See E Ellis, Turnbull Library, New Zealand, to T Hume, letter dated 18 September 1972, Archives

New Zealand, NS776/3/3.
17 *Wellington Independent*, 14 October 1846, p. 2; 'Proceedings of Court Martial Maori Prisoners Captured at Pari Pari', NM46/494, Archives New Zealand.

17 A merciful alternative

1 *Britannia and Trades' Advocate*, 19 November 1846, p. 2; CON37/3/765-69; CON16/3 pp. 312–15, TAHO; *Cornwall Chronicle*, 21 November 1846, p. 898.
2 Governor George Grey to His Excellency, the Officer Administering the Government of Van Diemen's Land, 31 October 1846, enclosed with Despatch 34, 30 November 1846, CO280/197, *ACJP*, Reels 545 & 546, pp. 408–11.
3 *Colonial Times and Tasmanian*, 13 November 1846, p. 4.
4 *The Britannia and Trades' Advocate*, 19 November 1846, p. 2; *Colonial Times and Tasmanian*, 24 November 1846, p. 3; 'New Zealand Prisoners', *Hobart Town Courier and Government Gazette*, 25 November 1846, p. 2.
5 'New Zealand Prisoners', *Hobart Town Courier and Government Gazette*, 25 November 1846, p. 2.
6 'New Zealand Prisoners', *Hobart Town Courier and Government Gazette*, 18 November 1846, p. 2.
7 Paffen, Paul, '"Forgotten Faces?": Portraits and other images of the Convict in Van Diemen's Land', *Tasmanian Historical Research Association: Papers and Proceedings*, Vol. 46, No. 2, June 1999, pp. 57–95; Hodgman, VW, 'Prout, John Skinner (1805–1876)', *Australian Dictionary of Biography*, National Centre of Biography, Australian National University, accessed 10 January 2012 at http://adb.anu.edu.au/biography/prout-john-skinner-2565/text3501; Ryan, Lyndall, 'Trugernanner (Truganini) (1812–1876)', *Australian Dictionary of Biography*, National Centre of Biography, Australian National University, accessed 11 January 2012 at http://adb.anu.edu.au/biography/trugernanner-truganini-4752/text7895.
8 Trott, Mary, 'Walker, George Washington (1800–1859)', *Australian Dictionary of Biography*, National Centre of Biography, Australian National University, accessed 12 January 2012 at http://adb.anu.edu.au/biography/walker-george-washington-2764/text3923.
9 *Colonial Times*, 27 November 1846, p. 3; Simmons, E, *A Brief History of the Catholic Church in New Zealand*, Catholic Publications Centre, Auckland, 1978, p. 27; 'New Zealand Prisoners', *The Hobart Town Courier and Government Gazette*, 25 November 1846, p. 2.
10 Thomas Mason to Dr Hampton, Comptroller General, 25 November 1846, Correspondence Files: Māoris, TAHO.
11 CJ La Trobe to Earl Grey, 30 November 1846, Correspondence Files: Māoris, TAHO.
12 CJ La Trobe to Earl Grey, letter dated 30 November 1846, NS776/1/4, Archives New Zealand; 'The New Zealanders', *Hobart Town Courier and Government Gazette*, 28 November 1846, p. 2.
13 Brand, Ian, *The Convict Probation System: Van Diemen's Land 1839–1854*, Blubber Head Press, Hobart, 1990, p. 16.
14 Colonial Office to La Trobe, letter dated 21 May 1847, NS776/1/7, Archives

New Zealand, Wellington.

15 'The New Zealanders', *Hobart Town Courier and Government Gazette*, 28 November 1846, p. 2.

16 'An Old Colonist' (Contributed), *The Queenslander*, 25 May 1901, p. 1019.

17 Smith, Dawn, 'The Strange Case of Dr JJ Imrie', *Journal of the Nelson and Marlborough Historical Societies*, Vol. 1, Issue 5, October 1985, accessed 11 January 2012 at www.nzetc.org/tm/scholarly/tei-NHSJ04_05-t1-body1-d9. html.

18 'Family Group Sheet' supplied to the author by Mr Greg Carlill, an Imrie descendant based in Brisbane, Queensland.

19 Brand, *The Convict Probation System*, pp. 133, 177, 236.

20 Imrie, John Jennings, 'A Copy of the Diary of Dr Imrie While he was in Charge of the Maori Exiles on Maria Island', N1093, TAHO.

21 Colonial Office to Governor George Grey, letter dated 7–8 May 1847, NS776/1/5, Archives New Zealand, Wellington; Colonial Office to La Trobe, letter dated 31 May 1847, NS776/1/6, Archives New Zealand, Wellington.

22 *Colonial Times*, 25 February 1848, p. 3; Bhabha, Homi, *The Location of Culture*, Routledge, 1994, p. 125.

23 Lieutenant Governor William Denison to the Colonial Office, letter dated 21 March 1848, Public Records Office, CO280/226(ii), Reel 564. Cited in Kepars, I, National Library of Australia, to Tim Hume, Launceston, letter dated 7 December 1973, Archives New Zealand, NS776/3/12; Transcript of the Diary of JJ Imrie while he was in charge of the Māori Exiles on Maria Island, 20 December 1846–25 March 1848, NS1093/1, TAHO.

24 Brodie, James, 'Mason, Thomas – Biography', from *Dictionary of New Zealand Biography. Te Ara – The Encyclopedia of New Zealand*, updated 1 September 2010 www.TeAra.govt.nz/biographies/2m38/1.

25 *R v Te Ahuru*, 'New Zealand's Lost Cases Project', Victoria University of Wellington, accessed 13 March 2012 at www.victoria.ac.nz/law/nzlostcases/CaseDetails.aspx?casenumber=00717; Te Ahuru Conduct Record CON37/1/7 and Description List CON16/1/4, TAHO; Burnett, Robert, 'Penal Transportation: An Episode in New Zealand History', *Occasional Papers in Criminology No. 9*, Institute of Criminology, Victoria University of Wellington, 1978, pp. 25–26; Green, Neville & Moon, Susan, *Far From Home: Aboriginal Prisoners of Rottnest Island 1838–1931*, Dictionary of Western Australians, Volume X, University of Western Australia Press, Nedlands, 1997; Lieutenant Governor Denison to Earl Grey, letter dated 15 January 1852 and enclosures, GO33/1/73, TAHO.

18 Repatriating Hohepa Te Umuroa, 1988

1 Baudin, Nicolas, Journal Entry dated 21 February 1802 (Transcription), *Encounter 1802–2002: Celebrating Flinders' and Baudin's Expeditions in Search of the 'Unknown' Southern Coast of Australia*, accessed 22 January 2012 at www.slsa.sa.gov.au/encounter/collection/ocr_text/B12582426_03.htm; Robinson, Anthony, 'Five Days on Maria Island', *Mercury*, 23 March 1876, p. 3.

2 'Special Correspondent', 'Through Tasmania, No. 54', *Mercury* (Supplement),

23 August 1884, p. 1.

3 'AFG', 'Is Maria Island to Stagnate? Neglected Tourism Asset', *Mercury*, 13 September 1938, p. 10.

4 Tattersall, John, *Māoris on Maria Island*, Hawke's Bay Museum & Art Gallery, Napier, 1973. See in particular NS776/1, NS776/2, NS776/3 and NS776/5, Archives New Zealand, Wellington.

5 *Maitland Mercury*, 11 February 1843, p. 2.

6 Sinclair, Karen, *Māori Times, Māori Places: Prophetic Histories*, Bridget Williams Books, Wellington, 2003, pp. 180–81.

7 Heald, Chris, 'The Lost Son of Wanganui', *NZ Listener*, 10 September 1988, pp. 33–34.

8 Heald, 'The Lost Son of Wanganui', p. 33; CE Foster to Hon. Koro Wetere, Minister of Māori Affairs, letter dated 8 August 1988, 16/1/12/2, Archives New Zealand; Wetere to Foster, letter dated 22 September 1988, 16/1/12/2, Archives New Zealand.

9 Creswell, David, 'Report on the Repatriation of the Remains of Hohepa Te Umuroa', 16/1/12/2, Archives New Zealand.

10 Heald, 'The Lost Son of Wanganui', p. 34; Sinclair, *Māori Times, Māori Places*, p. 186.

11 Margaret Weindenhofer to PR Eldershaw, Archives Officer, letter dated 13 February 1966, Māori Correspondence File, TAHO.

12 Sinclair, *Māori Times, Māori Places*, pp. 185–87; Heald, 'The Lost Son of Wanganui', *NZ Listener*, p. 34.

13 Darby, Andrew, 'A Warrior's People Return for his Spirit', *The Age*, 2 August 1988, p. 1.

14 Heald, 'The Lost Son of Wanganui', p. 34.

15 Mariu, Max, 'Te Awhitu, Wiremu Hakopa Toa – Biography', *Dictionary of New Zealand Biography. Te Ara – The Encyclopedia of New Zealand*, updated 1 September 2010, accessed 21 March 2012 at www.TeAra.govt.nz/en/biographies/5t6/1; 'Māori Warrior in Final Resting Place', *Wanganui Chronicle*, 9 August 1988.

Conclusion

1 *Melbourne Times*, 15 April 1843, p. 2.

2 Therry, Roger, *Reminiscences of Thirty Years' Residence in New South Wales and Victoria*, (London, 1863), reprint, Sydney University Press, Sydney, 1974, pp. 286–87, 459.

3 Ihimaera, Witi, *The Trowenna Sea*, Raupo Imprint, Penguin Books, New Zealand, 2009; 'Hohepa', *New Zealand Opera*, accessed 21 February 2012 at www.nzopera.com/operas/hohepa.

Index

Index

Index

Index